THE RACE
TO THE BOTTOM

THE RACE TO THE BOTTOM

Why a Worldwide Worker Surplus
and Uncontrolled Free Trade
Are Sinking American Living Standards

ALAN TONELSON

Westview Press
A Member of the Perseus Books Group

Copyright © 2000 by Westview Press, A Member of the Perseus Books Group

Published in 2000 in the United States of America by Westview Press, 5500 Central Avenue, Boulder, Colorado 80301–2877, and in the United Kingdom by Westview Press, 12 Hid's Copse Road, Cumnor Hill, Oxford OX2 9JJ

Find us on the World Wide Web at www.westviewpress.com

A CIP catalog record for this book is available from the Library of Congress. ISBN 0-8133-6817-0

The paper used in this publication meets the requirements of the American National Standard for Permanence of Paper for Printed Library Materials Z39.48–1984.

10   9   8   7   6   5   4   3   2   1

CONTENTS

PREFACE

I work in a funny business. "Policy analysis." "Public affairs." Sometimes I am not even sure what to call it. But one thing is certain—you have made it (at least momentarily) in this business when you appear on a top-line talk show. So I was pretty ecstatic when I got the call from the Public Broadcasting System (PBS) in February 1996 inviting me on the *MacNeil-Lehrer NewsHour* to talk about the new global economy and the presidential campaign.

There is no special reason for anyone else to remember anything about the actual segment or the other three commentators. However, one exchange I was involved in haunts me to this day. In fact, four years later, this experience and several others convinced me that something like this book—a comprehensive but clear layman's guide to the new global economy's impact on American living standards and to the controversy surrounding this subject—was very badly needed.[1]

A few minutes into the segment, moderator Paul Solman asked one panelist, former chief U.S. trade negotiator Carla Hills, a critical question: Intensifying economic competition from abroad and a flurry of corporate layoffs and international trade agreements were filling the news (remember—this was before the U.S. economy became the "Goldilocks Economy," where everything was "just right"). Therefore, would not even a strong supporter of long-standing U.S. international economic policies have to concede that "many people have a really good reason to feel insecure about their economic future here in America"?

Ambassador Hills granted the premise but also pointed to all the economy's undeniable strengths. Then she said something that pushed our debate off course. We were talking about trade and its effects on the economy and politics, not about the economy itself. What Ambassador Hills said was, "If you look at smaller businesses, those with under 500 employees, they've created 8 million jobs in the last half of the decade. That's incredible."

Ambassador Hills was right about the dynamism of small business. However, research I had done recently made clear that this dynamism had virtually nothing to do with trade. So to get the show back on track, I interjected, "And most of them don't export."

Without missing a beat, Ambassador Hills shot back, "That is absolutely incorrect. It's incorrect." Unfortunately, not expecting this particular issue to come up, I did not bring any documentation. So, Paul Solman did what any reasonable moderator would have done—he quickly got us past this deadlock.

The following morning at work, I went on to the Web to recheck my facts. Sure enough, a U.S. Small Business Administration study made them plain as day. The updated version is even more striking. Nearly four years after Ambassador Hills' emphatic denial that most small businesses do not export, it is still the case that fewer than one percent of America's small businesses do any exporting.[2] Clearly, something else is responsible for the outstanding performance of these companies in general.

I immediately called the *MacNeil-Lehrer* staff and told them that Ambassador Hills had completely misstated the facts. Either her memory simply failed her on this important point or she knew nothing about small business exporting, despite several years as top U.S. trade official, and decided to invent something to score a debating point. Otherwise, she knew that few small businesses exported and decided to mislead.

I was sure that the program staff would want to correct the record. Silly me. Yet I am still amazed that a news program that prides itself on its serious, substantive approach to the issues (as opposed to all those crass, commercially sponsored network newscasts) displayed absolutely no interest in correcting a major factual mistake by a high-profile public figure. Because I came inadequately prepared, because the moderator was inadequately informed, and because the staff was inadequately concerned about accountability, Ambassador Hills got away with it.

One month later, I had a similar, equally depressing experience. Corporate downsizing kept making news, and insurgent Republican Pat Buchanan and his opposition to the status quo in trade and other U.S. policies toward the world economy had won his party's New Hampshire presidential primary. James Glassman, then a *Washington Post* columnist, wrote an article expressing his astonishment and dismay at the immediate political fallout—office-seekers all over the map were running scared on the trade issue.[3] How could even politicians, Glassman wondered, be so shortsighted? After all, they must have known what all thinking people knew—that the current approach toward this globalization phenomenon was best for America and the world. And the critics' lightning rod—the North American Free Trade Agreement (NAFTA)—was a smashing success.

To make his NAFTA point, Glassman zeroed in on the experience of one allegedly typical U.S. multinational manufacturer—AlliedSignal. Yes, Mexico's currency and economy had collapsed only a year after NAFTA went into effect in 1994, but like other boosters of the treaty, Glassman dismissed the idea that an agreement that they had all described as a watershed had anything to do with these problems. Even more important, Glassman wrote, look at the fortunes of AlliedSignal—and its American workforce.

According to Glassman, AlliedSignal had exported 16 million spark plugs from the United States to Mexico in 1993, the last year before NAFTA. In 1994, NAFTA's first year, sales rose to 21 million. After the peso crash, AlliedSignal's spark plug exports dipped, but at 19 million, they were still higher than pre-NAFTA levels. AlliedSignal executive Paul Boudreau told Glassman that sales to Mexico would rise by 10 percent in 1997. More exports from the United States obviously meant more U.S. jobs and higher wages. According to Glassman, NAFTA was making this possible throughout the entire economy. Who but a Neanderthal would complain?

What Glassman apparently did not know, and what AlliedSignal did not tell him, was that spark plugs are not like the exports that traditionally—and rightly—have been associated with job creation and wage increases. Specifically, they are not finished products—like blue jeans or computers or jetliners. They are parts and components of finished goods—in this case, motor vehicles. Economists even have a special name for these and certain other products—producer or investment goods. The very existence and growth of trade in these products reveals one of the major features of the new world economy—the creation by giant companies of production systems spanning many different countries.

In some cases, the export of these producer goods can have the same positive effect on jobs and wages in the United States as the export of finished goods. However, as will be explained later, in current and foreseeable circumstances, these kinds of exports usually displace American workers and drive down their wages. Most of these exports simply represent the supplying of American-owned factories in foreign countries that have replaced factories once located in the United States—along with their workers.

In principle, many or most or all of AlliedSignal's spark plug exports to Mexico can have the same beneficial effects on American workers as exports of traditional finished goods. It depends mainly on whether these spark plugs are placed in cars sold and used in Mexico, or in cars sold and used back in the United States. Even though distinguishing these types of exports is vital in order to assess fully trade's impact today on U.S. living standards, such information is virtually impossible for citizens to obtain. The Commerce Department's Office of Automotive Affairs told me that it has no interest in finding out how U.S. auto parts exports are used in foreign countries. It simply wants to know the total export numbers. Nor do U.S. auto parts trade associations separately track exports for the export market and the domestic market for individual countries.

AlliedSignal—which has since merged with Honeywell—obviously has records identifying its Mexican customers and needs a very detailed idea of the main trends in various product markets. However, Paul Boudreau, the executive who gave Glassman his spark plug figures, failed to return seven phone calls I made to his office. I did, however, manage to get some figures from trustworthy sources indicating that my hunches about the ultimate destination of these spark plugs was right. For example, I found a February 1994 report from the U.S. embassy in Mexico City claiming that only 20 percent of all auto parts produced in Mexico were sold as replacement parts—and used in Mexico. Fully 70 percent were sold to auto assemblers in Mexico—who sell the overwhelming majority of their vehicle output to the United States.[4]

Still trusting in the American media's interest in simple accuracy—not to mention explaining some of the critical details of globalization to readers—I sent a response to the *Post* hoping it would run as one of the paper's regular "Taking Exception" articles. I was not overly hopeful: The *Post* has a long record of strong support for traditional trade agreements like NAFTA, but I convinced myself that the importance of my point combined with an elemental commitment to fairness on the *Post's* part gave me a decent chance with the paper's editors. Plus, I'd established some credentials as a trade policy analyst by publishing regularly in other nationally known newspapers and magazines.

A few days later my optimism rose. My continuing research found some additional information that virtually clinched my case. I called the *Post* editorial page staff and told a junior employee of this development. At her suggestion, I faxed over a short memo describing my findings and their importance.

The new material evidently had no effect on the editorial page staff, because a few days later, they rejected the article. I was not even offered the chance to boil it down to a letter to the editor. Frustrated but still determined, I called an editorial page staff member who had once expressed some admiration for another article I had previously sent in. In response to his suggestion, I sent a two-page single-spaced memo explaining the issue of trade in producer goods and describing Glassman's oversights in more detail. To no avail. My response never ran, and *Post* readers were left with a completely misleading picture of U.S.-Mexican trade.

Two postscripts to this story: First, over the next few months, Glassman twice invited me to appear on his talk show *Technopolitics.* He said that he had seen the material I sent to the *Post* (and eventually to him) on auto parts trade, and other articles, but he acknowledged no errors either in person in his studio or in print in his column. On the air, he spent much of our time attacking me as a "protectionist."

Three years later, after NAFTA had become so unpopular with the American public that Congress refused to authorize President Clinton to negotiate new, NAFTA-style trade agreements, the president spoke at the annual convention of the AFL-CIO (American Federation of Labor–Congress of Industrial Organizations). The unions were staunchly opposed to these new trade agreements, and the president knew that on this issue, his audience was unfriendly. In his plea for support for new negotiating authority (called "fast track"), he made a startling admission. He insisted that his position "is not about NAFTA or factories moving there to sell back to here."[5] In other words, he confirmed that most of America's NAFTA exports were nothing like traditional, job-creating exports at all. The president's concession was never reported in the *Post* or, to my knowledge, any other U.S. newspaper.

By June 1996, the trade policy wars in Washington were focused on China. From 1980 until 2000, the president needed Congress' annual approval to keep tariffs on Chinese imports to the United States at the same low levels as tariffs on most other countries. In the summer of 2000, as part of a worldwide agreement to admit China into the World Trade Organization (WTO), Congress began the process of voting to make China's low-tariff status permanent.

The annual battles over China were usually hard fought. Big American companies—mainly the ones that import goods into the

United States from factories they own or work with in China—spent millions of dollars each year buying votes in Congress to keep tariffs on Chinese-made products low. For them, losing the China vote would have meant that the U.S. market would be largely closed off to the Chinese output on which they increasingly relied. Others, like labor unions and my organization, the U.S. Business and Industry Council (USBIC), opposed low China tariffs but had much less money to spend.

Along with my colleague Kevin L. Kearns, USBIC's president, I was asked one day to speak at a briefing organized by the House of Representatives' Small Business Committee on how U.S.-China trade affects small companies. (Our organization is made up mainly of such companies.) Everything was proceeding normally as these meetings go, when a representative of the U.S. multinational companies that dominate U.S. trade with China and the rest of the world went a little too far for me.

Not only do big companies like GE and Motorola and IBM and Boeing export to China, he said. These companies are supplied by thousands of smaller U.S.-based businesses whose bottom lines—and the living standards of their workers—also benefit from increased U.S. sales to China. Of course, this speaker was right. Small companies (especially manufacturers) often depend on larger companies for much of their business. All the big U.S. exporters to China do buy parts and components and other inputs from smaller companies based in the United States. They also are supplied by service companies of all sizes, which also gain from higher export-generated profits.

But the U.S. supply base is not the whole story. As the speaker knew full well, the big U.S. exporters buy goods and services from companies large and small all over the world. Those that do business in China use a great many Chinese companies—in part because the Chinese government often requires foreign companies to use Chinese workers and products as a condition of signing a contract. In fact, companies like Motorola say they are "committed to identifying local suppliers for the key components of all equipment manufactured by the company's ventures in China." Motorola has said that it "expects to spend $1 billion annually [in China] on locally sourced products at the start of the millennium."[6] That is $1 billion worth of business that will not go to U.S.-based facilities and their workers—quite possibly for reasons having nothing to do with free trade or free markets.[7]

So the issue is not whether big U.S. exporters use smaller American companies and their workforces as suppliers. Of course they do. Nor is the issue that big U.S. exporters use foreign suppliers. Of course they do, and if the decision reflects free market conditions and standard business considerations, no one can rightly complain. The issues are what the trends are and why they are unfolding.

If the big exporters' representative really wanted to be informative regarding China trade's impact on small companies, he would have told the audience how the number of U.S.-based suppliers used by corporate giants like Motorola for export products has changed in the last decade or so. He would have told them how the number of Chinese suppliers they use has changed. He would have identified how the mix of products provided by the American and Chinese suppliers has changed. The corporate representative also would have discussed whether the Motorolas of the world use Chinese suppliers because they're the world's best companies with the world's most productive workers—or because in China they do not have to deal with independent unions and worker safety regulations and high wages and all the costs of doing business in countries like the United States. Finally, he would have disclosed whether Chinese suppliers are being used because Beijing has demanded this.

I asked the corporate representative this question and never got a straight answer. At every opportunity since, I have urged public officials and their staffs and ordinary citizens to ask these questions whenever they encounter a lobbyist or executive from a big U.S. company. I even still advise journalists to explore these questions, despite my experiences with the *NewsHour* and *The Washington Post.* Some of them actually have responded with impressive efforts, as the chapters ahead make clear, but not enough.

Fast forward to early 1999. The cluster of issues including NAFTA and China trade had inspired a new catch phrase—globalization. The momentum had swung over to the critics, who had halted in their tracks nearly all of the trade policy initiatives of the Clinton administration and its allies in Congress, big business, and the academic world. So supporters of these policies began striking back—redoubling their efforts to show that the trade agreements they sought were indeed enriching most Americans.

On February 4, 1999, the Cato Institute, a free-market-oriented think tank and strong supporter of traditional U.S. trade policies,

hosted a seminar with W. Michael Cox and Richard C. Alm, authors of a recent book challenging the view that any significant
number of Americans had become worse off economically in recent decades.[8] I had already finished the first draft of this book and
had not yet read theirs, so I went to the seminar hoping to learn
about the bases of their findings.

Cox, a vice president of the Federal Reserve Bank of Dallas, and
Alm, a reporter, focused on the lowest-income Americans in their
talk. The conventional wisdom about the poor, they insisted, is
completely wrong. Far from being the greatest victims of globalization and technological change, these Americans were major
beneficiaries. How did Cox and Alm know this? Even though they
were earning less and less, the statistics showed that these Americans were consuming more than ever—and more than they were
earning. Clearly, Cox and Alm concluded, the earnings data were
meaningless, and it was obvious to them that the impact of globalization and technological change on the poor had been misjudged
as well.

I was surprised to hear the two speakers identify consumption
as the most important measure of prosperity—rather than earnings or income. Did that mean that people could become rich by
maxing out their credit cards no matter how much they took in? I
was even more surprised to hear them suggest that the surprising
consumption levels of poor Americans vindicated free trade and
free market economics in general. To me, the real explanation was
obvious. More important, it should have been obvious to Cox and
Alm and nearly everyone else in the audience at a research institute highly critical of government intervention in the economy.

I asked Cox and Alm during the question-and-answer session:
Were the poor able to consume far more than they earned because
of the various forms of welfare they received? Of course, they
could buy more appliances and more leisure and live in nicer
homes than the poor of previous generations. Government at various levels, I pointed out, provided for all or much of their health
care, education, legal expenses, food, and housing— to mention
just a few items. I could not resist adding, "The organization hosting this event keeps telling us that these welfare programs and
their effects should be criticized, not praised."

Cox and Alm muttered something in response to the effect that
these kinds of government payments and programs are not the
most efficient way to help the poor. But that, of course, was not the

point. Most revealing to me was that analysts such as Cox and Alm are so determined to trumpet the virtues of current trade policies that they readily abandoned other deep policy convictions to make their case. Trade zealotry, in other words, was powerful enough to turn free market champions into cheerleaders for welfare.

These incidents and many others led me to three main conclusions. First, too many participants in our intensifying national discussion of trade and other international economic issues are unforgivably sloppy at best and possibly dishonest at worst. Second, although the public should be able to depend on the media for accurate information on these issues, as well as balanced assessments, too often they cannot. Too many journalists are ideologically hostile to critical views of current U.S. policies toward the world economy; others are simply too lazy to investigate economics and business very thoroughly. Third, as a result, the citizenry that is beginning to challenge the conventional wisdom on globalization urgently needs a guide to the policy wars it has sparked.

Americans need a guide to what is important and relevant and what is purely a distraction. They need a guide to whose work is generally trustworthy and who has a lot to answer for. (You really cannot tell the experts without a scorecard.) Most of all, they need to know that the seemingly super-difficult theories and concepts flung around by the politicians, the pundits, and the celebrity professors are not so hard to understand after all. This book is an attempt to meet these needs. It seeks to provide the public with a readable primer on the evidence of how U.S. globalization policies have affected the American people, on the noisy and usually confusing debate of these effects, and on the equally confusing welter of proposals for new U.S. approaches to globalization or for keeping the old approaches on course.

Not that I do not have my own point of view. More than a decade of studying these issues, as is no doubt already clear, has convinced me that current U.S. globalization policies have helped to make the vast bulk of Americans poorer, not richer for more than three decades. Because my main concern is globalization's effects on the U.S. economy and America's workers—not the world economy or the world's workers as a whole—I devote little attention to non-American voices in the international economic policy debate. This is not to suggest that developments abroad do not bear heavily on the U.S. economy. Indeed, the following chapters explore these effects in great detail. It is to hint at an argument made at greater length in the final chapter—that the United States is uniquely positioned in the world economy to control these effects and to control them in a way that benefits most of the American people. As a result, the ability of the United States to cope successfully with globalization will and should depend mainly on American policy—on decisions made by the American political system. Clearly, there is much that we can and should learn from the rest of the world. Yet because no one else will ever be as devoted to America's well-being as Americans themselves, American opinions need to be considered first. I make the additional argument, however, that in the long run, what is good for the U.S. economy will be good for the world economy as well.

This brings me to my final prefatory point. When debating globalization issues, I have developed the habit of responding to opponents who begin statements with words like "I think ..." with the admittedly provocative rejoinder, "It does not matter what you think. It matters what we know and can find out." In fact, I had become so sick and tired of theories and opinions and proposals detached from any observable reality that I sometimes told myself that it did not really matter what I thought, either. So when I began writing the book, I even toyed with the idea of not including a chapter with my own policy recommendations. My reasoning was that this would be the best way to keep the focus on the information I have discovered, not on my personal twelve-step program for saving the world.

Of course, everyone I mentioned this idea to told me that it was completely ridiculous and a shameless cop-out. So like nearly all public policy books, this one ends with policy recommendations. Do not get me wrong; I think they are extremely useful—even brilliant. Obviously, I hope that the next president and other policymakers will take them seriously. However, if readers who finish this book focus less on the rudimentary Tonelson plan than on the sheer amount of evidence presented indicating how much is wrong with our current globalization policies, I would gladly forgive them.

Alan Tonelson

ACKNOWLEDGMENTS

Works as research-intensive as the volume you are holding are rarely produced in splendid isolation, and I have benefited greatly from the expertise and hard work of many others.

First, and foremost are my colleagues at the U.S. Business and Industry Council, and its Educational Foundation. This book would not have been possible without the wise counsel, administrative skills, and faithful friendship of Kevin L. Kearns, president of both organizations. Along with Kevin, William R. Hawkins, Laura Walton Crouch, and Bonnie Moran not only provided a congenial working environment, but gave me much information, editorial and production assistance, and common-sense advice. I am also deeply grateful to the many members of the Council and contributors to the Foundation for their backing and their confidence in my work. Special thanks go to Roger Milliken, who has done so much to ensure that iconoclastic voices can be heard in our national economic policy debates.

This book began as a project undertaken with Thea Lee, then of the Economic Policy Institute and now with the Public Policy Department of the AFL-CIO. Her new responsibilities prevented her from continuing with the project, but I have continued to profit from her insights even when we have disagreed.

A figure who also helped inspire this project was the late Herman Starobin of the International Ladies Garment Workers' Union (which has since merged into the Union of Needle Trades, Industrial and Textile Employees). Everyone genuinely seeking to understand the global economy owes a major debt to Herman and to his dogged, pioneering efforts to expose myths about U.S. trade flows propagated by Washington, Big Business, and too many professional economists.

Numerous scholars at the Economic Policy Institute—especially Robert Scott, Jared Bernstein, Lawrence Mishel, and John Schmitt—have been extremely generous with their time in providing data as well as explanations and interpretations of major economic trends. Others who have patiently tutored me on the broad and fine points of trade and economics include David B. H. Denoon, Kathi Dutilh, R. Taggart Murphy, Jock Nash, Andrew Szamosszegi, and Charles W. Wessner.

Brad Botwin, Jaron Bourke, Tiffany Butler, Melissa Corcoran, Bill Frymoyer, and Doug Fuller helped me access information not available—at least not in timely form—to most researchers.

The U.S. Business and Industry Council and Educational Foundation also provided four excellent research assistants during my work on this project: Vanessa Fuhrmans, Elizabeth Lizut, Stephan Mercier, and Shay Gray, who set up my electronic filing system.

Many USBIC interns assisted me as well, especially Christopher Cahlamer, Darlena Stark, Kim Gabriel, Nicole Binkert, Bonita Wong, Katie Church, Lindsay Hall, Jocelyn Hall, and Lauren Ellis. Three other research assistants deserve special thanks—the Internet and Worldwide Web (without which this book never could have been written as quickly as it was), and my mother, Florence Tonelson, whose on-line skills turned up numerous sources of data.

John W. Wright not only did an excellent job of marketing the finished manuscript, but provided much expert advice on setting editorial priorities and articulating major themes. I greatly appreciate Robert Dallek's willingness to introduce me to this outstanding literary agent.

I am grateful, too, for the faith shown by Leo Wiegman of Westview Press in a first-time author, and to the copy editing and production team at TSI Graphics—notably Donna Cullen-Dulce and Reid Paul—for their meticulousness and professionalism.

Needless to say, I take full responsibility for any errors of fact or interpretation in this volume.

My greatest debts, of course, are owed to my parents, Emanuel and Florence Tonelson, and to my brother, Steven, who have given me everything worth having and asked for nothing in return save for my health and happiness. This book is dedicated to them.

1 INTRODUCTION—A TALE OF TWO CITIES

WAY BACK IN THE MID-1990S, NO TWO CITIES SYMBOLIZED THE new global economy and its promises of progress and prosperity like Seattle, Washington, and Bangkok, Thailand.

Hugging the picturesque Puget Sound and looking out at the teeming air and sea routes of the Pacific, Seattle seemed practically cast by Hollywood to provide both the software that runs most of the world's computers and the jetliners that help link its peoples and markets. Better yet, the broad appeal of the city's coffee bars, music, and affluently bohemian ethos, combining latte-tinged self-absorption with a social conscience, suggested that globalization could not only be wildly lucrative but hip and even progressive.

Bangkok, for its part, typified the most spectacular and encouraging success story of the burgeoning economic and information flows comprising globalization—the booming third world metropolis. Barely twenty years ago, Bangkok was best known to Americans as the capital of Anna's tradition-bound King of Siam—or possibly as the home of an almost unimaginably lurid sex industry. By the 1980s, Bangkok was the center of an archetypical "tiger" economy, whose mushrooming automotive and computer parts factories produced so much growth and so much wealth so rapidly that the city's streets became choked with legendary traffic jams.

Today, both cities still symbolize the new global economy, but in very different ways. Now they represent the shortcomings and dangers of this economy.

Just after Thanksgiving 1999, trade ministers from some 130 countries gathered in Seattle to try to break the logjams blocking the launch of a new set of negotiations to free up global trade even

1

further. The talks were organized by the World Trade Organization (WTO), a new international body set up by these national governments to help develop new rules for global commerce and resolve the disputes that heated international economic competition frequently produces.

The ministers attending the meeting and the U.S. officials and American corporate leaders who hosted them were no doubt expecting business-as-usual in the world of trade diplomacy—hardnosed but businesslike bargaining conducted behind closed doors, routine press coverage, and broad public disinterest.

What they got instead were the biggest, messiest street protests in America since anti-Vietnam War demonstrators rocked the 1968 Democratic convention in Chicago. Tens of thousands of protestors converged on Seattle, representing an astonishing variety of citizens' activist groups, including labor unions, environmental organizations, religious groups, and consumer lobbies. Joining them were small but often violent packs of anarchists. Thanks in part to a poorly prepared local police department, the result was four days of not only mass marches, rallies, teach-ins, and guerilla theater, but vandalism, civil disobedience, tear gas, and arrests.

The "battle in Seattle"—as President Clinton called it[1]—left national leaders, economic policymakers, and businessmen around the world in a state of shock. They had all brought ambitious agendas to the World Trade Organization meeting, reflecting the daunting obstacles still blocking their goal of a world where goods, services, money, and technology would be generally free to cross the globe in search of the lowest costs, the loosest regulations, the highest profits, and the loftiest returns on investment. High barriers still impeded trade in agriculture and in many service industries—like finance. Third world countries were pressing for more influence over the economic rule-writing process, and China, with its huge potential market, strange hybrid capitalist-communist economic system and deep-rooted protectionist ways, was knocking on the door, seeking entry into the WTO. Nonetheless, the Seattle negotiators and their supporters expected further progress on most of these fronts.

After Seattle, the global economy's powers-that-be were at a loss on how to proceed. The U.S. government faced especially big challenges. Domestically, globalization cheerleaders and critics disagreed sharply over how to cope with the relationship between protecting workers' rights and the environment on the one hand,

and promoting trade on the other. Should future trade agreements contain enforceable labor and environmental provisions, as most of the Seattle protestors demanded? Or as desirable as these objectives were, should they be dealt with in other arenas? Until this dispute was somehow settled, major progress seemed unlikely on globalization issues ranging from China to Latin America to new worldwide investment rules.

The Seattle protests also vividly showed the cheerleaders just how unpopular their policies were with the American public. Although many media commentators tried to dismiss the demonstrators as a small, unrepresentative coalition of lazy, selfish blue-collar workers, environmental extremists, and other chronic malcontents, many elected leaders and numerous business spokespeople recognized that the opposition was wider and deeper. Supporting this view were five years of consistent poll results showing vigorously growing public unhappiness with the trade and other globalization policies (like wide-open immigration) being pursued by Washington for so long.[2]

Internationally, WTO boosters faced an equally knotty dilemma. Most of the organization's third world members—or at least their governments—opposed including any labor rights and environmental protections in trade agreements. They viewed low wages and lax pollution control laws as major assets they could offer to international investors—prime lures for job-creating factories and the capital they so desperately needed for other development-related purposes. Indeed, they observed, most rich countries ignored the environment and limited workers' power (to put it kindly) early in their economic histories. Why should today's developing countries be held to higher standards? And would reaching these higher standards drive investors to put their resources in other locations that were more familiar and in many ways easier to operate in—like back home, in the developed economies of North America and Europe? So if Washington agreed to domestic critics' demands for new types of trade agreements, third world governments would be deeply antagonized, and third world governments made up the majority of WTO members.

Furthermore, at Seattle, these third world governments made clear their view that the WTO and current trade liberalization strategies had given them a raw deal. They complained about being forced to open domestic markets too quickly to imports—before their own industries could get off the ground. They observed

that the new trade talks being pushed by America focused on economic sectors where free trade would mainly benefit the United
States, such as agriculture and finance. Because of the WTO's egal-
itarian setup (unlike the United Nations, for example, where big
powers have veto rights), achieving U.S. goals would require
progress on at least some of these concerns.

Seattle may have given globalization a big public relations black
eye, but Bangkok became its victim. In June 1997, Thailand faced a
massive financial crisis. The investors who underwrote its factories, its gleaming new skyscrapers, and its glitzy Western-style
shopping malls suddenly began losing faith in the country's ability to repay them. Global financiers, meanwhile, sensing this eroding confidence, quickly began exchanging their holdings of Thailand's currency—the baht—for safer money, like U.S. dollars or
Japanese yen.

Currency nowadays is like any other commodity that is bought
and sold. When holders sell it, all else being equal (as economists
love to say), the supply increases and each unit of the currency
falls in value. When investors smell enough blood, the type of relatively limited, orderly currency trading that takes place every
day around the world can turn into a genuine panic. Since no one
wanted to be left holding the last (particularly worthless) baht,
powerful incentives built to cut losses by selling off as quickly as
possible. Just as bad, local banks and businesses that had to repay
loans they might have received in foreign currencies found that
whatever assets they held in baht were dropping rapidly in value,
too. And as their ability to repay or service their debts shrank, the
loss of confidence in the currency and country as a whole accelerated in a classic vicious cycle.

At first Thai officials thought they could defend their currency
on their own. Mainly they thought they had in their treasury large
enough holdings of foreign currencies to slow the baht's fall and
even stabilize it. Governments and national central banks (like
America's Federal Reserve and the Bank of England) can do this
by using their foreign exchange holdings to buy up their national
currency. If they could soak up enough of the worldwide supply
of baht, the Thais understandably reasoned, they could prop up its
value and even convince the most aggressive private speculators
that Thailand possessed enough foreign currency holdings to frus-
trate any short selling they might be capable of.

The Thai strategy ran into one fatal problem. The governor of
the central bank had been lying to the prime minister about Thai-

land's foreign currency holdings. Specifically, he had greatly exaggerated them. The Thai government, it turned out, had many fewer defensive weapons than it was counting on. At that point, the government realized it had lost the currency battle. Thailand had no choice but to let the baht "float"—to let the global currency market find a new natural value for it. Of course, at first this announcement greatly sped up private investors' flight to the baht exit doors, as everyone expected the markets to decide on a dramatically lower value for the currency.

Meanwhile, the governments of many of Thailand's neighbors and major trading partners started to grow genuinely alarmed. If the global markets' "run" on the baht continued, Thailand's economy might take a tremendous long-term hit—so tremendous that its huge borrowings from these countries' banks and other creditors might never be repaid. If major banks in East Asia and elsewhere could not count on repayments or at least debt servicing from Thailand, their own ability to repay some of their own borrowings from other creditors would be endangered. Indeed, some countries' banks had lent enough to Thailand—in other words, they were so leveraged—that Thailand's collapse could seriously damage their entire national economy.

As a result, these countries decided to throw Thailand a lifeline, in the form of a $16 billion loan. The loan was administered by an international agency called the International Monetary Fund, but it was no ordinary loan. It came with conditions—mainly that Thailand put in place reforms to enable it to start repaying its debts and to ensure that it never ran into this kind of trouble again.

Unfortunately, some of these conditions seemed to cause more problems than they solved. All of them combined seemed to doom Thailand to years of either recessionary conditions or sluggish growth. In order to repay its debts, the country had to go on an economic crash diet. Thailand had borrowed and spent too much; now its people would have to tighten their belts and use most of whatever new wealth they could generate not on the necessities of life but on paying off the nation's creditors.

Clearly, some kind of austerity was in order for Thailand. Unless it could reestablish its creditworthiness by strengthening its international balance sheet, it would never (or at least, not for many years) regain its access to foreign capital, and its dreams of becoming a modern, truly industrialized country would be put on hold. Nonetheless, the short-term impact was devastating—especially for a country that had become accustomed to record-setting progress. Thailand's economy shrank by 1.8 percent in 1997, and a whopping 10 percent in 1998, before rebounding by an estimated 3–4 percent in 1999. Real wages stagnated. Unemployment soared (although the official 1998 peak of 4 percent was, of course, low by global standards). Many Thais left the cities—like Bangkok—they had recently flooded into for the best jobs and greatest economic opportunities and went back to the farm.[3]

As Thailand's financial crisis helped touch off similar crises throughout the region, Bangkok became a monument to Asian hubris and folly. Office towers stood unfinished or largely vacant. Once thriving banks were shuttered. The shopping malls became miniature ghost towns. Even the city's traffic moderated. As the twenty-first century dawned, Bangkok, the rest of Thailand, and much of the rest of East Asia, were still digging out.

Seattle and Bangkok, however, symbolized more than just the new global economy's perils. They also symbolized how little our leaders in the public and private sectors (as well as citizens) actually know about this system, and when it comes to the leaders, the two cities symbolized how little they seemed to want to know.

This ignorance, whether willful or not, could not be more dangerous for America's future, or for the world's future. In his 2000 State of the Union Address—the last of his presidency—Bill Clinton called globalization "the central reality of our time."[4] He was right. Some of the signs are clear to everyone—the investments millions of us put into (and take out of) foreign stocks and bonds; the millions of us who work for foreign-owned companies, or companies that export or import or facilitate trade; the millions who have been displaced (temporarily or permanently) by foreign competition; and the low-cost, high-quality foreign-made goods we all see in our stores.

However, some of the signs are harder to see. For example, education recently has become such a hot-button political issue largely because American parents fear that public schools are not preparing their children well enough for the new global economy. The U.S. government has relaxed antitrust enforcement largely because U.S. companies claim they need to be big enough to compete against the giant conglomerates fostered for so long in Europe and Asia. Similar reasoning lay behind the major overhaul of Depression-era banking laws in 1999. Perhaps most important, over the long run, the international financial position of the United States— its status as either a net worldwide lender or borrower—greatly influences interest rates.

As will be seen, however, the U.S. government is rushing into the new global economy knowing too little about that system and the nations and business cultures comprising it; understanding too little about the effects of swirling, swelling global flows of goods and services and investment and knowledge; and hiding too much about what is known about globalization from the American people—specifically, about how many jobs multinational corporations have transferred from America to overseas factories, what kinds of products are made abroad, where they are sold, and what the workers in these plants are paid.

Those outside government—chiefly in academia and journalism—who discuss and debate the new global economy bear considerable blame for obscuring the effects of globalization as well. Their misdeeds go far beyond the dissembling and distortions that mark so much of our policy debates in general—though there is plenty of that. They also often demonstrate a remarkable lack of curiosity about their subject. They just as often prefer to spin out and manipulate theories rather than dig out and analyze facts. They turn logical and rhetorical cartwheels to defend ideologies that clash with reality. And they even make different arguments to different audiences.

One result of this often willful ignorance was the battle in Seattle—and the resulting astonishment expressed by the global economy powers-that-be. The Clinton administration and the World Trade Organization, as well as the corporate interests who actually paid for much of the meeting, clearly thought that in this high-tech Pacific port they had found the perfect site for a watershed event in global trade diplomacy.

However, at planning sessions for the protests that I attended starting in the spring of 1999, the main organizers could barely contain their glee that the WTO crowd had chosen a major U.S. city. The event was bound to attract mass coverage from the world's greatest national concentration of news media. The media factor was vital, because the critics understood something about the domestic politics of globalization that the WTO crowd had completely missed—that despite the so-called Goldilocks American Economy, the prevailing U.S. approach to globalization was deeply unpopular with the American people. As previously discussed, whether because they felt more economically pressed than the economic headlines suggested or because they disliked certain features of current globalization policies (e.g., the alleged neglect of human rights and environmental protection, the inevitable

weakening of American national sovereignty), the public's unhappiness with today's globalization policies had been growing for
more than five years, since Mexico's economy imploded right after
the controversial North American Free Trade Agreement went into
effect. Although the protestors were hardly a cross section of the
public, poll after poll showed that they spoke for most Americans
on international economic issues.

Bangkok had come to stand for another dimension of this widespread ignorance about globalization—the utterly misleading picture of rapidly developing third world countries painted by most
supporters of the globalization status quo. U.S. policy toward
globalization took a significant turn around 1990. Political leaders,
industrialists, and financiers began focusing many of their policy
initiatives and business planning on the developing world. Although U.S. trade and investment with the wealthy industrialized
countries still represented the vast bulk of America's global commerce, the globalization crowd observed that business with the
developing countries was steadily catching up. Indeed, Japan's
continuing refusal to import goods or capital, Europe's growth-
choking monetary policies and red tape, and the last American recession on the one hand, and the impressive economic advances
being made in Mexico to China, on the other, all helped create a
new conventional wisdom—that most of the world's best future-
growth opportunities were in developing countries.

Consequently, the highest profile U.S. trade policy efforts involved bringing Mexico into America's new Free Trade Agreement
with Canada and expanding trade with China. The Clinton administration greatly encouraged this shift in focus. The President
himself stated in 1995 that the United States:

> has hard limits on its growth; we have a mature economy and slow
> population growth. We have four percent of the world's population. To
> grow and prosper at home we must open the most lucrative markets
> in the rest of the world to U.S. exports—both in our historic trading
> partners in Europe and Japan, as well as the dynamic emerging
> countries in Asia and Latin America.[5]

Not surprisingly, his Commerce Department launched a major
campaign to intensify public and business interest in 10 third
world countries officially designated as Big Emerging Markets.[6]
The American financial community seemed to have already gotten

the message. Wall Street was reaping in emerging market stock holdings and other investments, and awarding solid credit ratings awarded to many developing economies.

So money from the industrialized countries and their savvy, no-nonsense financiers kept flooding into countries like Thailand—until it stopped in the middle of 1997. Within days, the conventional wisdom did an about-face. Emerging markets such as Thailand—and Indonesia and South Korea and Brazil and Russia—were not El Dorados in the making after all. They were hype. Their governments were not models of Confucian bureaucratic efficiency and their leaders' Ivy League economic degrees proved nothing about their honesty. Rather, these countries were sinkholes of crony capitalism. Their new factories and office towers and shopping malls were not can't-miss cash cows but white elephants, built not by strategic thinkers following rigorously engineered plans for national economic development but by crooked politicians extending favors to friends and family.

Worse, as the embarrassed and infuriated globalization cheerleaders suddenly pointed out, the emerging market countries lacked even something so basic as legal and regulatory systems that businesspeople could rely on for swift, speedy justice. Nor were these systems the slightest bit "transparent," a fancy way of saying that outsiders had no way of knowing why decisions were made, or even what these decisions were.

Countless investment professionals had made billions of dollars in the 1980s and early 1990s channeling vast sums into developing countries, and numerous scholars and political leaders had made sterling reputations by endorsing and encouraging such investments. However, as made clear by the Asian financial crisis, these experts were not describing emerging markets as they were, but as they wished them to be.

Perhaps the most important symbolic message carried by the battle in Seattle and the Bangkok meltdown is that today's globalization policies are driving both the American economy and the world economy toward a frightening crack-up. To be sure, expressing any serious economic concerns about the United States at this turn of the millennium can seem eccentric at best in the face of nearly hourly headlines about national economic success. However, breadth and depth of American popular opposition to this new global economy revealed at Seattle—despite all the signs of good times—could not have come out of nowhere. In fact, they in-

dicate that there is considerably less to this current American expansion than meets the eye. Most obviously, the protests and their
resonance point to a prosperity that is concentrated too exclusively
among the very wealthiest Americans, and to mounting economic
strains on a middle class whose vitality is essential to our nation's
broader success as a healthy democracy. Less obviously, the fallout
from Seattle highlights how much of the current expansion rests
on breakneck borrowing and spending, rather than rising real incomes and robust savings. As a result, it indicates not only that
this prosperity cannot last, but that it has already powerfully undermined our nation's economic future.

The Bangkok meltdown shows the wider global economy to be
on equally shaky ground. For nowadays, most of the world's
growth is based on the unsustainable growth of the United States.
Two fundamental problems are at work. First, since the Asian crisis first hit in mid-1997, the only major trading region to achieve
strong, consistent growth has been the United States. Japan has
been in recession for most of the 1990s, and European Union's performance has been sluggish for most of the past two decades. Second, as will be seen, even when the rest of the world has been
growing strongly, few countries are as open to imports as the
United States. Indeed, on every continent, countries large and
small are determined to grow mainly by exporting, not by stimulating demand at home.

Consequently, the United States has been the world's importer of
last resort. The good news is that the American economy still has so
much built-in strength and has been such a good place to do business that it has been able to play this role so far without apparent
cost. Because of America's vigorous growth, and because the dollar
plays a special role in the international economy, foreigners have
been willing to finance the nation's imports and consumption. The
bad news is that America's trade and investment deficits with the
rest of the world (i.e., the amounts by which it is spending more
than it is producing and borrowing more than it is lending) are
growing so fast that they threaten to place the United States in the
position of Thailand in 1997. That is to say, America's debts to the
rest of the world may soon become large enough that its creditors
could start wondering about the nation's ability to repay.

Should foreigners lose faith in America's creditworthiness, they
may start dumping dollars the way they dumped Thai baht. In
that case, the American consumer would face significant belt-

tightening to enable the country to start paying the debt down. Alternatively, the Federal Reserve could raise interest rates very high. This step would aim at persuading foreigners to keep up their lending by offering them higher rates of return on their loans, but it would also slow down the domestic economy by making the cost of money much more expensive for businesses and consumers. It would also add greatly to the total debt that would have to be repaid.

If the story stopped here, the problem would be relatively manageable. However, any significant reduction in American growth would reduce American imports, too. Obviously, other major economic powers like Japan and Europe could compensate by either jump-starting their own economic growth or lowering their trade barriers—or both. These steps would not only help America repay its debts through higher exports, but relieve America of the burden of importing so much of the third world's output—and help prevent these export-dependent economies from collapsing.

Japan, however, has tried just about everything except opening itself up to trade, and its gigantic economy is still stuck in neutral. Slow-growing economies like this, moreover, generally do not like to welcome imports even if they are naturally inclined to do so. After all, when mired in recession, they are already by definition having a hard enough time preserving business for their companies and good jobs for their own people. Europe is more open to foreign trade, but European economies have long been hamstrung by too much regulation (although this is starting to change) and a deep-rooted fear on Germany's part that any efforts to boost growth too easily lead to inflation—and a repeat of that nation's economic nightmare during the 1920s and 1930s.

A significant U.S. slowdown, therefore, would most likely leave the Japanese and Europeans (plus the Chinese and the rest of Asia and Latin America) with ever greater stockpiles of goods that no one could or would buy. These products would either languish on the shelf, or global price wars would break out, with each country trying to undercut the other in a frantic attempt to trim losses. Nations would either offer their goods for sale for much less than their production costs, or they would devalue their currencies, making them cheaper relative to other currencies. Thus their goods would automatically sell for less in foreign markets, and foreign goods would automatically become more expensive in their market.

History never repeats itself exactly, but it is scary (as well as useful) to remember that a sequence of events something like this helped make the Great Depression of the 1930s truly great. Political leaders and policymakers these days all over the world vividly recall this catastrophe, and since the end of World War II, they have created many international institutions and mechanisms for preventing a recurrence. However, none of the remedies they have been suggesting lately has any real promise of success. In fact, many so-called remedies—for example, helping the Asians back on their feet by promoting more of their exports (without making sure that they can sell someplace other than the United States)—can only hasten the day of reckoning. The only genuine solution involves balancing global growth patterns and global trade flows much, much better.

Supporters of current globalization policies, therefore, have amassed a record of whopping mistakes and wildly off-base predictions. They, too, fear that a global financial train wreck lies ahead. And they have clearly been losing political momentum since well before Seattle. As shown by their success in winning permanently lowered tariffs for China, however, these forces still control the main levers of economic power in U.S. politics. Much of their strength derives from the confidence they retain in their policy positions, and the compelling story they tell on media stages that they still dominate.

In fact, the globalization crowd literally claims a monopoly on economic wisdom. Its leading lights insist that everything known about economics demands ever faster progress in continuing to free up international commerce. The widely published Massachusetts Institute of Technology (MIT) economist (and recently annointed columnist for *The New York Times*) Paul Krugman speaks for many when he dismisses opponents as "entirely ignorant men" who are "startlingly crude and ill informed."[7] The globalizers further contend that six decades of such policies (the United States' first modern-style trade agreements were negotiated in the 1930s) deserve credit for much of the record prosperity enjoyed by most of the world since the end of World War II. In particular, they claim, lowering or breaking down barriers to international commerce has reenforced progress in transportation and communications that in and of themselves have been rapidly integrating the global economy. As long as these policies remain in effect, globalization optimists predict, they will continue to enable productive new technologies and new ideas to spread ever faster around the world and leave greater efficiency and higher living standards in their wake.

Even better, pressing further ahead with these policies will eventually benefit those currently hurt by globalization—by spurring the additional growth needed to provide them either with decent-paying jobs or with better social safety nets. The globalizers split on questions of whether economic inequality is growing in the U.S. and, if so, whether anything should be done about it. However, all agree that U.S. globalization policies are all but blameless, and that interfering with international economic flows would leave everyone everywhere in the world worse off in the long run.

Underlying the globalizers' case is a bedrock confidence that the U.S. economy, the new global economy, and their interactions are firmly governed by fundamental laws and principles known to scholars literally for centuries. These laws and principles comfortingly tell us exactly how freer global commerce will keep enabling workers everywhere to enrich themselves and enrich others—by pushing them into ever more challenging and lucrative jobs and thus turning them into avid consumers. All these workers need to do is to maintain cutting-edge knowledge and skills and elect governments that get their economic policies right—including money supply, budget balances, taxes, and regulations as well as globalization. Best of all, from an American standpoint, because most U.S. workers currently possess superior knowledge and skills and because the country's budget situation has recently been put in order, they are not only already profiting from the surging tides of global commerce but should be able to keep their edge.

However, for all the intellectual tradition and professional authority underlying this picture of the global economy and the United States' position in it, the globalizers get several vital pieces wrong and completely miss many others. As will be shown, mountains of empirical evidence that the globalizers inexplicably overlook or downplay reveal a much more widespread deterioration in U.S. living standards than the globalizers acknowledge. In addition, the evidence pins substantial responsibility on recent globalization policies. It sheds considerable light on the many and varied ways in which worldwide economic flows have worsened the quality of jobs available to U.S. workers and makes clear why remedies at the international level, not more talk about sending these workers back to school, are essential.

Just as much evidence shows why the globalizers' hopes for correcting dangerous international economic imbalances are in vain. In particular, it reveals the futility of expecting that third world populations will amass enough purchasing power soon enough and that their governments will give them enough freedom to import to sop up their share of world output, create sustainable global trade flows, and thereby enable U.S. workers to earn their way in the world again.

Much of this information comes from the U.S. government, foreign governments, and international organizations such as the World Bank. Additional hard information comes from academic research that has remained undeservedly obscure and from journalistic accounts so numerous that they cannot be dismissed as anecdotes. These data tell a story about where and why economic resources and know-how are moving around the world. They document how many of the industries that are the world's leading creators of high-paying jobs have long been leaving the United States. Just as important, they explain why this is likely to continue.

Admittedly, some of these data are suspect, especially concerning trends in developing countries. There, many governments lack ways to gather reliable economic information, and literally hundreds of millions of people live and work beyond the effective reach of any political authority. Some of the latest available information about globalization, moreover, is already considerably out-of-date. In addition, much of the most revealing information about globalization's course, impact, and probable future is locked away in the records of the world's multinational corporations. U.S.-owned multinationals have dissuaded the U.S. government from seeking much of the data and from releasing much of the information that Washington does possess. They emphasize that opening their books could reveal valuable business secrets to competitors. They also undoubtedly appreciate the public relations disaster that releasing their job-exporting activity would create.

The bottom line: A powerful case can now be made that, far from enriching most U.S. citizens and citizens of other countries, the combination of technological advance and current globalization policies is now exerting downward pressure on living standards. More specifically, governments and workers all over the world have been forced into a competition for productive investment that is most often won by scrapping or forswearing most of the laws and regulations that complicate business operations and lower short-term profits, but that also ensure that living wages are paid, that workplaces are safe, and that pollution is controlled. In other words, current globalization policies have plunged the great majority of U.S. workers into a great worldwide race to the bottom, into a no-win scramble for work and livelihoods with hundreds of millions of their already impoverished counterparts across the globe.

In addition, by sapping the earnings power of U.S. consumers, who are almost single-handedly propping up the world economy despite their sagging earnings, continuing this race could all too easily bring the global financial house of cards tumbling down.

The globalizers' problems start with setting the stage inaccurately. Most have failed to take into account the myriad channels through which the new international economy influences living standards around the world. By too often restricting their investigations to the impact of trade in goods and services, they leave mostly unexamined the effects of worldwide capital flows (which recently have been growing much faster than trade flows), as well as the effects of increasing legal and illegal immigration and accelerated worldwide transfers of technology. Globalizers also seem unaware that stagnant or falling wages and benefits have befallen the vast majority of U.S. workers—including the college-educated as well as highly skilled production workers—not simply the so-called dregs of our labor force.

The case for linking these developments centers on four features of the emerging world economy that have assumed decisive importance in roughly the past two decades. The first is the sudden entry into the global economy of countries like China and India. These giants not only contain vast, growing, often highly productive workforces whose wages are the barest fractions of those in the industrialized countries, they also suffer towering rates of unemployment and underemployment. The rapid but rocky integration of such developing regions into the modern capitalist world defines much of what the terms "global economy" and "globalization" mean nowadays.

U.S. globalization optimists apparently believe that labor markets are immune to the laws of supply and demand. Nonetheless, with workers far more abundant than job openings, employers around the world not surprisingly have enjoyed a buyer's market. Combined with the many and varied ways in which developing countries suppress domestic consumption and strive to grow by exporting, their vast labor surpluses mock the expectation that their populations will become major final customers for American goods in the foreseeable future.

These global labor surpluses undermine American wages in two principal ways. First, the bleak economic prospects of many emerging market workers have led millions to emigrate to their more prosperous third world neighbors or to industrialized countries like the United States. In the latter case, by artificially increasing the U.S. labor supply, these movements give U.S. employers the same options as their foreign counterparts of restraining wages—and not only for the unskilled and uneducated.

Second, the worldwide reach of U.S. multinational corporations also greatly expands the pool of workers potentially available to U.S. business. These companies perform much of their production abroad, either through affiliates they own in whole or in part, or through independent foreign subcontractors. As a result, many have foreign workforces that have long been significant percentages of their domestic workforces. In addition, multinationals can easily choose among either U.S. or foreign subcontractors in the numerous industries that supply them, thereby sending downward-wage pressure rippling far into the U.S. economy.

Multinational companies also figure prominently in the three other features of the new world economy that are eroding U.S. living standards. First, their operations have transformed the nature of much international trade—from exchanges of finished goods (like aircraft or television sets) between unrelated buyers and sellers, to shipments of parts and components of these finished goods among the assembly plants, factories, and other facilities of the same multinational company or its partners.

Many of the multinational production facilities that are now abroad, however, used to be located in the United States. As a result, although products shipped to these foreign facilities from their U.S. parents are counted as exports by official U.S. trade figures, they cannot possibly have the kinds of job-creating and wage-boosting effects in the United States that most Americans assume exports have. Quite the contrary: In many instances, these exports deserve to be associated with displaced U.S. jobs as surely as do imports that compete with American-made goods. In fact, this activity is not exporting at all in any meaningful sense; it is outsourcing. It is the supplying of the United States by factories that used to be in the United States. Worse, because the final market for much of this multinational production is the United States itself, such intrafirm exports tend to generate greater or more valuable flows of imports and contribute to that share of the enormous U.S. global trade deficit that is structural—immune to the policy tools that governments typically use to balance their international accounts, like slowing growth or devaluing their currencies.

Another reason for globalization's high net economic toll is that many of the jobs displaced by these imports and deficits clash with the stereotypes of U.S. "losers" from international trade. Not for decades have these casualties been limited to unskilled and uneducated workers. Once significant U.S. deficits opened with industrialized Europe and Japan in the 1960s and 1970s, the losers have increasingly included first workers in core manufacturing industries such as steel, autos, machine tools, and consumer electronics, and then workers in information industries such as computers, semiconductors, and telecommunications equipment. The resulting disappearance of high-paying manufacturing jobs has sparked ever greater competition for worse-paying service jobs—and thus further strengthened the buyers' market for quality American labor.

During the last 20 years, the flight of good jobs and the resulting fall in wages have been accelerated by two other globalization-related developments. The first has been the multinationals' determination to locate production facilities in a wide range of ever more advanced manufactures—including sophisticated information-technology goods— in low-income countries ranging from Mexico to the relatively small, rapidly developing economies along China's rim, like Malaysia, Thailand, and Singapore. These investments in low-income countries have also helped ambitious local governments and entrepreneurs to create impressive and growing high-tech production capabilities of their own, including a huge pool of world-class scientific and technological talent. Thus the United States' most skilled production workers and even many professionals are finding themselves competing for jobs not only with industrialized-country rivals who earn comparable wages— and who therefore can at least potentially consume U.S.-made products—but with foreign counterparts who earn orders of magnitude less and therefore cannot remotely balance their potent production with robust consumption.

The second multinational-related development has been the movement of many such factories and laboratories in turn to these countries' much larger neighbors with their even cheaper workforces and high unemployment rates—especially China itself, the Philippines, and, in the case of software development, India.

Finally, the spread of advanced technology, the mobility of corporate capital, and the abundance of inexpensive but highly skilled labor around the world means that the most popular U.S. strategy for reviving living standards—retraining and reeducating U.S. workers—is doomed to fail if unaccompanied by changes in globalization policy. Champions of the reeducation strategy, such as President Clinton and his former labor secretary, Robert Reich, argue that because the United States is an already developed country, its educated labor force is already one of its biggest competitive advantages in the new global economy. For decades, they argue, U.S. workers and their counterparts in other rich countries have been able to master rapid technological advances faster than workers in poorer, more backward countries, and ensure that they win the lion's share of the resulting high-paying jobs—both blue collar and white collar. U.S. workers can keep one step ahead of the foreign competition, they insist, by maintaining this educational edge. Achieving this goal, in turn, involves recognizing that technological change has become so rapid that a never-ending education and reeducation process is required to keep abreast.

For all their emphasis on change, however, the re-educators' view of U.S. international competition is surprisingly static. They grossly underestimate the knowledge and skill levels already attained by many workers in poor developing countries. Consequently, they also grossly underestimate the amount of high-tech production that has already moved to these countries. They ignore the fact that the industries that U.S. workers still dominate with their educational edge are too technology- or capital-intensive to be mass employers. And finally, they seem utterly unaware that governments and workers in low-income countries fully understand the need for continual, lifelong reeducation and retraining as well as they do. In more advanced developing countries like Malaysia and Singapore, they are already working frantically to move up the knowledge and skills ladder. Their main motivation—fear that they, too, will be priced out of ever-more sophisticated manufacturing industries by their gigantic neighbors and their equally gigantic and fast-learning workforces. With so much actual and potential labor worldwide flowing into industries with such relatively limited employment potential, most of today's high-wage jobs are already becoming lower-wage jobs, and this trend will continue whether U.S. workers go back to school or whether businesses offer them retraining or not.

2 | SOME BOOM

A. THREE QUARTERS OF A NATION

It is the greatest economy in U.S. history—and practically, by extension, in world history. Everybody says so—from President Clinton to all the newsreaders at CNBC to Republican politicians (who have had to ignore it so far in the 2000 presidential campaign) to Federal Reserve Board Chair Alan Greenspan (whose job it is to make sure that the economy doesn't get too good—i.e., inflation-prone). In addition, globalization enthusiasts point to it as proof positive that their policies are a slam-dunk success.

Yet the more closely one examines the current expansion—officially the longest our country has ever enjoyed—the stranger it looks. For example, the U.S. economy's growth rates during the 1990s were just at the average for all the decades of the twentieth century—no worse, but certainly no better. Nor by several critical measures has the U.S. economy outshone the economies of other major powers, either—at least not over a serious length of time. Although U.S. productivity growth has taken off in recent years after a two-decade slump—especially in manufacturing—productivity in Germany and Japan actually grew faster over the last ten years. Furthermore, although the U.S. economy remains by far the world's largest single national economy (representing about 28 percent of the world economy), when output is measured on a per-person basis, America's performance only matches Japan's and lags behind Germany's.[1]

Numerous features of the Goldilocks Economy, moreover, are far from being just right. After eight straight years of economic growth, 12.7 percent of Americans—34.5 million people—were still officially classified as living in poverty. The poverty rate for children was nearly 20 percent. More than 10 percent of U.S. households were considered "food insecure" in 1998, and half of the 26 million Americans who rely on food banks were two-parent working-class families. And despite the longest bull market in Wall Street's history, nearly half of all American families had a net worth of less than $25,000.[2]

Much more ominous, however, are the numerous signs that the current run of national prosperity is based largely on an unprecedented consumption binge. As widely noted, the country's net personal savings rate has been hovering around zero in recent years—and actually has dipped into negative territory. Accordingly, debt rose from about 48 to 55 percent of Americans' incomes from 1989 to 1995, and the typical household has changed from being a net creditor to a net borrower.[3]

Some globalization optimists note that statistics about personal savings rates are misleading, because they only count the new funds that Americans put into savings instruments, and leave out the incredible run-up in the value of the financial assets (like stocks) that they already own. However although nearly 50 percent of Americans currently own stocks, as of 1998, more than two-thirds of this stock was owned by the wealthiest 5 percent of the population.[4] Possibly the most revealing indicator that overconsumption has become a way of life in America: In 1970, only one in 50 Americans in poverty held a credit card; in 1999, more than one in four did.[5]

In all, however, by far the biggest problem with the expansion— and its most stunning feature—is how long it left the living standards of most Americans lower than when it began. The globalizers' insistence on celebrating the recovery even as living standards have fallen or remained low by every measure makes for an economic debate eerily detached from reality. After all, what can the ultimate purpose of economic policy be if not to help improve the lives of the many? Certain rates of joblessness, inflation, productivity, and of course, economic growth are indispensable means to this end, as are responsible fiscal policies and healthy financial markets. However, they cannot logically be ends in and of themselves. If these achievements are not producing more prosperity for most Americans, then economic policies cannot reasonably be judged a success. According to this definition, U.S. economic policy has been failing for the last quarter century.

It is essential to be specific here. The charge is not that living standards have stagnated for an unfortunate, hapless few, or mo-

mentarily paused or dropped for the many. It is not simply that income inequality has widened, with most Americans remaining
ahead of inflation but some merely keeping pace and a handful
falling behind.[6] It is certainly not that economic policy has failed to
guarantee affluence for all. The charge is that for more than 25
years, taking inflation into account, the living standards of the
overwhelming majority of Americans have either stagnated or
fallen, measured by the compensation they receive for every hour
of work they do. In other words, as the U.S. Census Bureau reported in 1998, for the first time in the country's history, a generation of Americans on the whole is doing worse economically than
its predecessors.[7] Nor does the slight uptick in real wages that finally began in 1997—entirely normal for this stage of a long recovery—show any evidence of decisively reversing this development.

Trends in living standards have been vigorously debated for
most of this decade. Experts in and out of government have filled
the media with a blizzard of clashing numbers that measure
wages, overall compensation (which includes benefits), income
(which includes welfare payments and financial gains), and wealth
(which includes financial assets). They have examined these trends
among the entire workforce (which includes CEOs and rock stars),
nonsupervisory production workers, and households (where income can rise when a second spouse or child finds employment).
They have studied average figures (which mask uneven distribution across any sample that is studied) and median figures (which
identify the most representative item in a sample). They have
tracked weekly earnings (which can be pumped up simply when
workers put in more hours) and hourly earnings (which more accurately assess a worker's value in the labor market).

Some analysts have gone so far as to say that the best measure
of living standards is how much Americans consume. The aforementioned team of W. Michael Cox and Richard C. Alm are the
most prominent proponents of such views these days. In their
Myths of Rich and Poor, they wrote, "If we want to know about
living standards, it is better to use direct indicators of what
Americans own, what they buy, and how they live, not some
proxy, whether it be earnings or income." Of course, the problem
with this reasoning is its suggestion that the most affluent among
us are not the ones accumulating the most new wealth, but those
who spend it fastest regardless of what they take in. In fact, if we
take these analysts seriously, we would wonder why anyone

bothers to earn new wealth at all, as opposed to simply running up debt.[8]

Any selective presentation of data can reasonably be accused of bias. But globalization optimists have not explained why so much evidence can be marshaled that points to such widespread erosion of U.S. living standards over so many years of supposedly excellent or solid economic performance. If the economy were stumbling or falling, heated debate over specific sets of numbers and their relevance or representativeness would be expected. The globalizers, however, are being forced to pull out all the methodological stops—and even veer into the absurd, as suggested above—to prove their case at a time when the economy supposedly is so strong that serious debate logically should not be occurring at all.

The problems with the rosy view of the U.S. economy start with the accomplishment many globalizers point to most proudly—the lowest U.S. unemployment rate in nearly a quarter century. In the first place, what these aggregate figures do not show is what many Americans by now know from experience: Employment is not what it used to be. Specifically, as made clear by the research of the Economic Policy Institute, in Washington, D.C., the relationship between official definitions of employment and the ability to make ends meet has changed.

For example, part-time workers (who attracted so much attention during the 1997 UPS strike) are counted as "employed" by U.S. labor statistics. However, the increase in part-time workers between the early 1970s and the later 1990s was hardly, as globalizers have claimed, solely the triumph of a U.S. labor market flexible enough to accommodate an increasingly diverse workforce and its increasingly diverse employers. An analysis of the Census Bureau's Current Population Survey by the Economic Policy Institute (EPI) shows that all of the increase in part-time workers from 1973 to 1989 resulted from an increase in the numbers of involuntary part-time workers. The trend seems to have moderated through 1997, though changes in the survey make direct comparisons difficult.[9]

In addition, significant numbers of temporary workers are becoming a permanent fixture of the U.S. labor scene. Between 1973 and 1997, the share of employed Americans falling into this category jumped eightfold, to 2.4 percent, and these workers earn substantially less than workers in comparable stable jobs. Further, as of late 1995, temporary agencies created 13.8 percent of all jobs generated by the 1990s recovery—up from 4.8 percent in the 1982–1990 period.[10] In a similar vein, moonlighters—Americans holding at least two jobs—increased from 5.1 percent of the workforce in 1973 to 6.3 percent in 1997. Most of the increase came during the growth years of 1985 to 1989, and nearly half of these workers cited economic hardship as their motivation.[11]

EPI research also completely invalidates the view that only the already poor have seen their living standards deteriorate. Most important, between 1973 and 1998, real hourly wages fell for the bottom 60 percent of the entire U.S. workforce. For the next highest decile (tenth) workforce, real hourly wages rose a miniscule seven cents during this period. The lowest income workers have indeed been hit hardest by this trend. The bottom 10 percent, for example, suffered a 5.2 percent decline in real wages between 1979 and 1998, whereas workers in the top two deciles experienced 5.9 and 10.5 percent increases, respectively. However, for 25 years, seven out of ten American workers failed to keep up or merely kept up with living costs, even though most of these were years of solid economic growth. This trend is a striking contrast to the pattern of most of the first three quarters of the twentieth century, when robust economic growth was accompanied by even greater wage progress by America's poorest. MIT economist Lester Thurow has provided some valuable new perspective on this point. Not since 1929, he wrote, have real wages fallen for most U.S. workers at the same time that output per worker was rising.[12]

Nor do the trend lines change much when benefits or stock options are factored in, as some globalizers suggest.[13] In fact, despite solid recent economic growth, workers' benefits are being squeezed nowadays from several sides. Many workers (even retirees) are being denied company-financed health care or retirement plans. Many others are being asked to pay more for the coverage they do receive. Moreover, because health care inflation is still high despite the spread of managed care arrangements, most Americans today receive considerably less per dollar of health expenditures than a decade or two ago.

From 1979 to 1993, for example, the share of private-sector workers with employer-provided pension coverage fell from 51.1 percent to 47 percent. And from 1975 to 1997, the share of those covered workers with defined contributions, in which they themselves bear most of the investment risk, jumped from 13 percent to about 42 percent. As a result, more and more Americans are being forced to rely on their own investments in financial markets, rather than on more secure private and public-sector pension plans, to pay for their retirements.[14]

The falloff in health care coverage has been more pronounced. Between 1979 and 1996, the percentage of private-sector workers receiving employer-provided coverage dropped from 70.2 percent to 62.6 percent, with the lowest-wage workers taking the biggest hit. A 1996 United States Health Care Association report projected that this trend will continue among the entire workforce (including government workers, who generally are guaranteed substantial coverage). By this measure, only 70 percent of U.S. workers will receive coverage in the year 2002, down from a peak of 77.7 percent in 1990. A report by the Labor Department shows that the share of premium costs paid by covered employees rose from 13.7 percent in 1987 to 16 percent in 1993.[15]

An increasingly prosperous economy also would appear amply capable of keeping promises to retirees. But since the late 1980s, more and more employers are curbing or simply ending health care coverage for former workers. From 1988 to 1994, the share of retirees enjoying coverage from a former employer fell from 37 percent to 24 percent. In 1994, companies paid the full premiums for only 42 percent of those pensioners still covered by health insurance—down from 50 percent in 1988.[16]

B. EVEN THE EDUCATED

Eroding living standards in the United States are almost invariably attributed to inadequate schooling. As former labor secretary Reich told Congress in 1996, "restoring wage growth and economic security for the majority of working families" requires helping Americans "get more education and build their skills." As evidence, he cited an "income gap" between the college educated and the non-college educated that has widened dramatically since 1979.[17]

Many of the leading economic reporters heartily agree. In the words of Bob Davis and David Wessel of *The Wall Street Journal*—who predict that globalization will soon help bring on a "golden age of broadly shared prosperity"—education "has always been the key to closing the income gap." *The New York Times* columnist Thomas Friedman dismisses those suffering wage decline in the new global economy as "turtles" and as "people who ain't too clever."[18]

The widening income gap is real enough, but the data belie the conclusion that Americans can bring back good times for themselves simply by graduating from college. From 1973 to 1997, the real hourly wages of Americans without high school diplomas did fall 31 percent, but the real wages of college-educated Americans—less than 25 percent of the population—fell by 2.7 percent during this period. Indeed, as made clear by University of Chicago economist Kevin Murphy, the so-called college premium for wages—the supposed payoff for receiving a bachelor's degree—has been shrinking since 1989, not growing.[19]

Even U.S. workers with advanced degrees—a mere 7.8 percent of the workforce, according to the latest reliable figures—achieved real wage increases of only 11.8 percent from 1973 to 1997. In fact, in 1996, the median annual income of U.S. workers holding just a bachelor's degree was only $34,000—meaning that half of the country's working B.A.'s earned less. In an especially disheartening sign of the times, between 1979 and 1992, the percentage of U.S. men holding B.A. degrees but earning poverty-level wages (about $13,000 per year) doubled, to 6 percent. A recent MacArthur Foundation study found that in Chicago, fully 9.2 percent of the working poor hold B.A.'s.[20] In fact, reading Friedman's definitions of "turtles"—people that "just don't have the skill sets or the energy to make it into the Fast World" of "high-tech entrepeneurs" and microchip makers—makes clear that those losing out due to supposedly inadequate educations include just about everyone.[21]

At the same time, discussing the impact of opening the doors of academe to the majority of workers seems increasingly academic. Not only are real wages for the noncollege educated plummeting, but the cost of college is skyrocketing. Between the 1988–89 and 1998–99 academic years, for example, the inflation-adjusted cost of room, board, and tuition at the nation's private colleges and universities rose by 28 percent, while the same fees for public institutions increased by 22 percent. As Robert Reich himself has noted, even at America's public schools, costs have risen three times faster than median family incomes. According to the RAND Corporation, if these trends continue, 6 million students "will be priced out of the [higher education] system" by 2015—nearly half the full-time college enrollment projected by then. Already, teenagers from the most affluent 25 percent of U.S. families are three times as likely to attend college as those from the poorest 25 percent—and the gap has been widening for more than 20 years.[22]

High levels of skills are not a sure bet for staying ahead of living costs, either. The Department of Labor's Bureau of Labor Statistics (BLS) meticulously tracks the month-to-month changes in hourly wage rates for the workforces of literally hundreds of domestic industries. For most of these sectors, the figures go back decades; even for the newest industries, like computer software, 10 years' worth of consistent data is now available. The wage data in this National Employment, Hours, and Earnings series take inflation into account only in the broadest categories, but converting the narrower sector figures into constant dollars is simple enough. These calculations show how sharply much of the human capital allegedly prized by the U.S. economy and the new global economy has been devalued over the last quarter century.

For production workers (that is, the roughly 75 percent of workers who are not managers or executives) in numerous high-tech sectors, the BLS figures show that high-skill levels are indeed associated with rising real wages, as the globalizers say they should be. In 1973, for example, the first year for which semiconductor industry figures are available, production workers earned $3.56 per hour. By 1999, their wages had risen 416 percent—higher than the 26.5 percent increase in consumer prices during that period. Measured in 1973 dollars, therefore, semiconductor production workers earned $4.89 per hour in 1999—a $1.33 per hour (37.4 percent) increase in real, inflation-adjusted wages.[23]

Figures for production workers in the computer programming services sector (again, simply meaning anyone who is not a manager or executive) go back only to 1988, but they have kept ahead of inflation as well. From 1988 to 1999 when the consumer price index had risen by just under 41 percent, their hourly wages rose 60 percent. Measured in 1988 dollars, then, these wages increased from $15.90 per hour to $18.07, or about 13.6 percent.

In the popular mind, aircraft industry workers stand somewhat lower on the technology ladder than software or semiconductor workers, yet they, too, have seen their real hourly wages rise in the past 25 years—from $5.09 in 1973 to $5.80 in 1999. In addition, despite fierce Japanese and other foreign competition (though perhaps partly because of import restrictions), U.S. auto workers also have slightly beat inflation since 1973 (though they have lost a bit of ground since 1988).

But not all high-tech workers have enjoyed such success. Production workers for computer integrated systems design companies—a subsection of the programming services category—earned $15.51 before inflation in 1988. No one can reasonably accuse them of lacking cutting-edge, information-age skills, but by the end of 1999, their wages had risen only 38 percent—just below the 41 percent inflation rate for that period. Therefore, these workers lost nearly 30 cents in their real hourly wage—a 2 percent drop—during those 11 years. For workers who make communications equipment—another supposed industry of tomorrow—the wage picture is grimmer. From 1988 to 1999, this workforce suffered a real wage drop of some 7.9 percent, to $9.96 per hour in 1988 dollars.

In fact, starting at this rung on the technology and skill ladder, and proceeding downward, it is almost impossible to find a category of production workers that has stayed significantly ahead of living costs since the early 1970s. And many workers in sectors considered the country's core manufacturing industries—such as transportation equipment (which includes the motor vehicle and aircraft industries), electronic electrical equipment (which includes communications equipment as well as electronic components and electrical engines), and industrial machinery and equipment (which includes machine tools and internal combustion engines)—have lost considerable ground.

Take transportation equipment. Although the workers in aircraft assembly plants, as mentioned earlier, have beat inflation for most of the last quarter century, their counterparts at most parts and components factories have been left behind. Aircraft parts and equipment workers (excluding those who produce engines) have lost 1.5 percent in real wages since 1973. Auto parts workers have lost nearly 16 percent of their real hourly wages during this period. Machine tool workers' real wages have slipped about 13 percent as well, while their counterparts in the electric and electrical equipment sector have experienced a real wage decline of 2.3 percent since 1988 (the earliest year for which figures are available).

Just as interesting as what these BLS wage figures say about the link between living standards and skills levels are some of the things they do not say. For example, different industries can employ vastly different numbers of workers. At the end of 1999, the total number of production workers in the U.S. private sector—services, manufacturing, mining, agriculture, and construction—numbered 88.9 million. Production workers in goods-producing industries totaled just over 18 million.[24]

The computer programming services sector, in which wages have significantly outpaced inflation rates, employed some 373,000 production workers at the end of 1999. Their counterparts in the semiconductor industry numbered 111,000. By contrast, the total electronic and electrical equipment sector—which contains the semiconductor industry, and in which real wages are generally dropping—employed slightly more than one million. In industrial machinery and equipment, where real wages are falling even faster (by about 13 percent from 1973 to 1999), the workforce totaled more than 1.3 million. In motor vehicles and equipment, where the parts workers' wages have fallen enough to put the entire sector well behind the inflation rate since 1973, the production workforce stood at 776,000 at the end of 1999. In manufacturing overall, where real hourly earnings have dropped by 10.4 percent since 1973, the production workforce totals about 12.7 million.

Thus, although many of the very highest-skilled U.S. workers have enjoyed real living standards increases over the last quarter century, they represent only a tiny fraction of the entire workforce. In fact, these inflation beaters are even only a minority of the total high-skill workforce.

In addition, evidence is accumulating that the same wage stagnation and deteriorating job quality that threatens the U.S. workforce as a whole is now appearing at the top of the job pyramid. In June 2000, a Commerce Department study reported that between 1992 and 1998, the median weekly earnings of computer scientists, computer engineers, and computer systems analysts rose 17.5 percent—scarcely higher than the 15.4 percent inflation rate and only matching the average weekly earnings increase for all occupations. Weekly earnings for computer programmers rose faster—by 23 percent—but that figure hardly puts them in the stratosphere.[25] A 1999 survey by The Washington Post found salaries in the major high-tech cluster rapidly developing around the nation's capital actually to be falling in several job categories, such as programmer/analyst and Web programmer. Salaries were flat or rising only sluggishly in several other categories, such as systems engineer, client server/graphical user interface system developer, and network analyst.[26]

More evidence of the surprising wage lag for information technology workers comes from three researchers at the Sloan Semiconductor Program at the University of California at Berkeley. Their research shows that in the U.S. economy as a whole, professionals with 20 years of career experience earned 73 percent more than professionals with no experience—up from a 48 percent premium in 1985. In high-tech industries, however, engineers and other professionals with 20 years of experience outearned new hires by only 59 percent, and their premium was up from only 55 percent ten years earlier.[27]

Indeed, the only report on information technology workers' earnings that claims outsized increases and premiums comes from the Information Technology Association of America (ITAA). In recent years, this employer group has convinced Congress that the nation is experiencing a severe shortage of information technology (IT) workers, and that admitting more foreign high-tech workers (who can usually be hired at a fraction of their U.S.-born counterparts' wages and thus boost the profits of ITAA companies) is desperately needed to fill the gap. Of course, the at-best modest pay hikes received by information technology workers in recent years completely belie this claim. After all, when so many jobs supposedly go begging for so long, it is clear that employers have decided that making do with what they have is better than taking the measures usually taken by companies truly desperate for workers—offering much fatter paychecks.[28]

In 1996, moreover, the labor union-funded group Working Partnerships USA found that the part-time high-tech workforce in Silicon Valley has grown 35 percent in recent years, and now represents more than 40 percent of the region's high-tech workers. The study also found that the real incomes of these workers had fallen 15 percent since 1989. Such results track with a BLS study reporting that fewer than 10 percent of these part-timers receive health insurance from their employers.[29] If high education and skill levels cannot guarantee an improvement in real living standards and job security in the current recovery, imagine how empty their promise will be when the business cycle turns down.

At the same time, even if the business cycle stays up in the foreseeable future, the most authoritative sources indicate that the living standards crisis will continue. In addition to tracking past and present employment trends, the Labor Department each year publishes detailed projections for the following decade. According to its latest study, between 1998 and 2008, the U.S. economy will create nearly 55 million new job openings. Some 20.3 million will result from expanded employment opportunities. The rest will be generated by the need to replace workers who leave the labor force or leave their current jobs for new jobs.[30]

The good news in the Labor Department's picture is that the jobs requiring the most training and education, and that pay the best, will increase at the fastest rates. The bad news is that there are so few of these jobs today that, even after 10 years of rapid growth, they will still be a small minority of all jobs. For example, the total number of Americans in 1998 who were classified as general managers and top executives, engineers of all kinds, computer science workers, lawyers, and doctors and dentists, equaled 5.2 percent of the total 140.5 million workforce. In 2006, such occupations are expected to comprise only 5.8 percent of a 160.8 million workforce.

Several different measures make the same point. Those 1998 jobs requiring a B.A. degree or above, plus some work experience—the jobs that generate the highest pay—totaled 21.9 percent of all jobs. In 2008, the Labor Department predicts that such jobs will represent 23.2 percent of the workforce—an increase, but hardly a dramatic one. In addition, jobs requiring at least a four-year college degree will make up only 23 percent of the total new job openings appearing between 1998 and 2008. By contrast, jobs requiring only one month or less of training to perform satisfactorily—the lowest education level on this Labor Department scale and the category with the lowest pay—represented 39.2 percent of the workforce in 1998 and will decline only to 39 percent by 2008.

In fact, many of the jobs likely to have experienced the greatest absolute growth between 1998 and 2008 are jobs that are literally dead-end jobs—like cashiers, retail sales clerks, janitors, and wait staff. Fully four of the top 10 occupations expected to generate the most job growth during this period are in the bottom 25 percent of the American pay scale and nine of the top 20 are in this category. Four of the top 10 and only six of the top 20 are in the top quarter of the pay scale. Measured by education levels, six of the top 10 and 12 of the top 20 job-creating occupations will require only short-term training. Only two of the top 10 and five of the top 20 will require at least a four-year college degree.

C. THE REEDUCATION MIRAGE

Blaming the victim is a popular tactic in politics and policy analysis, especially among the successful and comfortable. A leading contemporary example is the emphasis of globalization optimists on reeducation and retraining as panaceas for job loss and wage stagnation. Despite all the evidence of globalization's damaging domestic effects—even among high-tech workers—the optimists still implicitly blame the losers of global economic competition for failing to become winners. At best, the optimists suggest that inadequate government education and training programs have let the losers down. In the words of U.S. Trade Representative Charlene Barshefsky:

> Many fear, and not without some reason, that growing trade and technological progress, while creating jobs and raising salaries for the most skilled and educated among us, will devalue the work of those less fortunate. So we must integrate trade policy with the right approach to education and training. There is absolutely no reason that everyone should not have the skills to succeed in a new world.[31]

Similar points are made by the private sector. According to Leo Reddy, president of the National Coalition for Advanced Manufacturing, an industry group, "Global competitiveness and growing exports exert added pressures on the U.S. workforce. The only way in which our workforce can withstand these pressures is to continuously improve the skills it needs to produce globally competitive products."[32]

Although these views come from avowedly the most internationally minded Americans, at the very least they betray a surprising parochialism. Assuming these individuals really do regard reeducation and retraining as a cure-all for what ails the U.S. workforce, they seem to believe that only Americans understand the importance of such efforts, and that they are underway only in this country. Nothing could be further from the truth. Governments and workers all over the world are not only expressing as much awareness as their U.S. counterparts of reeducation's importance, they are vigorously acting on these beliefs. And though the relentlessly growing global labor surplus will probably prevent most of these efforts from significantly lifting incomes in the developing world, continuing reeducation and retraining in low-income countries will greatly increase the downward wage pressure on ever-more skilled workers in industrialized countries.

Although they still suffer a great shortage of highly skilled workers, developing countries—especially in Asia—have made an impressive beginning in building high-tech workforces.[33] The National Science Foundation has studied trends in higher education in five developing Asian countries—China, India, Singapore, South Korea, and Taiwan. From 1975 to 1990, these countries expanded enrollment in colleges and universities from slightly more than 3.4 million to slightly more than 9.2 million. The biggest absolute and percentage gains were in China, where enrollment more than quintupled during this period, to 2.65 million. Enrollments in South Korea nearly quintupled as well. While these increases meant significant rises in the percentages of college-age students enrolled in these institutions in the smaller countries studied, even more remarkable has been the ability of China and India to keep this ratio stable despite enormous absolute population growth. At the bachelor's degree level, the numbers of graduates grew especially rapidly in natural science in India, Singapore, and South Korea; India in fact graduated more B.A.'s in this field (146,774) than did the United States (105,021). The fastest growth in engineering B.A.'s was recorded in India and South Korea, although both were still well behind the United States. (China's records show twice as many engineering B.A.'s granted in 1990 as in the United States, but figures from 1975 to 1981 are not available.) Similar trends have unfolded at the graduate level, and the Asian progress is even more noteworthy because so many science and engineering graduate degrees awarded in the United States go to students from these five countries plus Japan.[34]

Since 1990, all the evidence points to more and more Asians gaining advanced technical education. India's main software trade association, for example, currently pegs the number of software professionals in the country at 340,000—up from 160,000 in 1997. Further, the country's hundreds of engineering colleges, technical institutes, and polytechnics are graduating as many as 200,000 students with technology-related degrees annually. An American high-tech business group estimates that Chinese universities graduate 33,000 software engineers annually, most adept in developing in Java and writing in HTML. In 1994, South Korean math and computer science graduates from the associate to the master's degree level topped 25,000, and enrollment in two-year technical schools jumped from 84,500 to 100,000. Singapore's two universities and four polytechnic institutes turn out 2,000 information technology professionals annually.[35]

However, leaders in emerging market countries insist that much greater challenges lie ahead. According to longtime Singapore Prime Minister Lee Kuan Yew, one of developing Asia's most durable and outspoken leaders, "Technology is changing so fast that, if we don't get our workers up to the mark, they may be out of jobs because they cannot work the new machines that come in." His successor, Goh Chok Tong, has warned that Singapore's workers must continually upgrade their skills precisely because companies are locating labor-intensive, lower-value work to lower-income countries. Sounding even more like President Clinton and Robert Reich is Malaysian government economic adviser Tun Daim Zainuddin:

> The skills of the general labour force are going to be the key competitive weapon in the twenty-first century. While brain power will create new product and process technologies, skilled labour will be the arms and legs that master them. Natural resources, capital, and new product technologies are going to move rapidly around the world. Skilled people will remain as the only sustainable competitive advantage. If a firm or country is to be successful, each and every worker must have high-tech skills.

The Taiwanese, too, talk as if they understand the importance of upgrading worker skills. Noted an editorial in the government-published *Free China News*, Taipei's major economic initiatives "all have one extraordinary need in common: a world-class workforce." Similarly, members of India's National Taskforce on Information Technology and Software Development concluded that India's "competitiveness in the twenty-first century will critically depend on the skill endowment of our citizens."[36]

The evidence shows that these statements are much more than just talk. Moreover, foreign—and especially U.S.—multinational corporations have been deeply involved in these reeducation and retraining efforts. In 1989, for example, Motorola and other foreign companies established in Penang state, Malaysia, the Penang Skills Development Centre. In line with the Penang government's official goal of moving into "higher-tech, higher-value-added, and capital and skill-intensive manufacturing," the center offers courses in robotics, electrical engineering, software development, and other areas. Similar courses are offered in the Selangor Human Resource Development Centre in that Malaysian state. Set up in 1993, the center represents another partnership between local government and foreign investors. Nationwide, Malaysia is aiming to increase the share of science and technology students in its universities to 60 percent from the current 40 percent by early in the twenty-first century. Singapore, meanwhile, has set a target for companies to spend 4 percent of their payrolls on training, and provides financial incentives to do so.[37]

3 WHAT'S GLOBALIZATION GOT TO DO WITH IT?

EMONSTRATING THAT THE LIVING STANDARDS OF MOST Americans are stagnant or falling is important, but it does not prove that current globalization policies deserve any blame. In fact, the globalizers insist that the very same accelerating worldwide flows of trade, investment, technology, and to some extent people that they themselves consider as defining realities of our time have had at best a slight impact on U.S. living standards. According to the President's Council of Economic Advisers (CEA), "recent research indicates that international trade is responsible for only perhaps 10 or 15 percent of the observed increase in wage inequality during the 1980s."[1] This formulation, as just discussed, defines the problem too narrowly. As has been documented, the vast majority of American workers has experienced declining living standards, not just a handful of losers. But the CEA's claim does accurately describe much of the academic research.[2] Other economists—or the same economists writing at different times—place even less blame on trade flows for either general wage deterioration or rising inequality to trade flows, or they place no blame at all. For example, an influential 1993 article by Robert Lawrence of Harvard and Matthew Slaughter of Dartmouth, for example, concluded that trade had "nothing to do with the slow increase in average compensation." Paul Krugman has even contended that the world is witnessing a "convergence between wages [in low-income countries] and in the West through a process of leveling up, not leveling down."[3]

Wall Street Journal correspondents Bob Davis and David Wessel put a similarly bright spin on the living standards effects of globalization. "When prices decline or products improve because of imports, American living standards rise just as much as they do when wages go up," they write. "That fact of economic life never gets the attention it deserves during the bitter and emotional debates about trade and job-killing imports."[4] A little common sense, though, reveals exactly why this argument is deservedly neglected. First, real wage figures by definition include the impact of inflation—in the case they cite, the effects of lower import prices on overall price levels. Despite these lower prices, American real wages are still falling. Second, the potential for improving living standards by raising wages is surely much greater than the potential for achieving this goal by lowering consumer prices—unless one believes that absolute prices often go below zero.

As indicated by this Davis and Wessel argument, the national media have by and large bought the experts' arguments about the benign impact of trade and globalization. Thus, columnist Robert J. Samuelson allows that imports have "destroyed some well-paid factory jobs" but announces, "as economists Robert Lawrence . . . and Paul Krugman . . . argue, this can't explain most inequality. Trade isn't large enough." His colleague Thomas L. Friedman of *The New York Times* somewhat petulantly complains that "the anti-globalization movement ... is still with us, arguing that free trade and global integration cause stagnating wages. (Wrong. What primarily hurts lower-skilled workers is rapidly advancing technology that replaces them with machines, computers, and voice mail, not free trade.)"[5]

Ironically, much of the most striking testimony to the contrary comes from the very same globalizers—and others who agree with them. Despite dismissing the link between globalization and wage deterioration as "questionable in theory and flatly rejected by the data," in mid-1997, Krugman acknowledged to a reporter that "continued growth in imports" from developing countries could indeed bring "greater disparity in the distribution of wealth in the United States, with a large number of educated and highly skilled workers doing quite well, but also a large number of unskilled workers experiencing further deterioration in their standard of living."[6]

In January 2000, Krugman went even further. Although globalization makes the world as a whole richer, he wrote, "the wealth it creates goes disproportionately to two sorts of people ... workers in developing countries" and "the rich and highly educated in rich countries." He concluded that competition from these third world workers is "one, though probably not the most important of the reasons that the real wages of many American workers have stagnated or even declined over the last 25 years."[7]

Columbia University economist Jagdish Bhagwati has been one of academia's staunchest champions of traditional trade liberalization. During the highly charged 1997 debate over granting President Clinton "fast-track" trade negotiating authority, he insisted that "nearly all economists who have examined the issue conclude the adverse impact [of trade with poor countries on U.S. wages] is negligible." He added, "I conclude that trade with poor countries has likely benefited U.S. workers." Yet two years before, he told a reporter, "You're definitely seeing an enormous integration of the markets and therefore a drag on the real wages here of the semi-skilled, of the computer programmers, of the skilled." Yale University dean Jeffrey Garten, who as one of President's Clinton's chief trade policy advisers had actively promoted expanded traditional trade with developing countries, wrote of such trade: "We can expect rising imports and severe downward pressure on wages in the industrialized world."[8]

Congress' defeat of fast-track in the fall of 1997 seemed to have prompted second thoughts on Thomas L. Friedman's part about globalization and living standards. Globalization opponents, he allowed, "are right that globalization . . . does churn new jobs and destroy old ones, it does widen gaps between those with knowledge skills and those without them, it does weaken bonds of community." In his 1999 book *The Lexus and the Olive Tree*, Friedman wrote of the way that globalization "squeezes jobs from higher-wage countries to lower-wage ones."[9]

In fact, many of the most prominent globalizers have acknowledged, directly or indirectly, that the worldwide race to the bottom is in full swing. *The Economist* of London is a newsweekly whose very origins are rooted in the great political and intellectual battles fought out in early nineteenth century Britain over international economic strategy. As such, it has always championed the freest possible global trade. In January 2000, however, even its editors acknowledged that multinational corporations have powerful incentives to seek the lowest wages and environmental standards. The nation's globalizer-in-chief, President Clinton, has warned that globalization "must not be a race to the bottom." But his plea just before the battle in Seattle to put a "human face on the global economy" and to launch "a new kind of trade round ... about broadly shared prosperity, about improving the quality of life and work around the world" can be read as nothing other than an admission that his warning has not been heeded.[10]

Perhaps most alarming of all are the predictions made by two Harvard Business School faculty members that appeared in a *Wall Street Journal* essay, urging American leaders to stay the course of current globalization policy. Michael C. Jensen and Perry Fagan argued that industrialized countries like the United States are feeling the inevitable dislocations of a "Third Industrial Revolution." Driven by the post-communist spread of capitalism to worker-rich developing regions as well as by continuing technological change, this global transformation would bring a "wonderfully optimistic future" if Western leaders were courageous enough to endure "the short-term costs of adjusting to the new world." What are these costs according to Jensen and Fagan? How short is the short term?

> The upshot . . . for Western workers is that their real wages are likely to continue their sluggish growth, and some will fall dramatically over the coming two or three decades, perhaps as much as 50 percent in some sectors. . . .

> The economic and social dislocations being caused by the Third Industrial Revolution [also] threaten to undermine the stability of societies— and governments—around the world. Before the revolution concludes, we may witness the failure of one or more Western democracies as extreme brands of political activism find their voice once again and rise up in a bid for control. Faced with a choice between anarchy and non-democratic governments, some societies will opt for the latter.[11]

In other words, the industrialized nations should risk as much as three decades of mass poverty and a widespread revival of fascism (this time, unlike in the 1930s, in a world full of weapons of mass destruction) because in the "long run we will be better off." With friends like this, today's version of globalization scarcely needs enemies.

A. CRISIS IN MANUFACTURING TRADE

Regardless of what the globalizers do or do not say in a given interview, speech, or article, solid—often overlapping—evidence abounds for attributing much of the living standards crisis to current globalization policies.

For example, the globalizers' emphasis on the relatively small scale of trade flows and deficits compared with the entire U.S. economy overlooks two crucial and closely related points. First, adverse trade patterns and their effects have been heavily concentrated in the nation's manufacturing sector, which creates on average the best-paying American jobs. Second, although globalizers often seem to forget it, economists have long agreed that there are many ways in which the price of any good or service (i.e., the price of a worker's labor) can be dramatically affected by even modest changes in the demand for that good (i.e., the share of that demand affected by foreign competition).

The United States may be turning into a service economy, but manufacturing industries generally pay significantly higher wages than service industries. Manufacturing has also been the only sector of the economy with a long record of paying good wages and providing good benefits to Americans lacking a four-year college degree or equivalent levels of skills—no minor consideration in a country where some three quarters of the workforce lacks such attributes. According to the Bureau of Labor Statistics, as of mid-1999, the typical manufacturing job paid wages 8 percent higher than the typical service sector job. The gap has closed somewhat since 1979, when it stood at 13.9 percent, but the reason is no cause for celebration: The gap has closed because median manufacturing wages have been falling faster than median service wages.[12]

International comparisons also reveal the contribution made by manufacturing employment to widely shared national prosperity. From 1980 to 1996, 12 advanced industrialized countries saw their people's incomes rise faster than America's. Eleven of these countries boasted greater shares of their total workforces in manufacturing than the United States. Davis and Wessel of *The Wall Street Journal* made a widely accepted claim when they wrote: "Workers don't have to *make* something to get well-paid, productive jobs." Yet even though this clearly is not true for every single worker, it remains all too true for the vast majority of workers in the United States.[13]

Despite the importance of manufacturing jobs, from 1979 to 1999, while the United States ran up a cumulative manufactures trade deficit of more than $1.85 trillion, more than 2.4 million U.S. manufacturing jobs were lost. Employment in the typically lower-paying service sector, however, jumped by some 37 million jobs, with the two biggest job-creating service sectors being the two lowest-paying: wholesale and retail trade and a category including business, personnel, and health services.[14]

In addition, productivity in manufacturing is much higher and rising faster than productivity in services. This point is especially important because most economists and others who scoff at blaming globalization for the living standards crisis have identified sluggish productivity growth as one of its prime causes—at least before American manufacturing productivity rates began their current rocket flight.[15] How can rising productivity create rising living standards for the vast majority of Americans if our most productive jobs are being displaced by global economic forces and ineffective policy responses?

For all the recent media talk of a great American industrial revival, the nation's trade policy problems are highly concentrated in manufacturing industries. In 1990, the U.S. manufactures trade deficit stood at 73.5 percent of the total $101.7 billion trade deficit in goods (also called the merchandise trade deficit). By 1999—after a supposedly long and impressive American industrial revival—the manufactures deficit stood at 82.2 percent of the much higher overall goods deficit of $330 billion—by far the highest in American history to that point. During the same period, manufactures imports as a share of total U.S. goods imports rose from 78.6 percent to 86.1 percent. (In 1980, they stood at only 54 percent.)

In fact, in late 1997, *BusinessWeek* reported that imports accounted for a record 31 percent of all the goods consumed by Americans (including those produced domestically) other than oil. As recently as 1991, when the current economic recovery began, this figure was only 19 pecent, and in 1980, it was less than half the current level—13 percent. In other words, a very rapidly growing share of the non-oil goods consumed by Americans are made by foreign businesses and workers, not Americans.[16]

There is nothing wrong with imports per se, and often they are highly beneficial. The globalizers are right: Imports can force U.S. companies to be more productive and innovative. They can provide them with cheaper and higher quality parts, components, and other inputs for their final products. They do help dampen inflation. There is nothing wrong with trade deficits per se, either. However, recent levels of U.S. imports and trade deficits show that it is possible to have too much of a good thing. As former labor secretary Ray Marshall has explained, an import tide this enormous has significantly held down American economic growth rates because most of the rising American demand for goods in the last two decades has been met by goods produced overseas, not goods produced in the United States. The trade figures show that most of these imports are manufactures.[17]

Worse, from the standpoint of American living standards, large and rising shares of these imports are coming from low-income countries. Not only are these countries with economies either too small to purchase anything close to a corresponding amount of U.S. products or with consumers too poor to do so. According to a cornerstone of mainstream trade theory—the so-called factor endowments model—they are the countries whose trade with industrialized countries like the United States must inevitably pull wages down toward their level.

In 1990, America's top 10 third world suppliers accounted for 25 percent of total U.S. goods imports. By 1999, this figure had risen to nearly 34 percent. Their share of U.S. manufactures imports is even higher, rising from 28.4 percent to 37.6 percent from 1990 to 1996. Moreover, since at least the mid-1980s, when President Reagan began to encourage closer U.S. economic ties with Mexico, promoting trade with these countries has been a top priority of U.S. foreign economic policy. As previously mentioned, the Clinton administration even gave this policy an official name: the Big Emerging Markets strategy.[18]

If the U.S. trade deficit—whether in manufactures or not, whether with low-income countries or not—were caused mainly by free-market forces, globalization critics would have less cause to complain about them. But as will be discussed in detail in Chapter 4, much of the deficit stems either from barriers that keep competitive U.S. goods out of foreign markets or from predatory foreign trade practices such as intellectual property theft and subsidization that hurt U.S. producers in domestic and world markets alike. In addition, the continued prevalence of these barriers and practices reveals that not only are the deficits themselves hurting American workers—so is Washington's failure to eliminate or significantly reduce them.[19]

A recent Economic Policy Institute (EPI) study has provided yet more evidence of the corrosive effect of U.S. trade flows on living standards and further documents the damage they have done to high-wage manufacturing employment. Globalizers often observe that wages in industries exporting a large share of their output exceed wages in industries facing heavy import competition. From these facts, they reason that overall trade flows are shifting U.S. workers from uncompetitive industries that pay relatively poorly to highly competitive industries that pay relatively well—something that all sensible Americans should support.[20]

EPI researchers found that between 1979 and 1994 imports destroyed 230,000 more of the jobs occupying the top 10 percent of the American pay scale than they created. The impact on the jobs occupying the top fourth of the pay scale was even more pronounced—a net loss of 475,000. For the manufacturing sector, the EPI report confirmed that industries exporting the biggest (at least 30 percent) shares of their output paid better than industries that lost the biggest percentages (at least 30 percent) of market share in the United States—partly, of course, because foreign competition had driven down wages in the import-heavy industries. At the same time, both sets of manufacturing industries made up only slightly under 21 percent of the total manufacturing workforce—which in turn represented only 16.4 percent of all workers in 1994. If this group was widened to include manufacturing industries with at least 20 percent import and export shares, the picture would change. The big export industries with these numbers still paid considerably better than the average wage, but the corresponding import industries also paid better. Still, even these latter two groups of industries comprised less than 42 percent of all manufacturing workers.

Industries whose import and export shares were growing rapidly employed many more workers—and here the picture changes even more dramatically. In particular, the fastest-growing export industries in the manufacturing sector (those with greater than 2 percent annual growth in their exports from 1979 to 1994) employed nearly 64 percent of the manufacturing workforce. However, these industries paid average wages of only $14.81 per hour, according to the latest figures available to the EPI. That was more than 50 cents per hour less than the average manufacturing wage of $15.38. Those industries whose imports were growing fastest (also at at least 2 percent annually between 1979 and 1994) employed 73 percent of the manufacturing workforce. They paid considerably better than the star exporters—$15.33 per hour—although slightly lower than the average manufacturing wage. As the EPI researchers concluded,

"Where trade is having its largest impact, imports have been destroying better-than-average jobs, while exports increasingly compete in markets using low-wage labor."[21]

B. WAG THE DOG

At the same time, total two-way trade in both goods and services (the United States has long run a healthy surplus in the latter, though not one nearly big enough to offset the goods deficit) still represents only about a quarter of the $9 trillion U.S. economy, even though this share has risen steadily in recent decades. Imports of goods represent only about 13 percent of that economy. The entire manufacturing sector represents only about 16 percent of all American economic activity and today employs fewer than 17 percent of all American private sector workers. How can even the most adverse trends in *these* sectors affect living standards for the entire population?[22]

Actually, the question that most economists should be asking is "How could they not have such effects?" Skepticism that trade has outsized effects would be perfectly justified if we were considering a purely additive relationship, like the relationship between the growth rates of parts of a national economy on the one hand, and the growth rate of the entire economy on the other. If, for example, a small industry increases its output tremendously, the effect on the overall economy will still be pretty small (although many economists correctly note that growth in certain kinds of industries—like high-tech industries—usually does have disproportionate effects over time).

Price levels are a different matter altogether because they result from the complex interactions between living, breathing, calculating human beings. One of the defining insights of modern economic analysis—the study of economics dating back 225 years to Adam Smith—is that relatively small changes in the supply and demand for any good or service tend to bring significant changes in the price of that good or service. Economists call these changes marginal effects. Laymen can think of them as instances of the tail wagging the dog. As prominent University of Michigan international economist Alan Deardorff has explained matter-of-factly, "Wages, like any other prices if they are determined in competitive markets, result from the interaction of supply and demand." As elaborated by economists Joseph T. Abate and

Ethan S. Harris of the Lehman Brothers investment firm—almost in passing, in a discussion of the Internet—the impact of trade flows on prices is limited to actual import levels:

> Perhaps the best way to think of the impact of the Web is to regard it as the opening up of a closed economy to foreign trade: while the inflow of imports may be a modest portion of the economy, the implicit or actual competition will ensure widespread downward pressure on prices.[23]

In other words, despite the fuss raised about the relative unimportance of trade flows and manufacturing workers to the much larger American economy, the theoretical case for major effects of trade on wages is completely uncontroversial, even in the mainstream economics community.

It is easy to see why changes at the margin become critical. After all, in any integrated economy (where workers can and do move among industries and the fortunes of many industries are closely related), changes in job availability in even a single industry will in theory change the supply of workers available to all other industries. (In reality, these changes cannot be nearly as sweeping because not all workers are qualified for all jobs.) Therefore, such changes will have especially significant effects on the value of workers—the wages they can command. It also logically follows that these marginal effects will be especially powerful when the wages in sectors gaining and losing significant numbers of jobs are especially low or especially high. Such actions at the extremes of the income ladder will, of course, pull more of the overall workforce the greatest distance up and down this ladder.

This is precisely what appears to be happening in the U.S. economy. Imports of manufactured goods have replaced very large percentages of the manufactures consumed by Americans. This trend alone has greatly reduced the numbers of Americans who work in manufacturing industries—the industries that generally pay the highest wages. As the nation's low unemployment rates show, most of these workers have found other jobs. However, these jobs clearly cannot be manufacturing jobs—which have been falling steadily for twenty years. The new jobs that have been taken by displaced manufacturing workers have overwhelmingly been in the economy's service sectors, which tend to pay significantly lower wages.

This movement of U.S. workers from high-wage industries to low-wage industries has hit U.S. wage levels with a double whammy. It has lowered wages by greatly reducing the numbers of Americans working in high-paying jobs. In addition, it has just as greatly increased the numbers of Americans competing for jobs in the lower-paying service sector. The result has been to pump up the supply of workers competing for service jobs but not the demand for these jobs—thus enabling service companies to reduce their low wages even further.

Economists, moreover, have identified another mechanism through which trade flows can exert an outsized effect on wages—by undercutting what they call the rents that businesses and workers are able to charge the market when they dominate their industries. Rents are the extra pay or profits—the rewards—that such businesses and workers obtain when they overwhelm competitors with superior quality or value, or the windfalls they enjoy when they simply do not face much competition in the first place. The lack of competition can be caused by several factors. For example, the companies and workers are protected by government actions, they conspire to prevent or stamp out competition, they enjoy natural advantages in their market, or competitors simply have not emerged.

Increased import competition has affected the rent-charging capacity of U.S. companies in several ways, and these effects can be difficult to sort out. On the one hand, companies no longer able to charge premium prices have less money to pass on to their workers if they so choose (whether they intend to share with the workers or not). On the other hand, as the rising stock market indicates, many of these companies have been able to maintain or even increase their profits. The trade deficit figures indicate that one important way they have done so has been by importing many of the parts and components of their products from foreign companies that can produce them more cheaply (often because they employ lower-wage workforces). Alternatively, they have set up their own factories abroad in order to realize these cost savings, and sent the parts, components, and even the finished products back to the United States for final sale.

Analysts at the prominent investment firm Lehman Brothers explain that access to cheaper foreign labor is one of the prime reasons that "big cap" companies have been much more profitable recently than "small cap" companies. No less than President Clinton himself (while he was still running for president, to be sure) has said that repression of labor rights in countries such as Mexico—which, of course, drives down wages—can encourage multinationals to outsource.[24]

Most U.S. workers, however, do not enjoy such options. They receive rents either by working for rent-creating companies, by joining unions strong enough to secure them premium wages, or by acquiring premium skills and knowledge themselves.[25] Unlike companies, most workers cannot offer their services to employers located overseas. Not only have American workers' wages consequently been reduced by the erosion of corporate rents, they have also been reduced by the import-induced erosion of their union-generated rents.

Thus, the effects of eroding workers' rents have been relatively easy to sort out, and they have resulted in less worker bargaining power, weaker unions, and lower wages. On the organized labor front, union membership in the United States fell from just more than 24 percent of the workforce in 1979 to 13.9 percent in 1998. In addition, labor has been falling even further behind in the most dynamic sector of the U.S. economy—the private sector. As of late 1996, unions only represented 10 percent of private sector workers.[26]

From the 1960s to 1994, the percentage of organizing elections won by unions fell from about 80 percent to less than 50 percent. The number of strikes in the country has plummeted from 317 in 1973 to 34 in 1998, and the share of working days in the United States lost annually to strikes fell from a 30-year peak of nearly 0.3 percent in 1970 to 0.02 percent in 1998.[27]

Although trade flows cannot be the only reason, the prominence of their role is suggested by how many countries around the world have seen their workers' bargaining power weaken in at least the last decade. According to the International Labor Organization's (ILO) latest survey, between 1985 and 1995, union membership declined in some 70 of 92 countries studied. Although the steepest percentage drops occurred in Central and Eastern Europe— mainly due to the end of compulsory membership in unions controlled by their former communist governments—union ranks also dwindled in Britain, France, and Germany, and generally remained tiny in areas such as Southeast Asia. As the report observed, "With greater locational choice [available to companies], the cost of labor is back on the table."[28]

Evidence is also available that companies have taken a much tougher line with their unionized workers in response to greater import competition and other globalization pressures and opportunities. General Motors, the largest industrialized company in the United States and in the world, has seen its share of the U.S. vehicle market drop in recent decades from 50 percent to slightly more than 30 percent. As a result, noted a *Wall Street Journal* reporter matter-of-factly, the company "simply needs fewer plants" in the United States. Two months earlier, the same reporter noted a related development at GM: The company's management had become determined "to reverse GM's reputation for caving into big labor." GM's prime motivation was the need to cut costs and improve its worldwide competitiveness.[29]

Unfortunately, the news gets even worse for American workers. It has become clear that foreign competitors do not even have to enter the U.S. market for liberalized trade arrangements to force down wages and reduce bargaining power. Even the possibility of greater import competition can alarm employers enough to cut costs and employees enough to swallow these cuts. For example, a *Wall Street Journal* survey in 1992 reported that one-fourth of almost 500 American corporate executives polled admitted that they were "very likely" or "somewhat likely" to use NAFTA as a bargaining chip to hold down wages.[30]

Nor does the impact of foreign outsourcing—of relying increasingly on industrial inputs made by American-owned or affiliated factories located overseas—on American living standards depend on the amount of foreign-made inputs actually used by U.S. companies. As with imports of finished goods, the mere availability of this option often gives the U.S. firms tremendous leverage over their workers. In a report commissioned by the Labor Secretariat set up by NAFTA, Kate Bronfenbrenner of Cornell University found that more than half the firms she surveyed used threats to shut down U.S. operations as weapons to fight union-organizing drives. By removing most obstacles and uncertainties connected with moving production to Mexico, NAFTA has added to the credibility of these threats. In fact, more than 10 percent of employers studied by Bronfenbrenner "directly threatened to move to Mexico," and 15 percent of firms, when forced to bargain with a union, actually closed part or all of a factory—triple the rate found in the late 1980s, before NAFTA.[31]

The intimidating effect on American workers of imports and outsourcing is now taken for granted by Wall Street analysts as a major force holding down wages. As economist Stephen D. Slifer of Lehman Brothers has written, "Both actual and threatened outsourcing is keeping wage demands under control." President Clinton, moreover, has made the same point with characteristic sugarcoating:

> American workers deserve a lot of credit [for the record U.S. expansion] because they became in the 1980s very sophisticated about the way the world economy works, and you haven't seen these enormous wage demands that would bring on inflation, even as the labor markets have tightened.[32]

Translation into plain English: American workers have learned that if they sought significant raises, their jobs would get imported or outsourced out of existence.

Conventional imports and outsourcing are not the only globalization-related forces depressing U.S. living standards. Even globalization optimists acknowledge that large influxes of legal and illegal immigrants into the United States have forced many of America's lowest-income workers into a race to the bottom of the wage scale.[33] The 1992 study by George Borjas, Richard Freeman, and Lawrence Katz—which had agreed with the economists' consensus on trade as a minor contributor to income inequality—also concluded that trade and immigration flows together might account for fully half the wage decline suffered by poorly skilled Americans in the 1980s. Several years later, Borjas contended that any 10 percent increase in the U.S. workforce lowers wages by about 3 percent—a sobering fact given that the 1990 Immigration Act increased annual U.S. immigration quotas by 40 percent. These findings were confirmed in 1995 by the U.S. Commission on Immigration Reform, chaired by the late Democratic Representative from Texas Barbara Jordan: "Curbing illegal movements into the country would ... benefit the wage structure, working conditions, and employment opportunities of U.S. citizens, legal permanent residents, and other authorized workers."[34]

More important, the idea that pumping up the U.S. workforce with immigrants will dampen wages has also been confirmed by no less than Fed Chair Greenspan. In January 2000, he told a Senate hearing:

> Demand is putting very significant pressure on an ever-decreasing available supply of unemployed labor. The one obvious means that one can use to offset that is expanding the number of people we allow in, either generally or in specifically focused areas. And so I do think that an appraisal of our immigration policies in this regard is really clearly on the table.[35]

What Greenspan did not mention—but which should be obvious—is that pumping up the supply of workers available to American businesses through outsourcing and other aspects of current globalization policies logically has the same effects.[36]

Looking at the actual immigration flows makes clear why their impact is so great, and looking at U.S. immigration policy makes it clear that, for more than 30 years, Washington has actively sought to boost these flows. Since 1965, some 27 million immigrants (including illegals) have come to the United States. Since 1970, the numbers have tripled. Moreover, the estimated population of 5.6 million illegal immigrants is reportedly growing by some 275,000 each year. This surge represents the greatest immigration flow in U.S. history—more than twice as big as the previous record wave of 1899 to 1914. Largely as a result, some 10 percent of the nation's residents today are foreign-born. This is the highest level since the 1920s—which of course followed the previous record immigration decades—and a figure more than twice as high as 1970.[37]

The recent immigrant surge is hardly an accident or byproduct of unfettered market forces. In 1965, U.S. immigration policies were significantly loosened for the first time since the 1920s, allowing foreigners with close relatives in the United States or possessing specific job skills to enter. Largely as a result, legal inflows rose to an annual average of 300,000 during the 1980s. In 1986, a major new immigration law provided amnesty to 2.7 million illegals and enabled them to bring in relatives once they became citizens after five years of legal residence. In fact, 65 percent of the 915,000 legal immigrants in 1996 were admitted for precisely this reason. Finally, the 1990 Immigration Act increased annual immigration quotas by 40 percent.[38]

All the same, many globalization enthusiasts complain that these numbers are not enough. For example, *Los Angeles Times* reporter Nancy Cleeland wrote that despite annual legal immigration of nearly one million, " ... in contrast with earlier periods of low unemployment, businesses today cannot easily turn to immigrants to fill the gaps.... Instead, more than a decade of restrictive legislation and policies that target legal as well as illegal immigration has come back to haunt the economy and threaten to pinch off growth." Not only has national economic growth kept accelerating, but regional and national media later reported that immigrants were flooding into California in hopes of landing jobs in labor-intensive industries such as apparel and electronics assembly that NAFTA had steadily been sending to Mexico—where most of the immigrants come from! In other words, the state was importing people while exporting their likeliest jobs.[39]

Not only are today's immigrants more numerous than their predecessors, they are also generally poorer. A study by the Center for Immigration Policy in Washington, D.C. reported that a tripling of the numbers of poverty-level immigrants from 1979 to 1997 boosted the percentage of immigrants in poverty from 15.5 percent to 21.8 percent—nearly twice overall U.S. poverty rate.[40]

Interestingly, American business keeps finding inventive new ways to access low-wage foreign workers. The Pacific island of Saipan, for example, is an American trust territory. Companies operating on Saipan are allowed to send their goods to the United States duty- and tariff-free. That is to say, they are treated just like U.S. companies. However, Saipan businesses do not have to treat their workers just like U.S. workers because they are not covered by many of the labor regulations U.S. companies have to comply with—like minimum-wage laws. As a result, Asian and Asian-American businessmen have lured up to 50,000 Asian workers to Saipan in recent years and employed them in no less than 32 garment factories at $3 per hour—just under half the U.S. minimum wage. These factories are now shipping $1 billion worth of apparel products annually to the U.S. market, while employing workers in conditions so dreadful that the Federal Equal Employment Opportunity Commission (EEOC) has filed a suit.[41]

Given the low earnings of most recent immigrants, it is understandable that researchers focus on how their arrival affects the wages of the lowest-income Americans. Yet wide-open immigration policies are affecting labor markets in the economy's highest-wage sectors as well. When immigration policy was reformed in 1990, Congress also authorized the Labor Department to launch a program designed to admit temporarily into the United States foreign workers with special skills that American employers claim they urgently need on a short-term basis. This program, known as H–1B program, originally allowed 65,000 such workers into the country every year and has since been expanded to 115,000 (with another increase likely).[42] Many of these workers have been foreign software and other computer industry professionals.

Labor Department regulations require companies hiring these workers to certify that their skills are not available in the American workforce and to pay foreign workers prevailing U.S. wages. But in April 1996, the department itself reported that neither goal was being achieved: "We found the program does not protect U.S. workers' jobs; instead, it allows aliens to immigrate . . . and then shop their services in competition with equally or more qualified U.S. workers without regard to prevailing wage." Specifically, the department's report found the certification process to be "perfunctory at best and a sham at worst." More specifically, labor officials found that 74.6 percent of the foreign workers "worked for employers who did not adequately document the specified . . . wage. . . ." Moreover, the Labor Department observed that the myriad ways in which employers and foreign workers evade the H–1B program's requirements mean that "the prevailing wage may be eroded over time."[43]

In addition, two recent private studies show that the heavy use of these H–1B workers is reducing the wages of computer and software workers in particular. Norman Matloff, a professor of computer science at the University of California at Davis, has conducted some of the most detailed studies available of the evolution of the high-tech workforce in California's Silicon Valley. His analysis of the 1990 census data shows that average salaries for foreign-born computer professionals in the area were nearly $7,000—about 15 percent—lower than average salaries among comparable U.S.-born workers. Paul Ong, a professor of Asian studies at UCLA, has found even wider disparities—of more than 30 percent—between immigrant and native-born workers' salaries in engineering as a whole." The British research group Oxford Analytica pegs the difference at as much as 50 percent.[44]

As previously discussed, the lack of dramatically rising salaries in the information technology sector as a whole proves that the shortage claim is bogus. So does the fact that, as of 1997, 6.1 percent of new computer science Ph.D.'s could not find stable, full-time employment. The rate was significantly higher than the jobless rate for the entire American workforce. In addition, the unemployment rate for computer programmers over the age of 50 was an astounding 17 percent.[45] The implications should be obvious: High-tech companies have not run out of workers. They just do not want to hire even experienced techies who have families that prevent them from working 100-hour weeks, or who might require more expensive health insurance coverage than 23-year-olds or foreigners. Thanks to their Washington lobbyists and a compliant Congress, they don't have to. Instead, they can reach into the third world and bring some of it to America.

4 The Global Workforce Explosion

A. LABOR, LABOR EVERYWHERE

Imports, immigrants, and even outsourcing have generated abundant evidence of globalization's corrosive impact on U.S. living standards, but this is hardly the only evidence. Even many critics of current globalization policies have not adequately considered four other major reasons for linking globalization with the living standards crisis: (1) the continuing, unprecedented surge in the number of workers around the world available to U.S. business; (2) the skewing of standard export figures by the corporate spread of manufacturing around the world; (3) the vastly underappreciated amount of high-tech manufacturing that has already been globalized in the past twenty or so years, as well as the startling buildup of advanced scientific and technological capabilities in low-income countries that it has helped to produce; and (4), as discussed, the determined effects by these low-income countries to retrain and reeducate their own workers in order to qualify them for the jobs and industries of the future.

The twentieth century's last two decades have witnessed history's most massive and sudden increase in the supply of industrial and technological workers participating in a genuine globe-spanning economic system. Until roughly 1980, the flow of workers into the international trading system was relatively gradual, and the wage and employment effects of much industrialization were mainly national, not global. The United States, for example, began its intensive industrialization after the Civil War, but U.S. producers manufactured mainly for a rapidly expanding internal market, and manufactured imports were tightly limited by high tariffs. Impressive industrialization began in Russia in the very late nineteenth

53

century, but after 1917, this system, too, was largely closed off to the rest of the world. Following World War II, of course, Moscow removed the eastern half of Europe from the capitalist economic world as well.

The Chinese industrialization begun in 1949 by the Communists was similarly isolated for its first 30 years. Meanwhile, during that same period, most of the billions of inhabitants of the old and new developing states remained economically inert or simply suppliers of raw materials—at least as far as the wealthy capitalist countries were concerned. True, OPEC (Organization of Petroleum Exporting Countries) oil exporters and Latin American government borrowers significantly influenced the world economic system during the 1970s. However, once Western Europe and Japan recovered from World War II's effects, the only major new productive forces that entered this system were from the four smallish East Asian "tigers"—South Korea, Taiwan, Singapore, and Hong Kong.

Starting in the 1980s, however, the world economy's labor supply began to explode. Most descriptions of the last two decades emphasize as their main characteristic the spread of market practices and institutions into economies where governments were the dominant actors. In retrospect, the demographics of the decade were at least equally important.

The late Deng Xiaoping literally opened coastal China for business, especially to Western capital and technology. A desperate, debt-strapped Mexico shortly followed suit. Meanwhile, Southeast Asian industrialization began spreading to a new generation of tigers—Malaysia, Thailand, and gigantic Indonesia. During the 1990s, literally dozens of other countries have begun knocking on the global economy's door. For all their difficulties, post-Communist Russia, the former Soviet republics, and Eastern Europe are poised to build major trading and investment ties with the rest of the world. Economic liberalization is catching on in South America's largest countries, Brazil and Argentina, and Washington has long-range plans to bring the entire hemisphere and its labor forces into a single trading community. Finally, Asia's last remaining major markets, India and a unified Vietnam, have begun—in fits and starts, to be sure—competing for foreign markets and capital.

The actual numbers involved are staggering. At present, seven countries with populations of 100 million or greater (as of mid-1999) are rapidly entering world markets—China (1.25 billion),

India (987 million), Indonesia (212 million), Brazil (168 million), Russia (147 million), Bangladesh (126 million), and Mexico (100 million). The former Communist countries of Eastern Europe—excluding the former Yugoslav republics—and the former Soviet republics represent two more roughly 100-million regions joining the global economy. Right behind them in size are Vietnam (80 million), the Philippines (75 million), and Turkey (66 million). Lagging these countries and regions in terms of global integration but looming on the horizon is Pakistan (147 million).[1]

Not only are these populations enormous, most of them are growing quite rapidly. None of these emerging giants and middleweights is adding population as fast as the numerous sub-Saharan African countries currently growing at between 3 and 3.4 percent annually, however, India, Bangladesh, Mexico, and the Philippines, with annual growth rates of about 2 percent, are all on course to double their populations in roughly 35 years. Populations are actually shrinking or stable in Russia and most East European countries. Several of the former Soviet republics, however, are still growing at nearly 2 percent.

Although China's population growth rate has been slowed dramatically—in part through draconian measures such as forced abortion and sterilization—its 1 percent growth rate represents an annual increase of some 12 million people. This amounts to roughly a new present-day Shanghai every year. By contrast, population growth in the industrialized world stands at one-tenth that level.

At least as important, the labor forces in most of these countries have been growing even more rapidly. Between 1980 and 1993, this growth reached 2.2 percent in Brazil, 2.5 percent in the Philippines, 2.3 percent in Indonesia, and 1.9 percent in India. China's labor force growth of 2 percent was twice as fast as its population growth. In Mexico, whose economy, and working population are becoming ever more tightly integrated with that of the United States, current estimates put annual labor-force growth at between 500,000 and one million. These labor-force growth rates are expected to taper off in the next decade, but the absolute levels are already so high that they will still result in tens of millions of new workers in these countries each year over this time span.[2]

Also pumping up the international labor supply recently has been an apparent sharp rise in the numbers of child laborers around the world. The ILO's latest estimates peg the global totals

at 250 million 5- to 14-year-olds, up significantly from earlier estimates of 73 million full-time child laborers. Many of these child
workers are not directly competing with adults—e.g., children
working on their families' farms, or employed as beggars or pros-
titutes. However, many do compete directly with adults. This
child labor expands not only the workforce in general, but the
number of workers most vulnerable to dangerous and exploitative
working conditions. Consequently, it drags down broad living
standards as well as wages. According to one South Asian labor
activist, Pakistan's carpet industry employed some 500,000 children as of 1996, while 600,000 adults in carpet-weaving regions
were unemployed.[3]

In all, countries with total populations of more than 3 billion
have been rapidly entering world markets since roughly 1980.
These populations are also rising at a fast pace. Just behind them
are Pakistan and the former Soviet republics, with a combined
population of more than 250 million. The result is that an estimated 450 million new workers from low-wage countries joined
an increasingly close-knit global labor force in the 1990s alone. As
business writers William Wolman and Anne Colamosca put it, in
1989, each American was competing with 2.8 inhabitants of the industrialized world. By 1994, each American was competing with
21 people from all over the world.[4]

During the next 30 years, according to the World Bank, this figure of 450 million new workers will rise to more than one billion.
Indeed, by the year 2000, fewer than 10 percent of the world's
workers will be living in economies still disconnected from the
world market. Further, 99 percent of the one billion new workers
will live in today's middle- and low-income countries—with per
capita incomes of less than $8,600 per year as of 1993. Conse-
quently, 89 percent of the world's total workforce in the year 2025
will live in these countries, and 61 percent will live in the very
poorest lands, where per capita income in 1993 was below $695.[5]

Even worse, from the workers' perspective, most of these countries suffer chronic and high unemployment and underemployment. The employment figures for the developing world must be
viewed with care. These countries tend to feature very large informal, or underground, economies, which are inherently difficult to
measure. After all, much of this economic activity exists in informal
form precisely to avoid tax collectors or regulators from governments that lack legitimacy in the view of most of their people. In ad-

dition, large percentages of third world populations simply live apart even from the mainstream of their own country's economy, let alone the global economy. Some, for example, live in remote locations. Others who are more accessible eke out a subsistence living, providing largely for their own needs, and simply do not interact with their country's or locality's more formal economic institutions.

These workers are often counted as "underemployed"—i.e., not working full-time. Yet underemployment is often voluntary, and just as often more than full-time. Nonetheless, few would dispute the general size of the world's informal workforce. According to the World Bank, nearly 85 percent of workers in low-income countries should be placed in this category. In middle-income countries, the informal sector employs nearly 45 percent of workers.[6] Therefore, few would disagree that these large informal sectors indicate that the formal sectors of these economies simply cannot provide full-time work to all who desire it.

Mexico is a case in point. The Mexican measure of unemployment most widely cited in the U.S. press is "open unemployment," a traditional measure that counts those who are out of work and who are actively seeking jobs. In 1995, at the height of the Mexican financial crisis, this figure was 6.25 percent. However, for several years, the U.S. embassy in Mexico City has considered another set of official Mexican statistics to be a much more accurate barometer—one that measures the portion of the workforce both openly unemployed and working less than 35 hours a week. In 1995, this measure stood at nearly 26 percent.[7]

The Russian government's unemployment figures—which among other failings do not count laid-off workers—are grossly understated as well. According to a February 1997 ILO report, the official Russian jobless rate for the previous year should have been 9.5 percent, not 3.4 percent. In addition, the ILO estimates that fully one-third of industrial workers should be counted as "suppressed unemployed." These surplus workers are officially kept on the payrolls of largely moribund state-owned enterprises in order to avoid tax and redundancy payments. They are permitted to retain their access to subsidized shops and hospitals, but millions have not received a paycheck for months. In March 2000, Russia's official jobless rate was up to 11.4 percent.[8]

Similar problems plague many other emerging market countries. South African unemployment stood at 30 percent as of early 2000—most concentrated in the black population. Although they

are down from their peaks in the early 1990s, jobless rates in virtually all of the former Communist economies of Eastern and Central Europe remain in the high single digits and even the teens.
Moreover, as in Russia, unemployment in many of these countries
is artificially and deeply depressed by the huge numbers of workers who officially remain on the payrolls of moribund state-owned
enterprises. In Latin America, which the Clinton administration
has targeted for a new Western Hemisphere Free Trade Agreement, the ILO estimates that joblessness hit 9.5 percent in 1999—
higher than in the 1980s, when the region was struggling with a
mammoth foreign debt crisis.[9]

Asia had been a relative bright spot in this picture, but even before the financial crisis hit, there were crucial areas of concern. Unemployment in India is pegged at 22.5 percent by the U.S. government, and has recently become an important political issue. In fact,
the International Labor Organization estimates that South Asia's
labor surplus might not be eliminated for decades.[10] Indonesia,
too, had been suffering from major employment problems. In
mid–1997, the U.S. embassy in Jakarta reported that, in contrast to
the country's official unemployment rate of 5 percent, underemployment stood at some 40 percent. Nor was higher education any
guarantee of economic success in that huge archipelago; the estimated rate of unemployed college graduates was 12 percent. Further, according to the United Nations Development Program
country representative, jobless has hit the mid-teens in Vietnam.[11]
All told, reported the ILO in late 1996, nearly 1 billion people
around the world were jobless or underemployed—30 percent of
the global workforce. According to the organization, the situation
has probably worsened somewhat since then.[12]

However, the big shadow hanging over the world employment
picture is China. The official *China Daily* newspaper recently reported that total joblessness in the People's Republic stands at 17
percent and that among city dwellers it has hit 11 percent. In July
1999, the Standard & Poor's credit-rating agency downgraded
China's debt precisely because of its jobs crisis. To make matters
worse, this performance is coming in a country that still claims a 7
percent annual growth rate. In the countryside, many scholars and
journalists have observed, the jobs situation is especially bad. An
estimated 100 million workers literally drift across China living
from one menial day job to the next. An estimated 100 million more
are underemployed—many, like their Russian counterparts, hold-

ing phony positions in hopelessly uncompetitive state-owned enterprises.[13]

Indeed, the shaky state of China's government-owned industries points to much higher jobless levels in the near future. Despite considerable privatization—a term that must be used guardedly in China—these businesses still employ roughly 140 million Chinese. Yet the state-owned sector is China's least competitive, and many companies are still alive only because they receive enormous loans from China's state banks. According to the World Bank, 35 percent of these workers may need to be fired for these companies to be considered viable. Already, nearly 20 million of these workers were furloughed between the beginning of 1998 and the middle of 1999—layoffs on a scale that Harvard University economist Thomas Rawlski contended "far surpasses the postwar experience of any major market economy." Small wonder that prominent Chinese leaders are openly calling unemployment a major threat to China's stability.[14]

B. Billions of Consumers?

Despite the world workforce explosion and a genuine jobs crisis in the biggest emerging markets, the belief that today's international *lumpenproletariat* will become robust consumers sometime soon is central to optimism about globalization. Professors Jensen and Fagan of the Harvard Business School, who predicted up to 30 years of wage stagnation and instability in the industrialized world thanks to globalization, also expect wages to recover—eventually. Why? "Remember, these 1.2 billion Third World workers and their families represent huge new markets as well as competitors." Similarly, as a *New York Times* correspondent reported, a recent Organization for Economic Cooperation and Development (OECD) assessment of globalization "found that the benefits far outweigh the negatives because of the enormous consumer buying power that will be unleashed [in emerging markets] for Western goods and services over the next 15 years."[15]

In other words, the globalizers see the enrichment of the emerging markets and the boost it will give to growth everywhere as the long-term payoff that justifies globalization's short-term pain—the pot of gold at the end of the process' long rainbow. Such a third world consumption boom would also bring global trade flows into more sustainable balance and help stave off future financial crises.

Moreover, *Financial Times* columnist Martin Wolf spoke for many when he insisted that "the rapid growth that reduces poverty" in the third world is possible only if current globalization trends are allowed to proceed. Anyone blaming these trends for further impoverishing developing countries is telling "the big lie."[16]

Just as important, the same confidence in enormous emerging consumer markets underlies today's U.S. globalization policy—to the point that these markets have been routinely portrayed as the domestic economy's ultimate salvation. As previously noted, President Clinton has argued that the United States is a "mature economy" with limited domestic growth prospects, and that exporting to these dynamic third world countries is the key to the future prosperity of the United States. Indeed, in the landmark 1993 NAFTA debate with Ross Perot over NAFTA, Vice President Al Gore cited Mexico as the quintessential example, emphasizing how Mexico's masses were already cleaning U.S. goods out of the country's newly opened Wal-Mart stores.[17]

Even though since Clinton's comments, the United States has established itself as the world's only major emerging market, the President's line remains unchanged. In December 1999, right after the Seattle WTO meeting, he repeated to a local audience an argument he and his aides have made into a mantra to justify their trade policies:

> Today, we have about 4 percent of the world's people. We enjoy about 22 percent of the world's income. It is pretty much elemental math that we can't continue to do that unless we sell something to the other 96 percent of the people that inhabit this increasingly interconnected planet of ours.[18]

The nation's business leaders seem to have stayed fully on board as well. Log on to the U.S. Chamber of Commerce's Web site, and you will learn that "the United States's dependence on world trade continues to grow" largely because "over 95 percent of the world's population lives outside the U.S."[19]

Thanks, no doubt, to incessant administration and corporate hammering on this theme, projections of enormous third world product demand are as common in the media now as before the Asian financial crisis. Breathless predictions continue to appear about the third world's multibillion dollar infrastructure needs over the next decade—roads, bridges, dams, power plants and energy grids, water systems, and communications networks that supposedly will be heavily supplied and built by Western companies and their workers and products. In addition, the emerging economies are still expected to account for most of the new global demand for products ranging from autos and auto products to medical instruments and computers to soft drinks.

Most hard evidence to date indicates that expectations of a new sustained global consumer boom that will benefit Western—and particularly U.S.—workers are greatly exaggerated for two main reasons. First, in large measure, precisely because the emerging markets' labor surplus is so huge, the abysmally low wages in those countries generally are not rising much. In fact, in many cases, even before the Asian crisis, they were falling. Further, the labor surplus will continue to depress wages for the foreseeable future. Second, governments in few emerging market countries have much interest in seeing big consumer markets emerge. In fact, the most economically successful have long been working overtime to squelch them. These governments believe that the best way to promote economic development over the long run is to reward savings and investment and to export prodigiously, not to consume and import. Many also remember colonial pasts or humiliating encounters with the West and are determined to avoid depending on foreign goods whenever practicable.

The spread of modern industry to low-income countries—much of it brought on by globalization but some resulting from home-grown development—has created wealth for many of their inhabitants. According to the World Bank, despite continued population growth that is overwhelmingly concentrated in low-income countries, the percentage of the world population below the poverty line (one dollar per day in 1985 U.S. prices) fell slightly between 1987 and 1993. Virtually all the progress, however, had been concentrated in Asia, where, between 1975 and 1995, the absolute number of poor people was cut by more than half, to just under 346 million. Since 1997, the Asian crisis has pushed world totals right back up again.[20]

Even if lost ground is made up any time soon, however, there is no reason to think that billions of people will become able to buy boatloads of American products—or will be even close to this point. In the first place, all the progress has been concentrated in Asia. Even where significant progress has or had been made, overwhelming majorities of the populations of developing countries

always remained and still remain far from the income level economists believe is needed to begin mass consumer purchases, about
$6,000 per year.

In China, this means that even if the country continues to grow
at near double-digit rates, it will take at least 20 years for a consumer society of any significance to develop. In more concrete
terms, it means that the cheapest passenger cars now being made
by Chinese industry cost 10 times more than the average urban
Chinese worker's annual salary of $600, and that even a roll of
Kodak film costs a day's wages for the typical worker. Indeed, one
of the most pathetic spectacles in international business recently
has been the opening in China of theme parks that started out
charging $12.50 per ticket in a country where the average monthly
paycheck hovers around $50. The tickets are now down to $2.50,
but the parks are still largely empty.[21]

In India, realistic assessments of purchasing power mean that a
middle class (by Western standards) often estimated at a quarter of
a billion people may be as small as one million. A more expansive,
Pakistani business assessment contends that between 6 and 10 million Indians can afford to buy the kind of "branded international
products" like autos and pharmaceuticals that industrialized
countries make.[22]

It is true that governments in low-income countries, not individuals, are expected to import many of these Western products, especially when it comes to infrastructure-related goods. However,
in the continuing wake of the Asian financial crisis, many countries of this region have been unable to sustain their consumption
and their purchases from abroad. Financial pressures, as will be
seen, will continue to depress their purchases.

Perhaps just as important, the crisis should be a reminder of
three troubling, crucial, and overlapping aspects of recent emerging market growth. First, much of it has been too fast, fueled not
by sound lending and borrowing, but by a burst of irresponsible
and unsustainable speculation. This speculation was triggered
largely by a combination of widespread global financial deregulation (which tremendously increased pressures to achieve the highest possible returns on investment almost instantly) and pervasive
systems of crooked, crony capitalism in emerging market countries (which permitted excessive short-term profits to be made).

Second, these countries were seen as major profit centers to
begin with mainly because of their stunning success in exporting.

These successes in turn rested on the naive expectation that foreign markets (especially in the United States and the rest of the developed countries) would keep opening wider and wider even as the super-exporters kept their own markets closed.

Third, entirely too much of the capital responsible for developing countries' growth has come from abroad, as opposed to coming from the earnings and savings generated by local populations. Successful long-term economic development, to be sure, nearly always requires low-income countries to import capital—to borrow from abroad. After all, if these countries could create enough capital on their own, they would not be low-income countries. The United States, for example, was a major net importer of capital for the first century and a half of its existence. Its main foreign banker was Britain, and the loans were used to build the most productive economy the world has ever known. However, the U.S. domestic market was big enough, and labor always scarce enough, that eventually much U.S. growth was also generated by rising incomes and demand at home.

Many emerging market countries, especially in Asia, have worked hard to raise domestic savings rates and keep them high. Nevertheless, because wages have not been rising high enough for enough workers, or because these domestic markets are too small to begin with, or because of some combination of these problems, few low-income countries—especially the most successful ones—have been able to finance their extraordinary trade performances and continuing ambitions through their own devices. In addition, their own independent wealth-creating ability is nowhere near sufficient to enable them to play the constructive global consumption role that their boosters expect.

Indeed, as will be seen in the next section, the main reason that the Asian developing countries have been able to create as much capital of their own as they have is that they have actively depressed domestic consumption. Latin America, by contrast, has permitted excessive consumer spending; therefore, it remains even more troublingly dependent on foreign capital than East Asia.

The discussion by Kemper-Zurich economist David Hale shortly before the Asian financial crisis of the emerging markets' imports is revealing. By buying most of the wealthy countries' most recent exports, he argued, the developing countries have become "an important growth locomotive for the whole world economy." However, this will not continue, Hale warned, "if they are unable to import capital." What Hale was really saying, of course, is that if the emerging market countries are largely or wholly cut off from foreign money, they will be unable to import because they have so little money—i.e., so little purchasing power—of their own, and such slight prospects of creating such wealth. Some engine.[23]

Even before the Asian crisis, moreover, it was never clear why lending massively to promising but risky and unfamiliar developing countries was viewed as a better way to sustain global growth than boosting growth or incomes in the industrialized world. All else being equal, it is easier to generate impressive relative gains and returns from a low base than from a higher base. However, the base in these developing countries was so low for so long that it should have aroused suspicions about their real potential. In other words, more investors should have been asking why these countries had fallen so far behind in the first place. Could their problems really be corrected so quickly?

In light not only of the current Asian crisis and its spread to Brazil and Russia, of the Mexican peso crisis of 1994, and of the Latin American financial crises of the 1980s, it should be increasingly clear that the current policy of lending third world countries enough to ensure continued servicing of their debts simply could build up an already shaky global financial house of cards even higher. Lending enough to restore precrisis levels of growth and trade seems out of the question, if not downright reckless.

In fact, debt servicing alone will require the third world debtors to boost exports and cut way back on imports for years. Without slashing their own foreign purchases and boosting exports, these countries will never continue accumulating enough foreign exchange to pay off creditors. This is why, in exchange for its International Monetary Fund (IMF) rescue package, Brazil, for example, agreed to run a $10 billion trade surplus in 1999 and a $2.6 billion budget surplus—both of which required major economic austerity.[24]

Moreover, emerging markets like India and Malaysia, which have escaped financial contagion, did so partly by following the IMF's prescription voluntarily—choking off growth at home, cutting way back on imports, and pushing exports even harder. In fact, Malaysia's austerity policies drew warm praise from former IMF managing director Michel Camdessus. The model in many respects is post-peso crash Mexico, whose then-president Ernesto Zedillo promised in the depths of his country's latest depression to turn his term in office into "six years of exports," and whose exports have tripled over the last decade—a rate of expansion much faster than Mexico's overall economic growth.[25] Consequently, manufacturers all over the world have watched new emerged markets throughout Asia and Latin America in particular shrivel up at a breathtaking pace.[26]

The Asian financial crisis also highlights a grim lesson being learned by a growing number of developing countries, but not yet by enough of the industrialized countries that hope to sell to them. Given the huge global labor surpluses and the ease with which investment capital and productive facilities can move around the world, countries where wages and living standards do rise significantly tend to get punished. In other words, improvements in people's lives are not only precarious, they are counterproductive. As business gurus put it, they make these countries less competitive.

Just as East Asia had been the single developing region of the world where poverty has been significantly reduced, it was also the only developing region in which industrial wages had risen significantly in real terms. U.S. Bureau of Labor Statistics figures show that from 1975 to 1996 hourly compensation for manufacturing production workers in Korea soared some 25-fold (without adjusting for inflation) and for decades Koreans enjoyed a virtual guarantee of lifetime employment. In Singapore, noninflation-adjusted manufacturing production workers' compensation shot up nearly tenfold. The same Bureau of Labor Statistics figures show non-inflation-adjusted U.S. compensation up 186 percent since 1975 (with progress slowing considerably after 1987) and Mexican compensation up only 19 percent.[27]

World Bank data show the same trend. From 1980 to 1992, inflation-adjusted manufacturing earnings per employee rose in South Korea, Singapore, Indonesia, and Malaysia. Less impressive growth occurred in India and the Philippines, but even their workers gained ground on their American counterparts.[28] Some workers in these countries (even India) have enjoyed even faster growth—with wages actually increasing more rapidly than productivity—mainly because shortages of skilled workers in high-tech industries have turned labor markets for skilled production workers, scientists, and technicians into seller's markets.[29]

However, for all the expectations of globalization optimists that the world living standards will increase robustly, these increases are often seen by financiers, businessmen, academics, and local governments themselves as problems, not progress. Commenting on rapid hikes in Indonesia's legal minimum wage (from $2.26 to $2.46 per day) in 1996, World Bank analysts fretted that the increases "have begun to reduce competitiveness in labour-intensive manufacturing." Similarly, rising wages in Singapore have been blamed for a loss in the city-state's export competitiveness vis-à-vis its neighbors, Malaysia and Thailand. Moreover, Singapore's leaders plainly agree. In November 1998, they cut the city-state's wages by 10 percent, with the deputy prime minister insisting that continuing wage restraint is crucial for its future competitiveness.[30]

These wage increases can backfire because the multinational companies that carry out so much of the developing countries' manufacturing can move on so easily. South Korea and Thailand, for example, need IMF rescue packages largely because increased labor costs led businesses to shift production to lower-income countries like China and India, or because their products could no longer compete with production that had already shifted to these countries. Singapore recently lost considerable computer disk-drive production to lower-cost Malaysia. Malaysia, in turn, which has been hit by the Asian crisis' backwash, lost circuit board and other computer hardware production to neighboring Indonesia— where despite the recent jump in minimum wages, companies can pay less than half Malaysian rates. Malaysia is even losing to Indonesia jobs that its own low wages only recently lured from more expensive Singapore. Further, Malaysia faces a threat in advanced electronics assembly and testing from the Philippines, where wages in the industry are 30 percent lower. As for South Korea, a 1996 report claimed that it was considering importing North Korean workers to bring down labor costs. In Latin America, Unilever, GM, Ford, and Tupperware all quickly moved production from Argentina to Brazil once the latter's devaluation drove down its relative wages.[31]

In fact, the more advanced Southeast Asian countries' share of foreign investment into Asia fell by half between 1991 and 1994, with lower-wage countries like China replacing them in many corporate plans. Even China, however, began to be undercut in the labor-intensive apparel industry by producers in Cambodia, Vietnam, and, in some cases before the crisis, Indonesia. [32]

In March 1998, Fed Chair Greenspan succinctly summarized how wage increases ultimately penalized export-dependent countries in a world of wide-open capital flows, and how these penalties were unavoidable:

> There was ... an *inevitable* [emphasis added] limit to how far this [government-directed] Asian economic regime could develop. As the process broadened beyond a few select applications of advanced technologies, *overall* productivity continued to increase, and the associated rise in the *average* real wage in these economies pressed export-oriented industries' wages higher and thereby blunted somewhat the competitive advantage they enjoyed initially. The consequent slackening of export expansion—aggravated by losses in competitiveness because of exchange rates that were pegged to a strengthening dollar—slowed economic growth somewhat, even before the current crisis.[33]

Especially interesting about Greenspan's explanation is his recognition that these wage gains created problems even though productivity kept rising—meaning that the gains were not inflationary.

At the same time, because wages in developing countries' rural areas are generally still much lower than in cities, foreign and domestic businesses do not always have to cross borders to find cheaper workers. In Thailand, apparel and shoe companies have recently started to move from Bangkok to small villages in the countryside. Chinese companies unwilling to pay workers in Shanghai $100 per month have been moving to nearby provinces as well, where wages are only $38 to $76 per month, and benefits are considerably lower as well. Third world governments like China and Indonesia, moreover, have been encouraging such moves in hopes of reducing the wealth gap between certain regions and thereby bolstering political stability.[34]

Even before the financial crisis, all this racing to the bottom has been having its predictable, if economically terrifying, result. Completely contrary to the predictions of the globalization optimists, current globalization policies are depressing, not raising, wages and living standards in enormous stretches of the developing world. In other words, the vision of the hundreds of millions of new third world workers righting the world's dangerous economic imbalances and helping to enrich their counterparts in the industrialized world is becoming more, not less, distant.

In Mexico, for example, economic liberalization and a policy of opening to the world economy have been gathering momentum since the early 1980s. Yet according to the World Bank, from 1984 to 1994—the decade before Mexico's latest peso crash—83 percent of Mexican workers suffered falling real wages.[35] Since the crash, Mexican wages have fallen even farther. And Mexico's lowest industrial wages are paid in that sector of the economy that is nothing less than a creation of foreign trade—the *maquiladora* sector, which consists of factories that almost exclusively turn imported parts and components into finished products for export. In 1999, real wages in both the *maquiladora* and domestic sectors rebounded, but still remain well below even 1994's abysmal levels. As of late 1999, these factories employed nearly 8 percent of all Mexican workers and nearly 30 percent of all Mexican manufacturing workers (up fourfold since 1983). In the first half of 1999, the *maquiladoras* generated nearly half of Mexico's total exports.[36]

In Mexico's neighbors in Central America and the Caribbean Basin, a similar pattern holds of falling real wages in thoroughly globalized sectors. Apparel is this region's biggest manufactured export, and since the early 1990s, sales to the United States from most of its countries are up tremendously. Yet even leaving out inflation, a major problem in this region, apparel industry wages actually fell in the Dominican Republic, El Salvador, Guatemala, and Honduras between 1996 and 1998. These wages only rose marginally in Costa Rica and Nicaragua. Workers outside the apparel sector generally have fared as poorly, or worse.[37]

Real wages also fell throughout the third world's superstar region, Asia, even before the financial crisis. In Indonesia between 1994 and 1997, they declined fully 11.5 percent. In the Philippines during this period, they fell 6 percent. In China, they dropped 5.4 percent (right in the middle of the peak of China's modern growth spurt). Many Chinese workers have also lost their guaranteed pensions. Further, two of the countries where real wages rose fastest in the 1990s, Thailand and South Korea, were two of the countries punished most severely when foreign investors touched off the financial crisis.[38]

Even more disturbing is the fact that third world wages have lagged far behind productivity growth in important countries. Productivity growth is almost universally regarded as a key to raising living standards on a sustainable basis. (Living standards can be raised by handing out money to people, too, but this approach is not sustainable.) Because higher productivity means more efficient workers, employers can raise wages and maintain or improve profitability without passing higher costs on to consumers. Wage and productivity levels almost never rise in lockstep—indeed, in the United States since the end of World War II, progress in the former has almost always trailed progress in the latter. Nevertheless, progress was made.

Productivity statistics are of questionable reliability even in the United States, and most economists seem to agree that U.S. government data are only beginning to capture the extraordinary gains made possible recently by information technologies, especially the internet. In developing countries, productivity data doubtless rest on even shakier ground. Yet what economists have been publishing shows not just a lag between productivity and wage increases, but in some major cases a shattered link.

In Mexico, whose workforce is becoming ever more closely integrated with the U.S. workforce, productivity rose 6.6 percent annually between 1988 and 1993, reported Carol Wise of The Johns Hopkins University and Manuel Pastor of the University of California at Santa Barbara. However, inflation-adjusted wages in Mexico actually fell during this period. According to the United Steelworkers union—a strong opponent of NAFTA—since the Free Trade Agreement with the United States, Mexican productivity has continued to grow by 36 percent. But Mexican wages have fallen 19 percent. Economist Stephen Golub of Swarthmore College made the same point in a slightly different way. He contended that in 1970, Mexican productivity was one quarter of U.S. levels—and so were Mexican wages. In 1995, however, Mexican productivity had risen to 30 percent of U.S. levels. But Mexican wages had sunk to 10 percent of these levels. Similar trends have probably unfolded in comparisons between the United States and China, according to U.S. government figures analyzed by economist James Burke of the University of Massachusetts.[39]

This unusual combination of high productivity and low wages is even recognized by Fed Chair Alan Greenspan.[40] The possible decoupling of productivity and wages in the third world has two especially troubling implications for U.S. workers. First, it would strengthen the case that the labor surplus in the developing world is so enormous that for the foreseeable future it will negate the effects of the only known recipe for achieving durable progress on living standards. As observed by the head of the official labor commission set up by NAFTA, despite impressive productivity gains, Mexico's "expected wage growth is being held down by the supply of labor and by the peso crash."[41] If major productivity improvements are not lifting wages in these countries, it is difficult to imagine what will.

Second, the combination of low productivity and high wages will make third world countries an ever more attractive site for new factories built by U.S. and other multinational companies, and make developed countries like the United States that much less attractive. Why bother with unions, regulations, and other hassles of doing business in the industrialized world if you can get low pay and high productivity without them in the third world? Why, in other words, not race to the bottom even faster?

From 1997 on, the idea that third world wages and consumption would in the foreseeable future begin catching up to levels in the industrialized countries has received what should have been a genuine coup de grâce—the steep devaluations of many Asian currencies against the U.S. dollar. As a result, from 1996 to 1999 overall purchasing power in these countries (including wages) has plummeted in dollar terms—by 46 percent in Thailand, by 51 percent in Malaysia, by 49 percent in the Philippines, by 48 percent in South Korea, and by a whopping 71 percent in Indonesia. Purchasing power in China has fallen as well in dollar terms, since the renminbi was significantly devalued in 1994.[42]

C. WHERE THE CONSUMER IS NOT KING

Yet even when wages in some of the rapidly developing countries were rising, it was unrealistic to assume that they would soon begin consuming proportionately. The reason is that most of their governments have long rejected the idea that they can consume and import their way to sustainable prosperity. Broadly speaking, they have followed the example of Japan, whose economic troubles are not so secretly delighting boosters of U.S.-style consumer capitalism, but which advanced from defeat, ruin, and starvation to economic superstardom in less than 40 years. Two key components of this economic strategy are promoting high savings rates and protecting domestic industries with trade barriers. For decades, these policies have combined to depress consumption and imports, and as explained earlier, the IMF bailout packages and austerity programs adopted voluntarily to avoid bailouts will keep both depressed for many years to come.

In the United States, and to a lesser extent, most other western industrialized countries, the consumer is king in economic policy-making. Providing U.S. consumers with the widest variety of goods at the lowest possible prices at a given moment in time has been the top priority of U.S. economic policy since the end of World War II.

Whatever the merits of this approach, however, it is not pursued by governments in most developing countries, and especially not by those in the most successful developing countries. Throughout East Asia, governments have focused on increasing savings, not consumption, and keeping savings rates high. Following Japan's example to varying degrees, countries like Singapore and Malaysia, for example, have long operated compulsory savings schemes. Certain shares of workers' earnings (21.5 percent as of mid-1997 in Singapore) are automatically deposited into government-controlled funds or state banks, and then typically channeled into the building of new productive capacity and infrastructure—e.g., factories, transportation and communications systems, schools, and research labs.[43]

Consequently, one of the world's greatest pools of capital today still is in East Asia—even after the financial crisis—and its countries boast the world's highest rates of savings and investment. In many places, quite literally, it is the law. The lion's share of this capital is in Japan, but the rapidly growing developing economies of the region have achieved savings rates averaging more than 30 percent of their economies over the last decade as well—for example, more than 40 percent in South Korea and Singapore, nearly 39 percent in Malaysia, 35 percent in China, and 33 percent in Thailand.[44]

The outsized role played by savings in East Asian economic strategies is also clear from their contribution to growth rates. According to economist David Hale of the investment firm Kemper-Zurich, investment spending in the region accounted for 30 to 35 percent of East Asia's growth during the 1990s, compared with 15 to 20 percent in the rest of the world. And even excluding savings-obsessed Japan, Asian capital investment rose from 30 percent of U.S. levels in the 1980s to 82 percent in 1996.[45] The Asian financial crisis, moreover, has convinced developing economies all around the world with lower savings rates that their current reliance on foreign capital is too risky. Thus the Philippines and bankrupt Thailand are both thinking of adopting Singaporean and Malaysian-style compulsory savings schemes. Meanwhile, broad programs to boost savings rates are being discussed or implemented in India, Mexico, and Brazil.[46]

Emerging market countries use tax policies to keep consumption down, too, regardless of whether the product is made domestically or abroad. Sales taxes on luxury goods and value-added taxes are especially popular. So are high taxes on vehicles, which are often considered luxuries and which most emerging market countries do not yet produce in great numbers. As of 1996, these stood at 12 to 36 percent in Brazil, 35 percent for most models in Indonesia, 25 to 65 percent (in the form of excise taxes) in Malaysia, and 32.5 to 45 percent in Thailand.[47] After their financial crises, Thailand, Argentina, and Brazil only managed to keep their auto industries on life support by reversing course and cutting these auto taxes. The new approach has worked while in place, but its potential is limited, for too much tax cutting in these countries could weaken their governments' financial position, and spook foreign investors all over again.[48]

The systematic and often violent suppression of labor unions in developing countries also keeps down wages and, therefore, consumption. One World Bank study has linked wage decline in Mexico to weakening union power. A fascinating report by Harvard University economist Dani Rodrik, moreover, found that wages are considerably higher in third world countries that are democracies (where unions are generally accepted), than in countries that are either partly free or full dictatorships. Rodrik also found that wages are most closely linked with productivity improvements in third world countries moving toward democracy.[49]

Suppressing consumption by erecting towering trade barriers has a long tradition in developing countries as well.[50] Many of these barriers are easily recognizable—the tariffs and quotas that countries have imposed on imports throughout recorded history. In the developing countries' cases, however, these barriers have reached genuinely breathtaking proportions.

Take China before the agreements it signed with its trade partners in order to secure entry into the World Trade Organization. Although it was the biggest potential emerging market, it was also one of the world's most protectionist countries. From 1996 to 1998, China lowered its average tariff from 42.1 percent to 17 percent, still a formidable level at a time of almost unprecedented global price competition in which literally every penny of costs counts. (In comparison, the U.S. average tariff is 2.9 percent). Yet tariffs have been much higher in sectors in which Beijing wants to develop a world-class Chinese presence—120 percent, for example on automobiles. In fact, individuals in China do not have the right to own imported automobiles; only institutions like government agencies and private businesses may do so. In industries like these (pharmaceuticals is another example), official Chinese policy explicitly aims to substitute domestic production for current imports.[51]

Tariffs, however, are not the only charge imposed on imports. Value-added taxes have been routinely imposed as well—and they have been based on the products' cost including their tariffs and any consumption taxes to which they are subject, not on their pre-tariff price. After China signed its WTO agreement with the United States, a Chinese automotive industry official announced that its remaining trade barriers would still keep Chinese auto costs four times world levels.[52]

In fact, despite nearly two decades of epochal economic reforms, China remains a largely communistic country in trade policy. Central government agencies, for example, have administered a comprehensive system of import quotas that effectively establish the level of demand in China for consumers and producers alike. For political reasons, Chinese officials also strictly limit the number and kind of foreign films and other entertainment products allowed into the country—products that are among America's most competitive. Indeed, in a recent study, economist Barry Naughton of the University of California at San Diego judges that China today is actually no more open to many imports than it was back in 1978.[53]

Another country that approaches China's record of protection is India. Even if many of its roughly one billion people were living above subsistence levels and enjoying rising real incomes, they would be prevented from buying numerous foreign products by pervasive trade barriers. Despite years of liberalizing economic reforms, India's maximum tariff still stands at 45 percent and was actually raised in the fall of 1997. Indian tariffs, moreover, tend to be highest for products that are also made in India and are often no match for their foreign counterparts. As a 1996 Indian government policy paper explained: "When it is required to face competition, domestic industry will be assured of a level playing field." Consequently, foreign producers face Indian tariffs of up to 40 percent on autos, air conditioners, and refrigeration equipment, and soft drinks; 20 to 40 percent on paper; and 10 percent on instant camera film. Like China, India also imposes a slew of additional charges on imports. In combination with tariffs, these charges can raise the consumer price of products like household appliances by 63 percent more.[54]

Even these often prohibitive tariffs , however, cannot even come into play unless exporters can penetrate India's import licensing system. For example, as of early 2000, New Delhi banned outright the importation of thousands of types of consumer goods. The importation of thousands of other kinds of products is either restricted to government monopolies or requires elusive licenses. The latter category includes all the consumer goods whose importation is not banned outright. Not surprisingly, the Indian government maintains a sweeping "Buy Indian" policy for government purchases. In January 2000, the U.S. government proudly announced a new bilateral trade agreement under which India would lift license requirements on 1,400 products. But India promptly moved to raise tariffs on these products to sky-high levels.[55]

Buying foreign goods was never easy for Indonesia's 200 million potential consumers, either, even before they lost nearly 80 percent of their purchasing power due to the financial crisis. Indonesia tariffs are falling steadily, but various import surcharges, value-added taxes, and the aforementioned luxury taxes are still pricing many key goods out of the Indonesian market. Indonesia maintains an active, though shrinking, import-licensing regime as well.

Even before its financial crisis in 1998–99, importing in Brazil was excruciatingly difficult as well—and becoming more so. The U.S. trade negotiator's office reports that in 1994, Brazil expanded government purchasing practices to give price breaks to domestic producers of telecommunications equipment and services, computers, software, and some digital electronics products. Brazil has been tightening up on auto imports, too. Most other Brazilian tariffs run between 20 and 30 percent, but importers must also pay federal value-added taxes, state value-added taxes, and high port and dock taxes. Brazil's import-licensing system has been liberal by developing-country standards, but in December 1997, the government tightened requirements on some 300 products. When the country devalued its currency in January 1999, it gained such competitive advantages over its neighbors that a series of disputes began roiling Brazil's trade relations with Argentina, a country with which it had signed a much ballyhooed trade agreement.[56]

Before the Asian financial crisis, South Korea was the world's eleventh largest economy. Moreover, personal consumption was growing by 8 percent annually. Except for farmers, however, foreign producers have had few meaningful opportunities to compete for this market. In fact, for many years it was so difficult for South Koreans to buy foreign products that they had to travel abroad to stock up—and typically spent half their travel budgets on shopping until Seoul imposed limits on credit card use overseas in 1996. South Korea imposes the standard array of tariffs and other discriminatory taxes on imports. In the case of autos, these levies can nearly double the price paid by consumers.[57]

Tariffs and quotas are only the tip of the iceberg of protectionism in developing countries. As observed by a recent report from the U.S. International Trade Commission about Asia, the impact of nontariff barriers—the myriad, often ingenious bureaucratic and regulatory practices designed to shut out foreign products—is "far greater in scope than the impact of tariffs."[58] Because the rule of law is at best weak in most of these countries, few of these barriers are written down in law books or other government publications. Instead, they are informally developed and administered almost exclusively at the discretion of government officials who usually are barely accountable to elected leaders (if such exist), much less consumers. Would-be exporters and foreign governments usually find these barriers difficult enough to identify and document, let alone negotiate away.

The Chinese, for example, have made a fine art out of keeping trade regulations a secret from foreign businesses. Despite a 1992 agreement with the United States, for example, no laws or regulations in the government procurement field have yet been publically revealed at all. In the Kafka-esque world of the Chinese trade bureaucracy, when regulations have been published, exporters often have found it difficult to learn whether they apply to their products or not. And when regulations have been written clearly, they often have been applied in a highly inconsistent, arbitrary manner.

For example, Chinese bureaucrats have had no qualms about excluding foreign goods failing to meet standards of quality and safety that the U.S. Trade Representative's office has considered "overly strict, unevenly applied, and not backed up by modern laboratory techniques." In addition, many Chinese standards "differ from international standards for no apparent reason." Beijing also has routinely forced imports to conform to standards not applied to domestic products.

China's most notorious nontariff trade barrier may be its toleration of massive intellectual property theft. Despite China's signing of agreements with Washington in 1995 and 1996 to reduce the infringements of patents, trademarks, and copyrights, the Software Publisher's Association, a U.S. industry group, estimates that the rate of Chinese software piracy is unchanged in recent years—at 96 percent. The Trade Representative's office adds that "Trademark piracy appears to be on the increase." One big problem hampering enforcement efforts has been that many of the counterfeit CD, video, and software operations are controlled by Chinese officials or their relatives.[59]

India uses its byzantine customs system as a major trade barrier as well. Voluminous documentation is required for imports, delays are frequent, goods are routinely misclassified and incorrectly valuated, and plain old corruption is rampant. In addition, India's food safety standards and government procurement laws are largely secretive, and some that are published do not pass the laugh test. For example, India has quarantined produce capable of hosting pests that are already present in the country. Like many of the emerging market countries, India is considered by the United States to be a leading violator of intellectual property rights. Similar intellectual property horror stories can be told about Indonesia, where counterfeit pharmaceutical products sometimes appear in local markets before the genuine article is registered by the government.

Brazil, hailed as Latin America's leading emerging market and an unusually promising customer for U.S. products, has claimed that U.S. agricultural products carry diseases that international scientific bodies certify have been eliminated in the United States. Like many other developing countries, it forces foreign producers in many industries to license their technology to domestic companies. In addition to not enforcing many of its existing intellectual property laws, Brazil sometimes requires a product to be made domestically in order to enjoy even nominal protection.

When it comes to nontariff barriers, however, Korea has been in a class by itself. Exporters' problems often have started at the dock. Korean customs procedures have been considered to be among Asia's most cumbersome—even perishable fruits and vegetables can be kept aboard ship or on the docks for up to five days. Seoul has required importers of processed foods to yield their most valuable trade secrets—their ingredients (including exact portions) and their production techniques. Many other manufacturing industries have been forced to submit blueprints and formulae to Korean officials, who have regularly leaked them to the press or directly to their Korean competitors. Customs inspectors have frequently barred imports because clearance forms contained erasure marks or were typed in the wrong font size, and they have arbitrarily changed tariff rates.

Korea's Ministry of Health regularly has required two years of testing before approving imports of American pharmaceuticals already certified as safe by Washington. As in China, many trade-related laws and regulations either have not been published at all or have been too vague to provide adequate guidance. Further, borrowing from the Japanese, Seoul has encouraged or tolerated the creation of huge industrial conglomerates—the *chaebol*—which, until the financial crisis, systematically refused to purchase supplies from competitive foreign companies and have operated equally exclusive wholesale and retail national distribution systems. Korea's intellectual property authorities even have passed a literal Mickey Mouse regulation—U.S. cartoon characters are sometimes denied trademark status if the Koreans judge that they embody no artistry or creativity.

But by far Korea's most innovative trade barriers have been the various anti-import campaigns either run openly or encouraged by the government. Since 1989, whenever Korea's imports approached what Seoul considered worrisome levels, the government has actually launched propaganda drives and sponsored bureaucratic and even physical harassment aimed at discouraging them. In mid-1996, for example, Korean government officials, journalists, and "consumer groups" embarked on a "frugality" campaign that included a flood of statements reminding Koreans that buying imports weakened the country's balance of payments. Although the Korean government denied involvement, Seoul refused for months to criticize the anti-import aspects of the campaign.

Automobiles have been a special focus of the anti-import campaigns. From December 1996 into early 1997, Korean tax authorities began to subject consumers who leased foreign cars to tax audits. Partially government-owned television stations have run public service messages featuring celebrities urging Koreans to buy small domestic vehicles instead of big imports. Some gas stations have refused to service foreign cars. In addition, import owners reportedly have been threatened, harassed, and even vandalized. As of March 1998, reports of "unofficial" harassment of foreign car buyers were still appearing.[60]

The final economic strategy of developing countries that will continue to prevent them from even roughly balancing their exports with imports is the premium they place on exporting. The tremendous gap between investment levels and growth rates in regions like Asia is enough to explain much of the export orientation. Even before the financial crisis, investment rates in the region were rising about three times faster than economic growth rates. If the surplus is not exported, many of these investments will be wasted. Much of this excessive investment growth, in turn, stems from the tension between the small size of some of the leading Asian manufacturing powers and the production levels needed to achieve scale economies in many critical industries. As a Korean businessman told a *Wall Street Journal* reporter in 1996, "Korea's market is so small, everyone relies on exports." At present, it would be impossible to run a world-class automobile industry, for example, that simply served the Korean market or a world-class semiconductor industry that sold only to Singaporeans. The necessary levels of efficiency would never be achieved.[61]

Because of these disparities, many governments in Asia and other emerging markets create numerous pressures and incentives to export.[62] China has provided Chinese exporters with cut-rate credit, tax breaks, and special access to supplies of energy and raw materials. Beijing also has imposed export quotas on Chinese firms as well as on businesses that include foreign partners. Sometimes these requirements have been quite onerous. Kodak, for example, was recently permitted to build a camera factory outside Shanghai, but only if it exported 100 percent of its output. In fact, China maintains a system of foreign trade zones throughout the country in which manufacturers are exempted from considerable red tape as well as most tariffs on imports provided the bulk of their production is exported. Since the financial crisis has lowered the price of exports from its Asian neighbors, China has countered by nearly doubling the level of tax rebates it provides to exporters.[63]

One of the largest and best known export processing arrangements is the *maquiladora* program. Since 1966, Mexico has encouraged the construction of factories along its border with the United States whose purpose is to receive parts and components from U.S. suppliers, turn them into finished goods or process them further, and send them right back to the United States for final sale. By early 1998, thousands of *maquiladora* factories accounted for 46 percent of Mexico's total exports and more than half of its exports of manufactured goods. As of 1998, they employed more than one million Mexicans, nearly 28 percent of the country's manufacturing workforce.[64]

India boasts a system of export processing zones, too. These not only permit participating businesses to operate free of the country's high tariffs and intrusive bureaucrats, but grant them five-year tax holidays plus exemptions from taxes on export earnings once the holidays end. Although the policy aims to reduce red tape for exporters, India's export mania is best revealed by the extraordinarily detailed requirements that companies must satisfy to receive these incentives. Producers inside these zones are permitted to sell to the Indian market, but only if they can obtain an import license. That is to say, their output is not considered by the Indian government to be domestically produced. India has also set up special export-oriented arrangements for software producers if they sell abroad 1.5 times the value of their equipment imports plus 1.5 times the value of the wages they pay.[65]

One of the world's most comprehensive and detailed systems of export promotion is run by Malaysia. It provides low-cost export financing not only to direct exporters (who make the final products that are actually shipped abroad) but to the "indirect exporters" that supply them with various raw materials, fuels, parts, components, and services. Double tax breaks are granted for the insurance of exported products, for advertising them, for overseas business research, for foreign business travel, for the costs of maintaining foreign sales offices, and for building the warehouses where export goods are temporarily stored.

Malaysia also permits exporters to import supplies duty-free if these materials cannot be obtained locally for a reasonable price. In fact, most machinery and equipment can be imported duty-free into Malaysia, because so much of the country's industrial base is geared toward exporting. Further, the more of its output a foreign-owned factory in Malaysia exports, the fewer local partners it must work with. Plants that export 80 percent or more of their production can be wholly owned by foreign interests.[66]

These anti-consumption, proexport policies have distorted the economies of many emerging market countries and world trade patterns in genuinely ludicrous ways. In 1995, for example, even before its financial crisis, South Korea produced more than 1.87 million passenger cars. Forty-two percent (nearly 804,000) were exported—a figure that does not count vehicles sent abroad as kits (full collections of parts) that are assembled in the exporting country. In 1996, as the first signs of major economic problems appeared in Korea, some 46 percent of the 2.13 million cars produced in Korea were sold abroad, and both production and exports grew at roughly the same pace in 1997 (again, excluding the kits). In 1998, the first year of full-blown financial crisis, Korean car production slumped badly—to just under 1.6 million vehicles. But exports kept rising—to 1.15 milion—and had jumped to an astonishing 73 percent of total production. Korea began to recover in 1999, with total car production rebounding to 2.16 million vehicles. Exports however, continued to grow as well, and still represented more than 64 percent of the total. Even after the crisis struck, Korean automakers were still talking about building new factories in South Korea and elsewhere in the world. In another industry, Korea also exported 90 percent of the semiconductors it produces.[67]

In 1996, Mexico produced 1.2 million motor vehicles and exported nearly one million. Mexico has also become the world's largest exporter of automotive engines. The overwhelming majority of this output is sent to the United States.[68] Taiwan, meanwhile, exports 90 percent of the millions of personal computers it manufactures each year, 88 percent of the semiconductors, and 75 percent of the textiles. On the other end of the technology spectrum, China exports 90 percent of the three billion pairs of shoes it produces annually.[69]

Finally, developing countries promote exports through currency devaluations, which make their products cheaper in foreign markets. China's devaluation of the renminbi in 1994 did much to spark the Asian financial crisis. It enabled many Chinese goods to undersell and crowd out the exports of other developing Asian countries in Western markets. South Korea was especially damaged in 1995 by Japan's devaluation of the yen. The Clinton administration has showered praise on China for maintaining its currency's value after its crisis-stricken neighbors permitted their own money to cheapen. However, through the aforementioned rebates, other subsidies, and even the domestic price deflation it has permitted for more than three years, China has reaped many of the benefits of devaluing without suffering either the economic costs or global criticism and retaliation.[70]

In all, the most important thing to know about the present and future of purchasing power in the developing world is what President Clinton told a Democratic party group in late 1999: "[Six] billion people on the face of the Earth. Half of them live on $2 a day or less; 1.3 billion live on $1 a day or less." This group is almost entirely found in the developing world. And where solid incomes progress is made, there can be little doubt that the interacting effects of the race to the bottom and heavy indebtedness will nip it in the bud.[71]

5 A NEW KIND OF TRADE

THE DRIVE OF DEVELOPING COUNTRIES TO PRODUCE AND EXPORT their way to prosperity not only makes for some bizarre export patterns, it makes for some bizarre import patterns as well. The total imports of these countries strongly indicate that, even though the effects of the financial crisis still linger, they are already becoming the huge markets predicted by the globalizers—if not huge enough net importers to rebalance world trade flows. Their total imports are so great that many even run merchandise trade deficits with the rest of the world, although not with the United States. (China is a notable exception. It has run a merchandise trade surplus with the rest of the world for much of the last decade.)

Yet the makeup of these imports is nothing like the makeup of U.S. imports. The vast bulk fits in perfectly with the production/exporting strategy, because these imports are comprised of what are called producer or investment goods. As opposed to finished or consumer goods (and the existing classification schemes make analysis tricky), they are not intended to be used in any way by individuals or by the businesses that cater to individuals. Their purpose is to build, operate, supply, and support industries. In the case of the developing countries and their anti-consumption bias, this means industries that mainly export. Producer goods consist of the machinery and equipment needed to construct factories for export goods, the energy and other infrastructure systems needed to run those factories, and the raw materials and parts and components needed to produce goods (usually finished goods but sometimes larger, more complex parts and components called systems or assemblies) that are shipped right back overseas. A large share of these investment goods comes from the United States, often through the investments and shipments of U.S.-owned multinational corporations.

The continuing buildup of production capacity in many key developing economies combined with their suppression of consumption at home will have increasingly profound effects on global trade patterns for decades. These trends are already becoming great obstacles to U.S. hopes of better balancing purchases from the developing countries with sales to these countries. In the first place, as new factories in developing countries come on line, these countries will maintain or further boost their already robust exports to the United States, and further widen their surpluses with the United States. In the second place, either because it is good business or because they value greater economic self-reliance for strategic reasons, most developing countries are striving to produce their own investment and producer goods. As they succeed in these endeavors, U.S. trade with these countries will become even more unbalanced, and hopes for the United States to earn its way in the world will become ever dimmer.

For now, however, the skewed nature of developing-country trade patterns is having another major effect—it is transforming the nature of many U.S. exports to these countries. Even more important, the impact of exports in general on U.S. living standards is changing dramatically. Once assumed to be unambiguously positive contributors to job creation and wage growth, the best evidence indicates that because they are increasingly dominated by producer goods, exports to emerging market countries have now turned into a little-noticed drag on U.S. living standards. Unfortunately, the national debate on globalization has not fully caught up with this reality, and U.S. multinational companies, with some help from American politicians and too many in the media, are doing their best to keep the public in the dark.

A. ALL EXPORTS ARE NOT CREATED EQUAL

Economists inside and outside of governments around the world are just starting to get their arms around the new trade in producer goods and the outsourcing patterns they reveal. One huge problem has been that the internationally used classification schemes for traded goods still do not always distinguish between intermediate and final products. Moreover, many developing countries did not begin even using revisions that were made to these categories until very recently. Nonetheless, published research reveals that this new trade has reached staggering dimensions. According to one World Bank estimate, it stood at some 30 percent of global two-way manufacturing trade, or $800 billion annually, as of 1995, and had grown steadily since 1978.[1]

The degree to which the imports of developing countries are dominated by producer and investment goods is impressive. Take the Asian debtor countries. South Korea, the world's eleventh largest economy before the Asian crisis, is a country in which real wages were rising healthily for most of the last 15 years. As of 1997, however, consumer goods were still only about 10 percent of total imports, and this share had actually fallen since 1980. In 1992, consumer goods totalled 2 percent of Indonesia's total imports. Figures from the U.S. embassy in Jakarta indicate that, as of 1998, producer goods still dominated Indonesia's foreign purchases. Thailand has been portrayed as the spendthrift of Asia, but as of 1996, raw materials and capital goods alone made up 74 percent of its imports. In addition, in the 1980s, as total annual import growth accelerated from 7 percent to 22 percent, the share of consumer goods imports actually fell, too.[2]

Even Taiwan, a genuinely advanced Asian industrialized country that largely escaped the Asian crisis, tightly concentrates its imports in the producer goods categories. Only 10.6 percent of its foreign purchases in 1999 were consumer goods, and imports of these products plunged by fully 23.4 percent.[3]

The rest of developing Asia displays similar trade patterns. In 1992, consumer goods imports represented only 13 percent of total Malaysian imports. By 1995, this figure had reached only 14.2 percent. However, producer goods also rose as a share of total imports. In fact, as of 1999, Malaysia classified 70 percent of its imports as producer goods. According to a governor of the Philippine central bank, his country's imports consist almost entirely of raw materials and capital goods for reexport purposes. And the meager share of total imports held by consumer goods keeps falling sharply.[4]

As for Asia's biggest potential market, only 4 percent of U.S. exports to China in 1996 were consumer goods, according to a study issued by the Federal Reserve Bank of New York. In fact, the authors estimate that only 20 percent of China's total imports reach China's domestic markets. The other 80 percent consists of capital goods and industrial inputs used in the country's vast network of export processing zones—and of course sold abroad.[5]

The role of such trade seems to be growing rapidly. The previously cited study by the University of California at San Diego's Barry Naughton contends that 58 percent of China's total world exports in 1998 consisted of imported inputs that were reexported as finished goods—twice the 1988 percentage. Further, the previously cited World Bank production-sharing report shows that China's imports of components alone (not including the capital goods that go into building and equipping factories) jumped five-fold from 1978 to 1995.[6]

The figures for individual industries often are even more striking. For all the talk of the booming Chinese market for computers, the latest figures show that only 10.4 percent of China's computer imports were completed machines. Fully 70 percent of these imports were components. As the official *China Daily* explained, "Only a small number of microcomputers were imported. Most big foreign companies had expanded their production facilities to factories within China." Indeed, in late 1999, an IBM executive openly told a reporter that the company now makes almost all the PCs it sells to China in China. Even two years ago, only 30 percent of the IBM computers bought by China were made elsewhere.[7]

By contrast, between 1992 and 1999, consumer goods as a share of total goods imports for the United States stayed constant at about 35.5 percent, and unlike developing Asian countries, the United States is an advanced industrialized society with a broad-based, state-of-the-art manufacturing base.[8]

The slight role played by U.S. consumer goods exports in U.S.-Asian trade was revealed in 1997 by Jonathan Menes, director of the Commerce Department's Office of Trade and Economic Analysis. No, Mr. Menes told a reporter, he didn't expect the financial crisis-induced fall in Asian demand to greatly affect U.S. exports to the region. Why not? Because "many U.S. exports to the region were computer parts assembled in other countries and then reexported to the U.S...." His analysis echoes one produced recently by the Federation of Swedish Industries, traditionally a strong supporter of open trade policies. According to the Swedish report, "Imports [in East Asia] are usually concentrated on necessary capital equipment and raw materials used in export industries."[9]

Similarly, two analysts at the Morgan Stanley Dean Witter investment firm have observed that Asia is not the final market for many of the electronics products it imports. Though they did not specify why, the obvious answer is that they are not finished goods. In addition, free trade enthusiast Barry Bosworth of the Brookings Institution wrote that U.S. firms use Asia "as a processing base for products that ultimately return for sale in the U.S. market. . . ."[10]

Given these import patterns, it should not be surprising that U.S. exports to these countries are dominated by the same producer goods. However, the ways in which these types of exports work to depress U.S. living standards has gone almost unnoticed. In fact, the almost universal failure to distinguish between different types of exports has produced a fundamentally misleading picture of how trade flows influence living standards nowadays. Exports are thought to boost employment and raise living standards for reasons economists and many businesspeople regard as rather obvious. As explained by a recent White House report, if companies can add foreign customers to their roster of domestic customers, they can earn more revenue, hire more workers if they wish, and afford to pay them higher wages and benefits.[11]

Unfortunately, this reasoning applies neatly only to exports of finished consumer products, like airplanes or personal computers or blue jeans. A substantial portion of U.S. goods exports—by some measures, most U.S. exports—do not fall into this category. For example, some 60 percent of U.S. goods exports consist of capital goods—usually the equipment and machinery used to build factories, and often the complete factories themselves, when American companies decide to move them abroad.[12] In other words, when a company decides to move one of its U.S. factories to another country and staffs it with foreign workers, this transaction is called an export—and this supposedly creates jobs in the United States just like the export of an airliner would.

To be sure, moving production facilities abroad can create more U.S. jobs than would otherwise exist, and thus drive wages up by increasing the demand for U.S. labor. For example, by manufacturing its product in a country where wages are lower than in the United States, a company can in principle increase its sales both at home and abroad, and use the profits to start making new, more sophisticated products in the United States that require higher-wage workers. Similarly, since many products consist of both relatively simple and relatively complex parts, companies can lower production costs by building the simpler parts in low-wage countries. Not only can the resulting cheaper final products in principle sell better both at home and abroad, the demand for U.S.-made parts and other inputs for these final products can increase in the process. President Clinton seemed to allude to this effect when he contended in late 1999, "Sure, if we buy stuff made somewhere else, where people don't have the incomes we do, it puts more pressure on our low-wage workers. But it also creates a lot more high-wage jobs."[13]

In addition, companies often find they can keep up better with new trends in foreign markets and therefore sell more goods there if they set up shop in those markets. The need to ensure that new products get onto store shelves ASAP is another powerful reason to manufacture abroad.

Finally, and especially important in terms of the changing nature of exports to low-income countries, companies can lower costs by sending U.S.-made parts and components of products abroad for further processing or final assembly. Turning these intermediate goods into finished products or turning them into systems or assemblies is often less advanced work than producing the original intermediate goods themselves. Therefore, this work often can be done by lower-skilled workers in low-wage countries. The result is lower production costs, and final products that are more price-competitive in foreign and domestic markets alike. In 1999, 20 percent of U.S. exports consisted of such "industrial supplies" (i.e., producer goods, a category consisting not only of parts and components but fuels and raw materials) if auto parts are added on.[14]

From the perspective of U.S. workers, however, the problem with exports of producer and intermediate goods to low-income countries is that little evidence can be found of their job- and wage-boosting effects at home. President Clinton and other globalization cheerleaders notwithstanding, the best available evidence indicates that such exports are not creating more good American jobs than they displace (by making American companies' final products or systems or assemblies more competitive and enabling them to win new customers at home and abroad).

It is undeniable that this new type of trading is indeed helping many individual U.S. companies reap such cost savings and increase their competitiveness around the world, thereby enabling them to employ more workers at better wages. However, the enormous, continually growing trade deficits piled up by the United States with every major area of the world, including most of the biggest developing country manufacturing powers, indicate that these results are not being achieved on an economy-wide basis.

That is to say, goods made in the United States with these imported inputs of various types are not winning as many new foreign customers as are the foreign goods they compete against. The deficits further indicate that foreign goods are winning more of the new domestic customers being created by strong U.S. growth rates.

In fact, the best evidence about this new form of trade indicates that all too few such exports are even geared toward helping U.S. companies serve new customers abroad—least of all in the emerging market countries. As has been discussed, not only do their governments suppress their individual citizens' consumption of all goods, but little of what they do import is bought and used and enjoyed by individual consumers. Instead, developing countries overwhelmingly use these imports as the building blocks and infrastructure for export goods. The best evidence—especially the huge, long-standing deficits—further indicates that, from the standpoint of U.S. workers, too many of these exports are geared toward helping U.S. companies hang on to the same domestic customers that they have always had (by substituting foreign factories and workers for American in their production chains). When this strategy works, it is clearly good for the companies. However, it is just as clearly bad for U.S. workers.

In this light, the export of parts and components is really little more than the supply of new foreign factories in a company's production chain that do work once done by domestic factories. The only reason that shipments to these new foreign factories are called exports is that they happen to be located abroad. Jeffrey Garten, formerly the top trade official in the Commerce Department, made this point in a 1994 speech: "In cases like the automobile industry, for example, talking about 'trade' between the U.S. and Canada makes about as much sense as talking about 'trade' between Michigan and Ohio." Of course, the only difference is that all the workers in Michigan and Ohio are Americans.[15]

B. The Mexican Example

These new kinds of trade patterns and their effects on U.S. workers are most clearly illustrated by recent U.S. trade with Mexico. This trade has of course been profoundly influenced by the North American Free Trade Agreement of 1993, and by the changes in economic policy and in production patterns on both sides of the border during the 1980s that paved the way for the treaty. Supporters of NAFTA and its blueprint for expanded U.S.-Mexico economic ties repeatedly predicted that its biggest effects would be on traditional types of imports and exports—sales of finished consumer goods between unrelated buyers and sellers. As mentioned earlier, Vice President Al Gore voiced these expectations memorably in his televised debate with NAFTA opponent H. Ross Perot. His words are worth quoting at length:

> Did you see the Wal-Mart that opened in Mexico City in the news? Largest one in the world, if I understand it. They have 72 cash registers ringing constantly with people in that—in Mexico taking American products out of that store. We have this image of them being so poor that they can't possibly buy any electronic equipment or anything else that we make. They are poorer than we are. But you know what? They spend more per person on American products than any other country except Japan. . . . If we lower those trade barriers and get rid of them altogether, we will have an export surge into Mexico. . . .

In Gore's view, the domestic impact would be clear: "When you sell more products, you make more products. When you make more products, you hire more people." For good measure, the vice president added that "the vast majority, 80 to 90 percent [of U.S. exports to Mexico] stay in Mexico and are bought there," not reexported to the United States.[16]

During NAFTA's first year, Gore's expectations appeared to be fulfilled, as U.S. goods exports to Mexico did surge. One year later, Mexico's economy crashed. The Mexican peso fell in value by 47 percent. The economy itself contracted by an almost unheard of 7 percent. Yet after the dust had settled, the drop-off in U.S. exports turned out to be modest. NAFTA supporters claimed vindication. According to the Clinton administration, "Comparing Mexico's recovey in 1996 with Mexico's recovery from its last financial crisis in 1982, when NAFTA was not in effect, reveals that both the Mexican economy and American exports recovered more rapidly following the 1995 crisis than the 1982 crisis, in part because of the economic reforms locked in by NAFTA." Similar arguments were made by NAFTA supporters in the media and academe.[17]

However, the idea of Mexico as a major traditional-style market for U.S. goods was always questionable. At NAFTA's signing,

Mexico's economy was only one-thirtieth the size of the U.S. economy. Moreover, as has been documented, the wages of most Mexicans remained abysmally low. Mexico did indeed experience a brief consumption boom in the early 1990s, but the peso crisis demonstrated that the boom was phony—fueled by a government-encouraged explosion of short-term borrowing. Indeed, the boom was disastrous, since the borrowing carried interest rates that Mexico could not possibly repay.

More important, even with the short-lived immediate post-NAFTA spike in Mexican imports of consumption goods, such products never rose above 10 to 15 percent of Mexico's total imports. In 1996, they fell to 7.4 percent and rose only to 8.4 percent in 1997.[18] These trends continued in 1999. The country's total imports fell by 1.5 percent, but intermediate goods and capital goods imports actually rose by 4.5 percent and 10.8 percent, respectively. Consumer imports fell by 18.9 percent.[19]

In other words, most U.S. exports to Mexico before, during, and since the peso crisis have been producer goods—in particular, parts and components sent by U.S. multinationals to their Mexican factories for assembly or for further processing. The vast majority of these, moreover, are reexported, and most get shipped right back to the United States for final sale. In fact, by most estimates, the United States buys 80 to 90 percent of all of Mexico's exports.

This is why U.S. exports to Mexico remained strong despite the collapse of Mexican consumer demand. Since such a big percentage of U.S. sales to Mexico is not consumed in Mexico, U.S. export levels have almost nothing to do with the health of the Mexican economy. Because the final destination of these U.S. exports is the U.S. market, U.S. companies can keep exporting vigorously to Mexico even when its economy shrinks.[20]

Although the U.S. government does not systematically track Mexico's reexports back to the United States, some idea of their magnitude can be gleaned from Mexican government figures. Mexico distinguishes between the different types of imports from the United States because the investment-type imports never reach the Mexican domestic economy. Many do not affect Mexico's international balance of payments, either, because they are paid for by U.S.-owned factories in U.S. dollars, not pesos. One of the most detailed studies of U.S.-Mexico trade—one commissioned by the U.S. Department of Labor—found that the recent increase in trade has been "driven almost entirely by an expansion of Mexican manufactured exports based on the processing of intermediate imports."[21]

As mentioned in the Preface, perhaps the most striking confirmation of the true character of U.S.-Mexico trade and its impact on U.S. workers was provided by President Clinton during the fast-track debate in the fall of 1997. Addressing a convention of the staunchly anti-fast track AFL-CIO, Clinton insisted that his request for new trade negotiating authority was "not about NAFTA or factories moving there to sell back to here."[22] Unfortunately, for U.S. workers, Clinton waited until after the agreement was four years old to make his confession.

C. SERVING CONSUMERS?

In the wake of the controversy stirred by NAFTA, numerous reports and studies have appeared purporting to refute the argument that producer goods exports to low-income countries destroy high-wage U.S. jobs on net. Their chief claims focus on the foreign and domestic activities of U.S. multinational corporations, which engage in most of this trade. Specifically, supporters of current trade policy argue that U.S.-owned or affiliated factories abroad sell most of their output abroad, not back to the United States. Thus, they contend, U.S. exports to these factories are indeed serving a growing list of new foreign customers, and therefore creating high-paying U.S. jobs on net. They add they are not substituting foreign workers for U.S. workers in efforts to hang onto the existing customers, or to hang onto them while earning higher profits. Similarly, many argue that the U.S. multinationals that own all the factories overseas nonetheless still rely overwhelmingly on U.S.-made parts and components for their finished goods, not foreign-made inputs. In other words, they imply, U.S.-Mexico trade is an exception to the pattern of most U.S. trade with emerging market countries.

This claim that U.S. investment in these countries is increasingly—and even mainly—serving new foreign markets is now routinely made and reported in the press. According to a study by the Deloitte & Touche Consulting Group, U.S. manufacturing companies are becoming more interested in establishing positions in large, prosperous markets than with accessing cheap labor when they invest abroad. A *Wall Street Journal* headline also announced, "Major U.S. Companies Expand Efforts to Sell to Consumers Abroad: Many No Longer Consider Emerging Nations Merely Sources of Cheap Labor." The new trade patterns, the article reported, contradicted "the general notion that American companies' foreign investments mainly finance cheap imports into the U.S."[23] These claims are also made by the most authoritative U.S. government study available on this subject, as well as in three recent reports on multinationals' activity at home and abroad by the Emergency Committee for American Trade (ECAT), the Economic Strategy Institute (ESI), and the Institute for International Economics (IIE).[24]

Yet these reports are more important for underscoring the positively surreal nature of the debate over producer goods exports than they are for clarifying trade flows and their implications. After all, the government agency publishing the multinationals report—the Commerce Department's Bureau of Economic Analysis—is aware of just how little its data actually reveal. The BEA, for example, does not track some of the most important journeys taken by producer goods, especially parts and components, as they travel across national borders through the production systems of multinational companies. Another shortcoming of current data is that U.S. (and other) multinationals have developed types of business relationships in low-income countries that are completely missed by the BEA statistics.

Finally, BEA data suffer a significant time lag. The latest data only cover multinational operations up to 1997, even though the late 1990s saw a continuing upsurge in U.S. investment in low-income countries whose effects on trade flows and living standards are just beginning to be understood. As the factories built by this investment rev up, their sales to the United States (and, in principle, to other markets), will surely rise. In addition, few very recent statistics provide enough details on specific industries or regions to shed much light on corporate activity in sectors where outsourcing is relatively easy (e.g., manufacturing), as opposed to those where outsourcing is more difficult or impossible (e.g., many services).

The BEA is also legally prohibited from publically releasing any data that could shed light on the activities of individual firms. The result is that the companies' trade secrets are protected, but the people of the United States and their leaders are denied information they need to evaluate the real domestic effects of globalization.

The Economic Strategy Institute, the Emergency Committee for American Trade, and the Institute for International Economics are in an even more awkward situation as they are mainly funded by precisely those U.S. multinational companies that generate most of the exports in question. These companies know exactly which factories they own or contract with. They know which ones handle which specific phase of the production processes for the goods they sell. They know why they place factories in particular locations, how many foreign workers they employ, what they do, what they earn, and where the final products are sold. How could any company make money without this information? Although the U.S. government is barred from releasing company-specific data, the companies themselves are not. They could end the debate over producer exports tomorrow, simply by opening their books to the think tanks they have hired. However, they claim that, in the process, they would reveal valuable trade secrets to competitors, so they keep the information to themselves.

All, for example, look at BEA figures showing where the products made by the foreign facilities of multinationals are sold. According to the IIE report only 10 percent of the sales of all enterprises known as majority-owned foreign affiliates (MOFAs—foreign businesses that are more than 50 percent owned by U.S. corporations) are made to customers in the United States. The rest of this output is sold to foreign customers. The figures for low-income countries in Asia and Latin America—where private consumption is much lower, local markets less lucrative, and therefore trade with the United States is less balanced—are higher, but not overwhelmingly so. And the even higher figures for countries like Singapore and Malaysia are offset by lower figures in countries like the Philippines and Thailand.

As the IIE report observed, the implications seem clear: "The picture that emerges is one of U.S. [investment] undertaken more to service high income markets than to exploit locally cheap labor." This finding, moreover, is portrayed as strongly supporting the conclusion that "U.S. investments and exports are complementary"—i.e., investment is not substituting for U.S.-based production and U.S. workers.[25]

However, these figures tell only part of the story. By lumping together investments in manufacturing on the one hand, and finance and wholesale businesses and other services on the other, these figures lump together investments in products that can be traded in the first place with investments in products that generally are not traded internationally at all. The picture in manufacturing—which does produce tradable goods, and which, of course, generates the best-paying U.S. jobs on average—is somewhat different. According to the latest (1997) BEA data, 10.2 percent of total worldwide MOFA sales are made to the United States, but the figure for MOFA worldwide manufacturing sales is nearly 15 percent.[26] Even this figure, however, masks big differences between the operations of affiliates in high-income and low-income countries. It also masks big differences among different industries operating in these low-income countries.

For example, only 4.8 percent of the sales of manufacturing MOFAs in Western Europe are made directly to the United States. This figure, moreover, has been growing. Since 1982, however, the inflation-adjusted output of all U.S. manufacturing MOFAs in the rest of the world—mainly developing countries—has been growing much faster.[27] In addition, fully 22.2 percent of the sales of these affiliates in Latin America and the rest of the Western Hemisphere (excluding Canada) are made directly to the United States—nearly five times the levels for Western Europe. For Asia (including Japan, which is a high-income country but one that buys relatively few manufactured goods not made by Japanese-owned companies), the figure is much higher than for Europe as well—18.8 percent.

The figures for individual countries are even more revealing. Manufacturing MOFAs in Mexico, the Latin American country whose economy is most highly integrated with the U.S. economy, make 43 percent of their sales directly to the United States. Manufacturing MOFAs in Malaysia, a major site of U.S. industrial investment, sell more than 42 percent of their output directly to the United States. Their counterparts in Singapore sell 41 percent of their output directly to the United States. In fact, the Lehman Brothers investment firm reports that these products constitute 99 percent of total U.S. goods imports from Singapore.[28]

The data for specific industries in these countries shed still more light on outsourcing. Singapore-based MOFAs in industrial machinery and equipment make 52 percent of their sales directly to the United States. Mexican MOFAs in the electronics and electrical equipment sectors sell nearly 70 percent of their output directly to U.S. customers. In transportation equipment (mainly cars, trucks, and their parts), where massive U.S. investments have been made in the last decade, the figure is 63 percent. U.S. auto industry figures show that the numbers for vehicles alone is far higher. According to the Big Three's former trade association, the American Automobile Manufacturers Association, fully 94 percent of the 210,198 cars and trucks exported by Chrysler, Ford, and GM from Mexico in 1997 were sold to the United States, and most of these non-U.S. exports were generated by GM. Three years after NAFTA's passage, Ford did not export a single one of its Mexican-made vehicles to a market other than the United States. Chrysler sold a grand total of 647. So much for the argument that NAFTA would make major U.S. manufacturers more competitive in global markets.[29]

Even thse data are incomplete and surely understate the dimensions of outsourcing that substitutes for U.S. labor. One main reason is that the initial sales made by U.S.-owned factories abroad—whether majority or minority-owned—often say little about the final destination of the product. Nor do they say much about a related question—whether the final customer is a net new customer of the company in question. Many of the products made by multinational corporations today are so complex that a number of different steps are needed to produce them. Therefore, because of the big differences in economic conditions and technological capacity among different low-income countries, it often makes sense for these companies to locate different phases of the production process in many different countries.

Consequently, goods that are traded, especially parts and components in various combinations, often make several trips back and forth across national borders before they are finally consumed. If the final consumption of products sold by U.S. multinationals takes place in the United States, particularly by customers the companies in question already have, then even much of the exporting among different foreign markets by these companies ultimately will have the same effect as sales directly back to the United States. It will merely substitute foreign labor for U.S. labor.

For instance, look at semiconductors. Chips are typically designed in the United States, and many of the most advanced components are made in the United States as well. These parts are often exported to East Asian countries like Malaysia or Singapore. In combination with other parts made in these countries or other foreign factories, they are often further processed or assembled into the final chips. After assembly, they are often sent to yet another country for packaging or for testing. Sometimes the final chips are exported directly back to the United States to be placed into the countless final industrial or consumer products (like machine tools or automobiles) that incorporate semiconductors today. However, often these products themselves are manufactured outside the United States. Therefore, completed chips are just as often sent to factories outside the United States, where they are inserted into various final products.

If these final products are sold outside the United States, especially to a brand-new customer, chances are that their manufacture abroad is good for U.S. employment and living standards. The U.S. government once collected data distinguishing between exports for consumption and exports for assembly, but despite the greatly increased importance of such trade in producer goods, these efforts were stopped several years ago.[30] Nonetheless, even though no reliable data exist, it is clear that most of the final products are sent back to the United States. The business press, for example, often reports this as a reality too obvious to belabor.[31] Sometimes in unguarded moments, the companies admit this, too. Texas Instruments, for example, told *USA Today* that it expected to weather the Asian financial crisis handily because "its customers in Southeast Asia often export their finished products [described as PCs, cellular phones, and other electronics products] to other countries, making their businesses more dependent on [foreign] economic growth than local conditions."[32]

As suggested previously, the importance of the United States—as opposed to foreign countries—as a final consumption market can also be deduced from the overall trade balances in goods between the United States and emerging market countries. The enormous size of these deficits—more than $100 billion annually—and their persistence indicate that, when the effects of all the intricate trade flows generated by multinational corporations are toted up, the lion's share of goods traded winds up in the United States. Moreover, the size and the rapid increase in these deficits (a growth rate considerably faster than even the U.S. economy's recent growth rate) indicates that the foreign production of multinational companies is displacing, not complementing, the work being done by U.S. laborers.

One example of how these trade flows work is suggested in a recent publication by the Malaysian Industrial Development Authority. In the December 1996 issue of its monthly magazine, the agency reported that the U.S. firm MEMC Electronic Materials had entered into a joint venture to set up Southeast Asia's most advanced facility for manufacturing the silicon wafers used in semiconductors.

The wafers, the Malaysians reported, "will be supplied to factories in Japan, Malaysia, and other countries in Asia."[33]

United States government figures will report these shipments as sales outside the United States. However, just because the factories will be putting the chips into products such as computers, autos, defense systems, and consumer electronic products, there is no reason to assume that most of these goods will be consumed locally in Malaysia, or even in Malaysia's Asian neighbors. In fact, given the official discouragement of domestic consumption in these countries, chances are they will be exported outside the region—many to the United States. More compelling evidence comes from the Malaysian government itself. Trade statistics it has provided reveal that in numerous types of semiconductor devices, its exports to tiny-to-small neighbors such as Singapore, Taiwan, Korea, and even the Philippines are either comparable to or greater than its exports to the United States. Either Singaporean consumers collect or horde semiconductors the way Americans eat ice cream, or the city-state is not the final home for most of these goods.[34]

The auto sector provides an even clearer example. Delphi Packard Electric, the main auto parts company, has set up a factory just outside Shanghai that produces the wire harnesses that form a motor vehicle's "electronic circulatory system."[35] The factory exports nearly one-third of its output to Mexico. However, the wire harnesses are not consumed in Mexico. Instead, they are finished in GM-owned factories in Juarez and then forwarded to GM assembly plants in the United States and Canada. Most of the vehicles they produce will be sold in the U.S. market. Yet the BEA figures will record Delphi Shanghai's shipments to Mexico as exports to Mexico that are assumed to serve a Mexican market.

Figures about the U.S. content of goods manufactured by U.S. multinationals in the United States suffer two major problems of their own. First, there is no reason to believe, as the Economic Strategy Institute and Emergency Committee on American Trade reports suggest, that the U.S.-made products used by multinationals in the United States are made entirely in the United States even if they are parts and components. As discussed previously, parts and components themselves are often made of parts and components. In fact, the steep increases in imports as a share of all the goods consumed in the United States indicate that many of these products are not entirely, or even primarily, U.S.-made. As the ECAT report itself observes (way back in the footnotes), the BEA

figures simply assume 100 percent U.S. content.[36] Thus the upward
bias in U.S. content figures could be enormous, along with the upward bias in the argument that U.S. multinationals rely mainly on
U.S.-made components.

In addition, the "imported materials" used by U.S. multinationals that are counted in the raw data include only "materials, parts,
components, containers, etc." They explicitly leave out the "cost of
products bought and sold as such" along with "contract work
done . . . by others." This methodology, however, misses two big
trends in corporate outsourcing. First, U.S. multinationals are increasingly outsourcing finished products—"products bought and
sold as such." For example, Nike imports finished sneakers from
its Asian factories, not just the laces, soles, or tongues. GE imports
finished microwave ovens from South Korean manufacturers to
sell under its brand name.[37]

Second, especially in the microelectronics field, U.S. companies
are relying more and more heavily on independent foreign companies, not affiliates, to manufacture the parts and components of
their products, as well as the finished products. According to
Michael Borrus of the Berkeley Roundtable on the International
Economy and the University of California at Berkeley, the use of
independent, locally owned electronics manufacturers in Asia has
been vital in the successful recent efforts of U.S. multinational
companies to recapture world leadership from Japan in most com-
puter-related products. For example, as early as 1983, nine local
Singaporean companies were contract manufacturing PCs for
Apple. By 1990, Apple Computer Singapore, the company's main
Asian affiliate, had 130 independent local contractors—mainly in
Singapore and elsewhere in Asia.

Taiwanese electronics companies have become particularly important in this regard. Before marketing products in the United
States under its own name, for example, Acer was building whole
notebook computers as well as monitors—for Apple, NCR, Data
General, and Japanese and German firms. Tatung supplies entire
PCs as well as motherboards and monitors to Compaq, Dell, and
Apple. The larger Taiwanese firms, themselves sit atop large local
supply bases of thousands of smaller design, component, parts,
subassembly, and assembly houses throughout Taiwan, Hong
Kong, China, and Southeast Asia.[38]

Even stronger evidence for the importance of foreign inputs
comes from the Washington lobbying efforts of U.S. multinationals

and the responses of government agencies engaged in activities like export financing. The Export-Import Bank of the United States provides publically guaranteed low-cost financing for exports of U.S. products, largely to emerging market countries. Because these countries sometimes take a long time to pay their bills, or sometimes don't pay them at all, private lenders are often reluctant to take on these deals without charging big risk premiums. Yet because competition for emerging market contracts can be so fierce, the ability to offer competitive interest rates (often well below market levels) is often essential to closing deals. Ex-Im's work is also important because many of the United States' foreign competitors assist their companies with public export financing. If Washington did not play, too, U.S. companies would no doubt lose out on many contracts for reasons having nothing to do with their real competitiveness or with free-market forces.

Because public guarantees are involved, Ex-Im had been congressionally mandated to ensure that the benefits of its loans are products made entirely in the United States by U.S. workers. However, this requirement recently has been relaxed. In 1987, in response to companies that were moving production offshore, Ex-Im agreed to finance deals for products with 15 percent foreign content. In spring 1996, journalist William Greider reported that the multinationals had been lobbying Ex-Im to ease these foreign content rules even further. Greider quoted minutes from meetings of the Bank's Foreign Content Policy Review Group in which officials from firms such as Caterpillar, GE, Boeing, and Fluor Daniel insisted that the bank acknowledge the new realities of international production networks. AT&T's priority, according to its representative, Angel Torres, "is to increase the allowable percentage of foreign content." One executive quoted anonymously in the Ex-Im documents explained, "We believe the current policy does not reflect the de-industrialization of the U.S. economy and the rise of Western European or Asian capabilities to produce high-tech quality equipment." Although the U.S. content roles have not been relaxed even further, the corporate lobbying continues.[39]

6 HIGH-TECH JOB FLIGHT

EVEN THOUGH CORPORATE OUTSOURCING TO LOW-INCOME countries appears to be a major contributor to U.S. trade deficits, these practices can still boost living standards for most Americans, at least potentially. As indicated in Chapter 5, such outsourcing could result in cost savings for U.S. companies through farming out labor-intensive work that pays relatively poorly anyway. Consequently, the U.S. employees of these companies would be able to concentrate on more sophisticated, better-paying work, and the overall cost savings would presumably boost worldwide demand for the final product—and for the U.S. workers.

The few analysts who focus on outsourcing generally seem convinced that this worker-friendly story is indeed unfolding. According to the United States International Trade Commission (ITC), by "shifting generally more labor-intensive operations to lower-wage countries," U.S. companies can "improve the relative price competitiveness of their product lines" and "are able to retain higher production and employment levels in the United States than might otherwise be possible." More specifically, the ITC noted, the U.S. companies involved regard production sharing as a way to "help keep higher-wage jobs and value-added production in the United States...."[1]

Similar company arguments have helped lead Laura D. Tyson, former chair of President Clinton's Council of Economic Advisers, to similar conclusions: "Lots of big firms will tell you that even if they do move part of their manufacturing process [to Mexico], doing so helps make their overall operation more efficient; they can sell more to Germany because they've kept their costs down." Colgate University economist Jay Mandle made comparable arguments recently in a published debate over which trade positions are truly "liberal":

> Trade relations with poor countries have become a sensitive issue only because the latter have increased their productive capability, particularly in the manufacture of products using relatively unskilled labor, to a level at which they can compete successfully in metropolitan markets.[2]

Further, according to *The Wall Street Journal* reporters Bob Davis and David Wessel, the higher-wage, higher-skill jobs will remain safely in the United States "because this is where innovation is greatest." Most globalization-induced job flight, in other words, is low-wage, low-tech job flight, and is therefore not to be condemned, but actually applauded—at least from the U.S. workers' point of view. In fact, whatever racing to the bottom will be done in the world will be confined to the developing countries, which will often compete by lowering wages and exchange rates for low-skill jobs like "sewing shirts."[3]

Unfortunately, even leaving aside the big questions of how "low-tech" and "high-tech" jobs are defined, and how many U.S. workers actually have jobs in knowledge-intensive information industries, this comforting outsourcing story is largely and increasingly inaccurate. A substantial share of outsourcing-produced job flight is high-tech job flight, and not even the most sophisticated U.S. industries—and workers—have been exempt. Just as important for U.S. living standards, much of this high-tech job flight has had little or nothing to do with free-market forces or been based on purely business decisions. Instead, it has been encouraged—sometimes even extorted—by government policies in low-income countries ranging from trade barriers to powerful investment incentives and performance requirements.

At the same time, U.S. and other multinational corporations are not the only engines of this high-tech job flight. Scientists, technicians, and businesses in low-income countries, often decisively aided by governments, have tremendously increased their technological capabilities through their own devices. In fact, a veritable revolution in technology development is occurring in low-income countries, and it shows no signs of petering out. Quite the contrary—these countries and their workers are likely to continue closing the technology gap with most of the workforce in the industrialized world, thanks to their own ongoing efforts and to major investments in their laboratories and universities made by U.S. and other foreign companies. Moreover, even though developing countries will continue to lag the United States in sectors at the very top of the technology ladder, their ongoing progress is certain to sop up many of the job opportunities created near the top.

A. Hewers of Silicon

In both the popular imagination and the experts' studies, low-income countries are still overwhelmingly seen as "hewers of wood and drawers of water"—societies lacking the technological know-how to be competitive producers of anything more complicated than raw materials and light, labor-intensive manufactures like apparel and shoes and toys.

Viewing developing countries as relatively backward is also absolutely central to one major case for optimism about current globalization trends and policies. Specifically, it dovetails with the comforting notion that if market forces are allowed to operate freely, an international division of labor will naturally result, keeping the best jobs in the wealthy countries and the rest in the developing world. In addition, this division of labor would theoretically help limit the imbalances in trade flows caused or worsened by the developing countries' inability or unwillingness to consume. After all, according to this version of globalization optimism, if these countries are not importing and consuming their share of world output (because their economies and workers stay stuck in primitive industries that cannot generate much purchasing power) at least they are not increasing the problem by competing with wealthy countries and their workers as producers and exporters in the so-called industries of the future.

Yet this view of developing countries is already literally decades out-of-date. Not only in East Asia, but throughout Latin America and increasingly in the former Communist countries of Europe, factories each year are churning out tens of billions of dollars worth of many of the most advanced products available today. The list ranges from automobiles and their parts to aircraft and their parts to pharmaceuticals to telecommunications devices to computers to semiconductors and even software and biotechnology products. As a 1994 *BusinessWeek* report put it, "Practically anywhere you go in Asia these days, local workers can be found doing the same highly skilled tasks you would expect in Palo Alto, Boston, or Tokyo."[4] In other words, developing country workers today are nearly as likely to be hewers of silicon as hewers of wood.

American multinational companies have greatly accelerated the developing countries' technological revolution. Indeed, the output of these companies in the developing world reads like a What's What of advanced, high-wage goods and services, including not only manufacturing but engineering, design, and research and development. As shown in Chapter 5, many of these investments are not producing for the U.S. market—and therefore generally do not destroy U.S.-based jobs the way that overseas factories exporting back to the United States generally have been. Even when these products are sold locally or elsewhere abroad, however, the investments that have made them possible ensure that serving these foreign markets will create relatively few new U.S. jobs. Moreover, they are likely to preclude the possibility of creating many more future U.S. jobs through exports from the United States and its workforce. U.S. multinationals, in other words, stand to profit enormously if emerging markets do indeed take off. U.S. workers, however, will largely be left out of the picture.

Motor vehicles are an excellent example. Often still thought of as a "smokestack" industry, auto design and manufacturing entails such a heavy use of microelectronics for computers, sensors, and controls that it obliterates the idea of neat distinctions between low- and high-tech industries. As of 1998, the typical passenger car contained more computing power than the lunar module that carried the Apollo astronauts home from the moon.[5] Nonetheless, U.S. and other automakers are spreading all aspects of vehicle production from the simplest to the most advanced far beyond their traditional sites in industrialized Europe, North America, and Japan.

Largely in response to tariff barriers designed to discourage imports of finished vehicles and build up local auto production, General Motors and to a lesser extent Ford and Chrysler have for decades set up factories in countries ranging from South Africa to Egypt, from Croatia to Russia, from Turkey to Taiwan, from Indonesia to Ecuador, and throughout Latin America. According to its Web site, GM is by far the most global of the Big Three U.S. automakers and currently assembles vehicles in 21 low-income countries.

Today, the same types of tariff and other trade barriers are also drawing more sophisticated U.S. auto investment, along with the better-paying jobs it creates. Low-wages, highly skilled laborers, and the very growth of increasingly sophisticated manufacturing and supplier bases have played big roles as well. GM, for example, does more advanced, genuine manufacturing work in seven developing countries: Egypt, China, Taiwan, Thailand, Brazil, Mexico, and Turkey. The Big Three's operations in Mexico are especially impressive. Thanks to their investments plus the facilities of Nissan, Honda, and Volkswagen, Mexico sent more than four times more autos to the United States (just over $10 billion worth) than the United States exported to Mexico in 1999. Including trucks in the picture yields an even more lopsided ratio. Mexico has also become the largest exporter of internal combustion engines in the world.[6]

Nor is Mexico the only developing country in which U.S. automakers are performing their most advanced work. Despite the slump in Brazil's auto market, GM opened new assembly and parts plants in the country at the end of 1999. Moreover, these investments have been designed by Brazilian as well as German teams of engineers.[7]

Meanwhile, GM is building a new integrated auto factory in addition to an assembly plant in Poland. The facility will perform metal stamping and body welding, along with lower-value final assembly. The share of Polish parts used in the vehicles is expected to reach 60 percent three years after production is launched.[8]

GM is also proceeding with a worldwide campaign to develop local suppliers for its factories in developing countries by bringing them up to its domestic quality standards. Although the Asian crisis has forced the company to suspend its plans for a $750 million assembly plant in Thailand, the nosedive taken by Asian currencies and the liberalized investment rules introduced by several Asian countries created a regional fire sale on sophisticated auto production facilities. GM is greatly boosting its Asian outsourcing as a result.[9]

The Big Three are becoming active in Asia's biggest markets as well. In February 1996, Ford announced a $418 million joint venture with an Indian partner to build 100,000 Fiestas annually in southern India. Indeed, partly because of India's still high tariffs on finished vehicles, when U.S. auto executives, like Ford President Jacques Nasser, asked New Delhi for increased access to the Indian market, exporting from the United States was the furthest thing from their minds. Instead, they were talking about greater scope to manufacture in India.[10]

A year later, GM won a contract to build Buicks in Shanghai. Originally supplied by made-in-America auto parts, the new factory is required by Chinese law to achieve 80 percent Chinese content in its vehicles five years after start-up. In addition, Chrysler has for several years produced Jeep Cherokees in a joint venture with Beijing Auto Works, and in October 1997, Ford entered a joint venture with Yuejin Motors Group Corporation to manufacture multivalve engines.[11]

Some of GM's most advanced overseas work is done by the Big Three's Delco Electronics in Singapore. Its $200 million facility produces radio systems, climate controls, semiconductors, and engine control systems, and the company continues to enter new regions. In fall 1996, GM and a group of Saudi industrialists formed Middle East Battery Company. The firm's new plant, GM's first in Saudi Arabia, will manufacture one million Delco Freedom maintenance-free batteries. Its output will replace the importation of 500,000 such batteries annually from the United States and South Korea.

The Big Three, however, have no monopoly on high-tech auto parts manufacturing abroad. Motorola, for example, produces antilock brakes and advanced electronic auto components in the Chinese joint venture with the Shanghai Instrumentation Group. AlliedSignal, which has done so well in the Mexican spark plug market, also produces auto parts in China.[12]

Usually there is no simple one-to-one correspondence between new U.S.-owned manufacturing investments in the United States and abroad, much less between production closed down in the United States and opened abroad (though particular facilities regularly do cross borders).[13] Too many different models and versions of too many different products are manufactured for too many different sets of customers. The 50 U.S. states, moreover, regularly attempt to tilt the playing field, too, by offering tax breaks and other incentives to manufacturers as they race to the bottom themselves.[14]

However, when it comes to any company that has finite resources—that is to say, any company—there is always some trade-off between resources used in one area and those either taken from another or not available for another. This is especially true for U.S. jobs given the huge U.S. trade deficit. Therefore, there is surely some relationship between the fact that while GM was making investments around the world during the 1980s and 1990s—and in the process, building up a workforce of some 83,600 in Mexico—it cut 14.5 percent from its U.S. payroll of 262,000, and its U.S. factory capacity remained flat.[15]

Although many Americans may still consider the automobile industry to be a smokestack industry and not a desirable high-tech business, few Americans would place pharmaceuticals in this category. However, as of the late 1990s, the pharmaceutical giant Pfizer had invested $80 million in China on projects such as a multi-functional organic synthesis plant, a formulation factory to manufacture bulk pharmaceutical ingredients and finished dosage forms, and a joint venture to manufacture and market the world's leading antifungal medication and other medicines.[16]

Given the Boeing-Airbus near duopoly in commercial airliners and the dominance of U.S. and European firms like Lockheed Martin, Northrup Grumman, General Dynamics, Dassault, and Saab in military jets, aerospace is understandably viewed as a preserve of the industrialized countries. However, U.S. firms have outsourced a significant and rising share of production of many aircraft to low-income and emerging market countries.

AlliedSignal, now a division of Honeywell, is a prime example. AlliedSignal was "positioning itself as an integral part of local industry," the company explained in a late 1996 press release describing its Asia strategy as changing from being "simply a distant global aerospace player." AlliedSignal has launched a joint venture with China's state-owned aerospace manufacturing company to produce aircraft climate control systems. Across the Taiwan Straits, AlliedSignal manufactures propulsion systems for Taipei's Indigenous Defense Fighter aircraft in a joint venture with the International Turbine Engine Company. AlliedSignal is also teaming with Singapore Technologies Precision (as well as with Japanese and European firms) to build parts for the new auxiliary power unit it is marketing for long-range executive jets. It expects that a new global alliance with India's Hindustan Aeronautics will result in "straight subcontracting arrangements" as well as joint ventures to manufacture specific products.[17]

GE, too, has signed on Indonesia's Industri Pesawat Terbang Nusantara to assemble and test small jet engines. IPTN also produces verticle fins for the F–16 fighters Indonesia buys from General Dynamics. In Russia, GE is making jet engines for wide-body aircraft in a joint venture with Rybinsk Motors, and it has been actively pushing its aircraft engine parts suppliers to relocate to Mexico in order to help cut production costs for the entire supply chain.[18]

GE's main rival in the jet engine field, United Technology's Pratt and Whitney division, has agreed to manufacture jet engine parts in a Chinese joint venture, and Rockwell International is building a global positioning system in a team-up with Shanghai Avionics and Shanghai Broadcast Equipment Factory. Before it was bought out by Boeing, McDonnell Douglas procured wings and nose sections for its MD–95 jetliner from Korea's Hyundai and a division of Korea Airlines, and had bought landing gear doors and nose sections for the MD-80 from China since 1985.[19]

Boeing itself has become a leading outsourcer. Much of its overseas work is done in Japan, by manufacturing giants such as Mitsubishi, Kawasaki, and Fuji, which provide large and growing shares of the fuselages, wings, and electronics in Boeing jets. Hyundai of Korea, meanwhile, has made wings for the 717 since 1996. Boeing also manufactures in Indonesia (e.g., wing flaps for 737s and overhead storage bins for 767s), and procures fuselage work that the Indonesians have secured from Mitsubishi. In addition, Boeing has announced plans to assemble 737s in Turkey.

Boeing has been sourcing aerospace components in China since 1980 and boasts on its Web site that it has 3,100 planes in the air "that include major parts and assemblies built by China." It currently procures from the Xian Aircraft Company tail sections (once made in Wichita, Kansas), vertical fins, and horizontal stabilizers for the 737, and vertical fins, horizontal stabilizers, and some access doors for the 757. These parts, plus trailing edge ribs and cargo doors, also are made for Boeing at three other Chinese aircraft factories. Meanwhile, the company has just started to produce composite parts for interiors and secondary structures for commercial aircraft in a joint-venture operation in Tianjin.[20]

Nevertheless, Boeing's outsourcing operations pale next to those that had been set up by McDonnell Douglas. A key part of McDonnell's ultimately unsuccessful last gasp for survival was its decision to manufacture 40 MD–82s and 20 MD–90s in China. The latter were slated to incorporate 85 percent Chinese content.[21]

According to the prominent consulting company DRI/McGraw-Hill, this aerospace outsourcing is having increasingly damaging effects on the aerospace workforce in the United States. Through the early 1990s, DRI/McGraw-Hill concluded, a downturn in the industry's business cycle plus continued low relative levels of defense spending destroyed most of the 270,000 jobs lost by the industry. However, of the 100,000 additional jobs DRI projected will have been lost between 1994 and 2000, some 60 percent will be the result of foreign competition.[22]

Nowhere, however, has U.S. corporate-led production in developing countries been as impressive as in the biggest, most future-oriented high-tech field of all—electronics. Some observers even consider an enormous chunk of the electronics industry—consumer electronics—to be too primitive for industrialized countries to produce economically. However, much of the most spectacular progress made by U.S. multinationals in globalizing production has come in what everyone would consider the high end of the electronics industry, including telecommunications, advanced consumer electronics, computer hardware, semiconductors, and even software. These are the industries that are supposed to make Americans—and especially U.S. workers—forget all about the loss of sectors like autos and steel and textiles and apparel. Yet they have been no less vulnerable to job flight than their more traditional relatives.

In cutting-edge consumer electronics and telecommunications, two of the most aggressive globalizers have been Lucent and Motorola. The former Ma Bell presently operates nine joint ventures in China, which produce the company's flagship switching system, the 5ESS, along with optical fiber, fiber-optic cables, digital transmission equipment, program-controlled switching systems, cellular communications systems, and lower-end products. In addition, Lucent assembles digital switching stations in Russia.[23]

Motorola produces a wide variety of advanced telecommunications products in China, too—pagers, digital cellular telephones, two-way radios, and components for communications equipment, including mobile systems. In October 1997, the company announced plans to build a second major production base in China that would turn out, among other items, large plasma screens. Professor Yasheng Huang of the Harvard Business School estimates that Motorola's factories alone generate as much as 25 percent of China's electronics exports to the United States. Motorola also manufactures pagers in Mexico, and its Advanced Messaging Group has chosen Singapore to produce the first Asian-manufactured two-way data pager.[24] Moreover, three major U.S. companies—Loral Space and Communications, Hughes Electronics, and Lockheed Martin—have gone to China to manufacture advanced broadband telecommunications equipment known as Synchronous Digital Hierarchy equipment.[25]

Production of computer hardware and peripherals (keyboards, mice, monitors, disk drives, printers, etc.) have been far more globalized than production of advanced telecommunications equipment. Since the mid-1960s, U.S. multinationals have rapidly increased both the sophistication and the volume of the computer products they manufacture in low-income countries. IBM was the pioneer. Some 30 years ago, the company began to move the wiring of core frames for its 360 System mainframe computers first to Japan and then to Taiwan. Taiwan's labor costs were so low that not only was moving this meticulous, labor-intensive work to the island cheaper than employing U.S. workers, it was even cheaper than automating the U.S. production lines.[26]

Another major wave of computer industry outsourcing began in the late 1970s. First came Tandon, a U.S. company founded by an Indian with a Singaporean passport, which moved production of hard disk drives to the city-state. In 1981, Apple Computer opened an assembly plant for printed circuit boards for the Apple II personal computer in Singapore. Michael Borrus of the Berkeley Roundtable on the International Economy has described how such investments steadily led to the transfer of more advanced manufacturing—and high-wage jobs and job opportunities—from the United States.[27] By 1985, as Borrus noted, Apple Computer Singapore (ACS) was responsible for final assembly of Apple IIs for the world market. In 1990, ACS was assigned final assembly responsibility for Macintosh PCs and was manufacturing the system's monitors. By late 1994, the company was assembling the Mac LC630 PC multimedia system—again, for worldwide export. Today, Apple outsources its iMAC desktop and notebook production to Taiwan, and the iMAC desktop monitor to South Korea.[28]

Compaq began assembling printed circuit boards (from components also manufactured in Japan and elsewhere in Asia) for desktop PCs in its Singapore factory in 1986. At that time, the computers themselves were still assembled in the United States. By 1994, however, Compaq was manufacturing all of its notebook computers and portable PCs in Singapore, as well as all the desktop PCs it sold in the Asia-Pacific region. Hewlett Packard started out in Singapore assembling calculators. Today, its Singapore affiliate produces portable printers as well as Pentium desktop PCs and servers. Compaq also announced at the end of 1999 that it would boost its procurement of Taiwanese products by 20 percent, to $8.5 billion annually. These purchases will include servers and new-generation information appliances.[29] Motorola's Singapore operations started out with the simplest printed circuit board assembly, and have progressed to manufacturing double-sided six-layer boards.

Computer equipment manufacturing has spread beyond Singapore, however. Intel, for example, manufactures motherboards in Malaysia. An especially popular location for U.S. multinationals has been China. Xerox produces desktop printers in the People's Republic—along with copiers and fax machines. Motorola joint ventures in China make personal computers and motherboards for systems based on RISC chips. Dell and Gateway, meanwhile, have both recently announced the opening of Brazilian production facilities, with the latter specifying that these facilities will account for all of its Brazilian sales. In other words, no imports from the United States need apply.[30]

No aspect of computer and peripheral manufacturing has become more globalized than disk-drive production. In 1985, 93 percent of U.S.-owned disk-drive production was located in the United States. By 1990, two-thirds of these companies' assembly was being performed in Southeast Asia, and three-fourths of all disk-drive parts were starting to be made in the region. By 1995, more than 60 percent of all global jobs in hard disk-drive production were created in Southeast Asia, including a rapidly growing share of sophisticated parts like motors and heads.[31]

Seagate Corp., for example, had located 14 of its 24 factories around the world in developing Asia—five in Thailand, four in Malaysia, three in Singapore, and one each in Indonesia and China as of 1995.[32] These Asian factories employed more than 85 percent of the company's global workforce. Seagate had kept much of the higher-end work in disk-drive manufacturing in the United States and Europe—principally the assembly of high-end drives and most component manufacturing, product and component development, prototyping, and initial process engineering. Even the low end of disk-drive manufacturing, however, is sophisticated work by any reasonable measure, and virtually all of this work is done in low-income Asia. Seagate's simplest assembly is performed in Indonesia. More advanced assembly is done in Thailand and Malaysia, and Thailand is handling most of the final assembly of all types of drives, including the highest-end drives. Even some of the highest-end manufacturing work has been moving to low-income Asia. Seagate is now even making a wide variety of advanced components in Southeast Asia, and its Penang, Malaysia, facilities reportedly are producing MR heads, which incorporate the most complex technology in current disk-drive manufacturing. In addition, a McKinsey & Company Study of Seagate's globalization showed that its moves into new Asian countries has been heavily influenced by the lower labor costs offered.[33]

Seagate's strategy has reflected its position as a merchant manufacturer of computer parts—a company not part of a major computer manufacturer. IBM has long made most of its parts in-house, but a major cost-cutting and decentralization drive in the 1990s led it to transfer disk-drive production from the United States, Japan, and Germany throughout the developing world. The company presently produces drives in Singapore, Mexico, and Hungary, and contracts production out to an independent Thai manufacturer.[34]

The globalization of sophisticated manufacturing has also spread to the products and technologies at the heart of the computer revolution—semiconductors and software. According to the Semiconductor Association of America (SIA), the U.S. chip makers' main trade group, as of 1993, nearly 30 percent of the manufacturing facilities (as measured by factory square footage) and half of the employment of U.S.-owned semiconductor firms were located abroad. Half of these jobs, in turn, had been created in Southeast Asia. Although the association could not provide more recent figures, the numbers undoubtedly have risen significantly in the last half decade.[35]

SIA echoes conventional wisdom when it contends that most of the semiconductor work done abroad by U.S. companies is low-end work, meaning assembly, packaging, and testing, as opposed to manufacturing the silicon wafers on which microcircuits are etched, the lithography process that performs the etching, as well as research and development, engineering, and design. Facilities handling the lower-end tasks have indeed become common in developing Asian countries. Intel, for example, opened a small assembly operation in the state of Penang, in Malaysia, in 1972. Today, Penang hosts large Intel assembly and test facilities, and the company recently has built similar factories in Shanghai and just outside Manila in the Philippines. In April 1997, Intel broke ground for a new assembly and test plant in Costa Rica. As of January 2000, the Costa Rica facility was exporting $2 billion in finished chips annually. In May 1998, Intel opened its first manufacturing site in China, a facility in Shanghai that assembles and tests flash memory products. As of mid–1998, the company pegged its total manufacturing investment in Asia at $2 billion over the previous 25 years.[36]

Texas Instruments and National Semiconductor both moved assembly operations to Singapore in 1968. Four years later, both companies set up integrated circuit assembly lines in Malaysia. Much more recently, TI has built a chip packaging plant in the Philippines. Motorola established semiconductor production lines in South Korea and Hong Kong even earlier, in 1967. Today it assembles semiconductors in Malaysia, as does Hewlett Packard.[37]

There are several problems, however, with the picture of American semiconductor companies confining their work abroad to the lowest-value activities. In the first place, the lowest-end work in this high-tech sector is considerably more sophisticated and knowledge-intensive than most of the service sector jobs becoming so numerous in the United States, especially those that require virtually no specialized training. In fact, Texas Instruments requires a high-school diploma for even the most basic positions in its Philippines factory.[38] Second, these ostensibly low-end chip production jobs are steadily becoming more sophisticated themselves. As observed by Dieter Ernst of the Berkeley Roundtable on the International Economy, "chip assembly is no longer the uninspiring 'back end' of the semiconductor industry. Assembling and packaging technologies in this industry have become highly complex and play an important role for yields and peformance features of leading-edge devices."[39]

Third, assembly, packaging, and testing hardly exhaust the list of U.S. semiconductor operations in developing countries. In Penang today, Intel manufactures Pentium and Pentium Pro microprocessors, and the company opened a plant in Kulim, in the nearby state of Kedah, to produce Pentium IIs. Advanced Micro Devices manufactures in Malaysia as well—notably its latest microprocessors, the K6 and the Athlon. In Singapore, Hewlett Packard produces gallium arsenide wafers for semiconductors (one of the highest-end manufacturing tasks in semiconductor production), as well as integrated circuits, while Delco produces semiconductors.[40]

Motorola announced its first semiconductor joint venture in China in 1995, and later that year began construction of a wafer fabrication plant near Tianjin. This factory is producing chips with circuits narrower than one micron, a hallmark of highly advanced semiconductor manufacturing. In 1996, Texas Instruments joined with South Korea's Anam—the world's dominant chip packager and tester—to build a factory for digital signal processors, a type of logic chip at the heart of wireless communications devices like cell phones. They also announced a technology alliance to produce specialized semiconductors to run multimedia products. TI, which has recently cut domestic production and employment, has also produced wafers on Taiwan with Acer since 1991 and is upgrading its facilities to produce highly advanced 8-inch wafers. MEMC Electronics Materials is also producing 8-inch wafers on Taiwan, in a partnership with China Steel. In addition, the world's leading manufacturer of semiconductor production equipment, Applied Materials, produces these machines on the island and plans to use Taiwan as its global supply center for components. In another branch of high-end computer manufacturing, 3Com recently opened a new factory in Singapore to produce a full line of high-volume networking hardware products.[41]

The spread of multinational-led software production to developing economies has been even more remarkable. China and India have been especially important in Texas Instruments' plans. TI was the first big U.S. firm to recognize the ocean of programming and engineering talent available in India. In 1985, it opened a development center in the city of Bangalore for writing software used in computer-assisted semiconductor design. By spring 1997, TI's Bangalore facility was employing 300 engineers and was expecting the figure to reach 500 by the year 2000. Informix's software research and development center in India may become its second largest laboratory in the world, and Novell's facility in Bangalore has been given the complete responsibility for producing such key software components as NDS for Solaris and developer tools for Netware 5. In August 1997, Cisco Systems, the world's largest networking equipment manufacturer, opened its largest development center outside the United States in Chennai, India. With a staff of 75 Indian engineers, the lab will design new generations of networking software. Also working on network management software, and other projects, in India is Sun Microsystems.[42]

Three months later, Microsoft announced plans to build its own software development center in India. Microsoft chairman Bill Gates has predicted that India will eventually provide the company with its "largest base of software professionals," and Microsoft's vice president for international operations has described

Indian software skills as unparalleled. Oracle and Motorola have large software development sites in India as well; indeed, Microsoft's Indian engineers wrote software for U.S. space shuttle program. In addition, IBM is using a joint venture with India's enormous Tata conglomerate as a key link in its new worldwide network for creating Java-based internet software components. Other links in the network will be located in Belarus, Latvia, and China. Small wonder that by 1994 Bangalore had become the world's second largest software producer, after Silicon Valley.[43]

In 1996, IBM created a software venture with Tsinghua University (often called China's MIT) to develop reusable, object-oriented software components and application packs that are marketed over the Internet. The new company, the Advanced Systems Development Corporation, will also produce Java applets, "intelligent dialers" for mobile workers, and other so-called OpenDoc components. In July 1998, Lucent opened the Asia-Pacific Communications Software Regional Technical Center in Beijing. This facility, affiliated with its world-renowned Bell labs unit, will develop products for worldwide markets. Novell also plans to set up a software development joint venture in the People's Republic of China.[44]

B. THE BRAIN WORK, TOO

Some globalization optimists try to shoehorn even the flight of the highest-tech manufacturing jobs to developing countries into their own comforting portrayal of third world workers as a *lumpenproletariat*. Take Secretary of State Madeleine Albright. On a summer 1997 trip to Asia, Albright visited one of Seagate's disk-drive plants in Singapore. Talking to reporters following her tour, Albright called Seagate "a perfect example" of globalization's capacity to benefit workers everywhere. However, her remarks left no doubt as to which workers she thought benefited most. Seagate's operations, she explained, represent "an interaction between a product designed and begun in the United States and produced and manufactured in Asian countries."[45] In other words, the brain work—e.g., the design—was still being done by Americans. The Asians remained stuck with the heavy lifting.

Even if the flight of high-tech manufacturing could properly be viewed with indifference, however, the division of labor cited by Albright and others is as obsolete as the image of third world workers specializing in shoes and toys. Just as high-tech manufacturing jobs are being transplanted to developing countries, the most sophisticated, highest-tech work created by multinationals— engineering, design, and research and develpment—is becoming globalized as well. Indeed, as of early 1995, the consulting firm Dataquest was reporting that "the most important trend in Asia/Pacific [is] the newfound local capability of Asia/Pacific-based OEMs (original equipment manufacturers) to both design and build their own equipment."[46]

The Seagate Singapore operations cited by Albright are an excellent example. The secretary of state might have been visiting one of Seagate's manufacturing operations in the city-state. On the other hand, she also might have been visiting the Seagate Singapore facility that develops high-volume production processes, or even the facility that designs the software used in the company's disk-drive testing operations. Had she come back two years later, she might have been visiting the Seagate Singapore facility that designs advanced disk drives.[47]

In fact, in virtually every industry where U.S. multinationals have exported production jobs to low-income countries, they have exported even higher-value work as well. GM, for example, is not only building auto factories throughout the developing world, it is using engineers from Brazil (along with Germany) to design these state-of-the-art facilities. GM also runs a Materials Engineering Lab in Sao Paulo, Brazil. Delco Electronics, which manufactures advanced automotive components in Singapore, also performs research and development for new products and manufacturing processes, and designs power trains as well. AlliedSignal performs research and development on brake systems, components, and turbochargers in Brazil while its Russian joint venture not only manufactures aircraft wheels, brake, and brake control systems, it designs them.[48]

GE has recently announced that outsourcing the brain work has become a major feature of its globalization strategy. According to its annual report, its new approach goes beyond "sourcing products and components . . . in a price-competitive deflationary world . . . to capitalize on the vast intellectual capital available around the globe." Accordingly, the company has plans to:

> move aggressively to broaden our definition of globalization by increasing the intensity of our effort to search out and attract the unlimited pool of talent that is available in the countries in which we do business—from software designers in India to product engineers in Mexico, Eastern Europe, and China.

Previously GE had announced that its joint venture with Russia's Rybinsk Motors was likely to develop new designs for aircraft engines as well as manufacture them. Schering-Plough, meanwhile, is building a biotech plant in Singapore that will not only make a new hepatitis C drug, but develop entirely new production processes for new products.[49]

The same trends are apparent in telecommunications equipment. Lucent not only manufactures its most advanced switches in China, it is designing these systems in China. Cisco is setting up 15 networking technology institutes in China. And Texas Instruments plans to have 100 labs in the country working on digital signal processors before 2002. Motorola Electronics Singapore has designed several cutting-edge pagers and conducts research in wireless and radio frequency technologies. The company also chose Singapore to handle the product development—from drawing board to manufacturing—for the first two-way data pager and the first 280/900 megahertz voice pager produced entirely in Asia. In addition, the company performs research and development in Malaysia on two-way radios, "smart" batteries for personal computers, and cell phones. Motorola also is performing research with a Chinese joint-venture partner on programmable switches and wireless base-station equipment. In addition, Rockwell is working with the Shanghai Rockwell Collins Navigation and Communications Equipment Company to design as well as manufacture a global navigation system for China.[50]

In computer hardware, Intel's Kulim, Malaysia facility contains not only motherboard manufacturing, but what the company calls "world-class R&D capabilities in board manufacturing operations." Apple Computer has been designing Macintosh desktops in Singapore since 1993 and began designing the motherboards and tooling systems for multimedia computers in Singapore in late 1994. Compaq began designing all of its notebook and portable PCs in Singapore that same year, and Hewlett Packard Singapore now handles process design and tooling development for all the company's portable printers and Pentium desktop PCs and servers. Motorola, meanwhile, designs and develops as well as manufactures printed circuit boards in Singapore.[51]

Motorola also has been especially active in transferring such work to China. In December 1995, the company opened its Asia Manufacturing Research Center in Beijing, the first Motorola manufacturing research lab located outside the United States. The center has signed a joint manufacturing research agreement with Tsinghua University's Computer Integrated Manufacturing System Engineering Center. In March, 1996 Motorola opened a Joint Development Lab for Advanced Computer and Communications Technologies with the Chinese Academy of Science's National Research Center for Intelligent Computing Systems in Beijing. In a similar vein, IBM is cooperating with Tsingua on massive parallel processing.[52]

The spread of semiconductor design and research and development seems nearly as widespread as the spread of advanced semiconductor manufacturing, and the biggest U.S. electronics and computer giants are again at the forefront. Motorola's Asia Pacific Semiconductor Products Group employs hundreds of systems design and applications engineers in design centers in Hong Kong, Taiwan, and Singapore. The group has pioneered such technologies and processes as the use of metal oxide semiconductors for advanced computer display screens, handwriting input and storage systems for displays, and new techniques for semiconductor assembly and testing.[53]

Intel's Penang facilities include Malaysia's first research and development center with leading-edge semiconductor design capability, as well as projects in developing chip packaging technologies. Advanced Micro Devices has just opened its own integrated circuit design facility in Malaysia. Hewlett Packard Singapore is involved in chip design as well as production, including a joint venture with Texas Instruments, Canon, and the Singapore Economic Development Board for developing advanced memory chips. TI has, as previously noted, been engaged in chip design in India since 1985, and its Bangalore facility is working on application-specific integrated circuits along with dynamic and flash memories. Korea and Taiwan also host TI integrated circuit development centers. Meanwhile, joining TI in chip design in India, among others, are Analog Devices, which is developing digital signal processors, and Cypress Semiconductor, which is working on advanced memory chips. In 1995, IBM chose Shangdi, just outside Shanghai, to place one of its few non-U.S. research laboratories, and its first in a third world country. The facility will cooperate on chip design with Fudan University and the Chinese Ministry of the Electronics Industry.[54]

Software design as well as production also has become thoroughly globalized. In addition to the research and development and design activities of TI, IBM, Microsoft, Oracle, Novel, Informix, and others, Motorola is working with Apple, IBM, and several Chinese partners to develop a Chinese-language operating system and application software based on the Motorola PowerPC hardware platform. IBM's joint research with Fudan University and the Chinese government also covers speech recognition and electronic filing systems. S3 performs software design in Bangalore, too, and Cadence Design Systems is expanding its Indian facility for creating electronic design automation packages. Further, Lotus and Xerox have set up software development as well as production operations in Singapore, and Sybase has established research and development facilities in Hong Kong as well as Singapore. Asia is not the only developing region where U.S. software companies have found productive new homes; IBM operates an Open Systems Center in Sao Paulo, Brazil, to develop networking solutions and internet tools.[55]

Corporate U.S. third world software research and development efforts have extended into advanced communications and internet applications as well. Intel's new research and development facility in Beijing is working on internet and speech recognition software projects, while its Shanghai center is investigating e-business applications. In 1998, Lucent established a Global Design Center in Qingdao, China, for the software used by its 5ESS switching system. The company envisions that its Asia-Pacific Center will become "one of the major research and development centers for communications software in the world."[56]

All told, U.S. corporate research and development conducted abroad has been increasing faster than domestic corporate research and development—according to one U.S. government study, rising from 6.4 percent of all such U.S. expenditures in 1985 to 11.6 percent in 1996. The bulk of these expenditures are made in industrialized countries, but their share of the worldwide total has fallen slightly since 1985—from 85 to 82 percent. These figures also show that within the developing world U.S. research and development expenditures have been increasing rapidly in Brazil and Singapore.[57]

The definitive interpretation of this data has come from none other than Craig R. Barrett, CEO of Intel: "Just as with the move of manufacturing overseas, you're going to see an increasing flux of technical jobs out of the U.S. We don't have any protected domains anymore."[58]

C. THE INVISIBLE HAND IS NOWHERE TO BE FOUND

American multinationals have sent good jobs overseas for a wide variety of reasons. Often these decisions make good business sense. The search for cheap, highly educated and productive labor is one such motive for companies. However, U.S. multinationals outsource massively to high-wage countries, too. Sometimes, for example, they are trying to prevent getting victimized by sudden shifts in exchange rates, which can dramatically affect the profitability of exporting from a country with a relatively strong currency to one with a newly weakened currency. Sometimes it is easier to identify foreign consumer tastes and manufacture for them when both market researchers and production facilities are located close to the consumers. Sometimes factories need to be located near supplies of important raw materials, parts, or other inputs, especially if they have adopted just-in-time production systems that seek to save on the costs of maintaining parts inventories by arranging for supplies to arrive exactly when they are needed. It is also significantly easier to supply wholesalers and retailers when the goods do not have to be shipped long distances.

Often, however, outsourcing decisions have nothing to do with business considerations. As indicated by the multitude of ways in which countries try to depress domestic consumption and boost exports, in today's world economy, government interference with trade and investment flows is nothing less than pervasive. Advanced industrialized countries are responsible for much of this interference. The European Union, for example, has lured a considerable amount U.S.-owned semiconductor production to its shores by maintaining high tariffs on semiconductor imports until very recently.[59] In the 1980s, the United States accomplished the same goal in the auto and steel industries when U.S. tariffs and quotas were instituted in response to decades of European and Japanese protectionism and other predatory trade practices that threatened the very existence of these sectors.[60] In fact, the big differences in trade policies among industrialized countries have also become a major force in pushing American multinationals offshore. Because U.S. companies often have to compete against European and Japanese counterparts that enjoy protected home markets, they often face more price-cutting pressures than their rivals. Since many Europeans and Japanese do not have to play defense as well as offense, they have many more opportunities than the

Americans to reap *scale economies*—the production cost savings for each unit of a good that results from making great amounts of that good. Given Washington's feeble responses to these foreign trade barriers, one of the few serious price-cutting options available to U.S. firms is sending production to low-wage countries.

Yet efforts to interfere with free-investment decisions also have become commonplace in low-income countries, and their popularity adds significantly to the special problems posed by these economies and their productive capacities for U.S. living standards. Some of the developing country interventionism is relatively passive—for example, tax breaks to encourage investments. One of the most highly developed tax incentive systems is found in Malaysia. The Malaysian government grants five-year tax holidays and exemption from taxes on 70 percent of statutory income to companies awarded Pioneer Status—companies whose activities dovetail with the official economic development priorities. The Malaysian Ministry of International Trade and Industry has identified some 260 product areas and industries that qualify, ranging from tea cultivation to silicon wafer fabrication. On top of these tax breaks, high-tech companies, which are rigorously defined, can receive an Investment Tax Allowance of 60 percent of certain capital expenditures incurred within any five-year period. "Strategic projects" can receive an Investment Tax Allowance of 100 percent. Generous tax incentives are also offered to perform research and development in Malaysia.[61]

In addition, Malaysia has offered 10-year tax holidays plus preferential status in bidding for government infrastructure contracts to companies that invest in the vaunted "multimedia super-corridor" project unveiled in August 1996. The project was conceived to build a Malaysian version of Silicon Valley, although its progress has been slowed by the country's recent financial troubles.[62]

As mentioned in Chapter 4, despite Indonesia's financial crisis and huge resulting shortfalls in tax revenues, Jakarta continues to offer 10-year tax holidays to large investors. In 1999, moreover, Indonesia unveiled yet more tax incentives in the chemicals and information technology industries. Thailand's Investment Promotion Act allows eight-year tax holidays for investment. Businesses in Singapore can be exempted from 50 percent of taxes on new fixed investments for five years, and existing businesses spending a certain amount on new machinery or equipment can receive five years of relief from the 31 percent tax on profits over and above pre-expansion profits. In order to attract auto manufacturing, Poland has exempted GM from its 40 percent corporate profit tax for ten years and granted it a 50 percent reduction in this tax over the next ten years. In addition, India's Tamil Nadu state has attracted substantial auto investment in part by exempting manufacturers from state sales taxes on locally made inputs and finished vehicles.[63]

Some Asian governments are also heavily involved in providing foreign companies with research grants. Malaysia's Penang state, for example, has created a venture capital fund to help local companies change from assembly to research and development operations by paying foreign companies to launch research projects with Malay partners. In 1996, Singapore doubled the level of research and development grants it was offering to foreign and domestic companies to a target of $2.8 billion of disbursements through 2001. Singapore's government also enters into partnerships with foreign and domestic companies to share the costs and risks of new high-tech endeavors. Funded by a Cluster Development Fund, these projects include a large joint venture by Texas Instruments, Canon, Hewlett Packard, and the island's Economic Development Board to produce advanced memory chips. Meanwhile, Western Digital, a disk-drive maker, and SCI Manufacturing, a contract manufacturer, are among the U.S. companies that have received grants from Singapore's Innovation Development Program.[64]

Low-income countries also actively manipulate the terms of trade to attract high-tech production and know-how. As mentioned previously, China, India, Malaysia, and many other developing countries allow products used in manufacturing export goods to be imported duty-free or at very low tariff rates. More aggressively, many developing countries have adopted for numerous products the same approach used by the European Union to attract semiconductor investment—low or no tariffs on parts and components, high tariffs on finished products.

These trade policies are especially common in the automobile industry. In March 1995, for example, Brazil increased its tariffs on finished autos from 32 to 70 percent, and in December decreased them to 35 percent for companies that produced vehicles in Brazil. Largely as a result, Brazil has received an estimated $17 billion in pledges of auto investment from nearly all the world's major vehicle makers. In the 1980s, foreign investment in the Brazilian auto sector was running only at about $500 million annually. GM and Ford insist that they would manufacture in Brazil regardless of its tariffs. However, they have also acknowledged that their invest- ment decisions have been influenced not only by Brazil's trade barriers but by the barriers erected by the South American trading bloc to which Brazil belongs—Mercosur.[65]

Poland's auto industry also partly owes its existence to trade barriers. Warsaw has maintained a 35 percent tariff on finished ve- hicles and in 1996 decided that only companies that assemble more than 100,000 vehicles and move from assembly to full manu- facturing in Poland (or at least significant parts production) would be exempted from import duties on parts, components, and auto- making machinery and equipment.[66]

Back in 1994, China designated autos as one of several sectors that would become "pillars" of its industrial development, and therefore eligible for special treatment. China's 1994 auto plan is a blueprint for using high tariffs and other official carrots and sticks to create a domestic industry that can serve most of the Chinese market. Beijing has aimed to produce 90 percent of its auto demand by the year 2000 and to completely displace imports by 2004. The plan also calls for a largely self-sufficient auto parts industry (specifically, 90 percent local content in all vehicles produced in China), for promoting auto exports, and for linking state support for manufacturers to their progress in achieving these goals.[67]

Perhaps the most serious interference with market forces in- volves a practice called offsets—globalization's version of outright extortion. An offset is any type of compensation that governments impose as a condition of buying a product or service. Offsets often entail demands that a seller farm out part of the production of its product to businesses and workers in the purchasing country. However, they can also consist of requirements to transfer technol- ogy, to provide investment capital for other parts of the buyer's economy, or to purchase goods completely unrelated to the origi- nal transaction.

Offsets are especially common in trade deals involving weapons and other defense-related goods. A 1997 Commerce Department report found that "virtually all U.S. defense trading partners im- pose some type of offset requirement, and at times the stated value of the offset exceeds that of the sales contract." In 1999, Commerce reported that over the last 20 years, "the number of countries that have formal offset policies has increased." Other U.S. government studies have also concluded that offsets are increasing in numbers and scale.[68]

The U.S. government seems divided on the subject of offsets. Their popularity indicates that the consumers of defense goods and services have much more leverage than the sellers. Industry representatives typically argue that they have no choice but to accept offsets if they want to continue winning sales. Companies that stand on principle could easily lose out to foreign competitors.[69] The relatively small absolute level of military offset deals (some $19 billion in new agreements from 1993 to 1997) has apparently convinced some U.S. officials that, for all the injustice it suggests, the problem is negligible—indeed, a small price to pay for maintaining high levels of U.S. exports.

According to Commerce Department aerospace official Sally H. Bath, offsets appear to play a fairly small role in aerospace industry employment overall. She has added, "Many more U.S. jobs are created through U.S. aerospace exports than are lost by U.S. manufacturers sourcing components from overseas. New trade measures which could cause our trading partners to restrict access to their markets would have obvious repercussions for American aerospace workers."[70] However, Bath's colleague at the Department of Commerce, undersecretary for export administration William A. Reinsch, has expressed serious concerns. Offsets, he told a reporter in 1996, "have the consequence of shifting production jobs overseas, and the long-term effect of creating competitors."[71]

The Commerce Department offsets report shows that the great majority of military offsets are imposed by European governments, but developing countries frequently use military offsets as well. Turkey, for example, recently agreed to purchase $4.3 billion of F–16 fighter jets from General Dynamics (now part of Lockheed-Martin). Although most of the sale was financed by U.S. government grants and loans, Turkey demanded—and got—$760 million worth of coproduction contracts for Turkish companies and workers. Moreover, the Turkish factory assembling the F–16s has sold some to Egypt, in a transaction again financed largely by U.S. taxpayer dollars.[72]

General Dynamics agreed to an even more onerous (for its workers) deal with South Korea, another country protected militarily by the United States. Seoul agreed to purchase 120 F–16s, but only 12 would be made by General Dynamics workers in Forth Worth, Texas. The rest would be manufactured or manufactured and assembled in South Korea. At the time, 3,000 American machinists at the Fort Worth plant were on layoff.[73]

Offsets occur in civilian industry as well, and no one plays the game more effectively than the Chinese government agencies that control commercial aerospace trade. Like automobiles, commercial aviation is a sector that China has identified as a "pillar" of future Chinese industrial development. Remarks by a senior Chinese aviation official at a 1996 Washington, D.C., conference made it clear that China (along with other Asian countries) wishes to develop its own aircraft industry and has no intention of leaving this matter to the free market:

> Attracted by the market opportunities and economic benefit [of commercial aviation markets], the rapidly developing countries will not be satisfied with being buyers only. This competitive trend is subject to the laws of economic benefit and resources movement. Aircraft manufacturers participating [in] the competition and hoping to lead the trend can only adapt to it, but can by no means change it. The winner of the competition will be the manufacturers who make correct cooperative strategies.

For good measure, the official added a definition of comparative advantage that market economists should find astonishing: ". . . the existing manufacturers have their basic advantages in design, production, and marketing, while the new comers within the region have their natural advantage in geographic position, human resources, and governmental supports."[74]

Notwithstanding the Chinese official's puzzling claim that China has a natural advantage in aircraft production personnel, offset demands, not market forces, explain why Boeing has outsourced significant work to the People's Republic of China. As Boeing official Newton L. Simmons told journalist William Greider, "We have a very onerous countertrade agreement in China, based on a percentage of the airplane price. They are asking 20 to 30 percent of the price in local purchases. That's the way the game is played." In the words of his colleague, Boeing president of commercial airplanes Ron Woodard, "The correlation is clear: work placement has opened markets for us where they might otherwise not be accessible."[75]

U.S. businessmen in other industries are reporting similar pressures from China. George Sollman, then president of the American

Electronics Association, an industry group, led a business delega-
tion to China in late 1996. After returning, he told a reporter, "On
many occasions, I was questioned either by ministers or staff regarding whether U.S. high-tech companies would be willing to
give up intellectual property rights in return for market share."
Sollman called the requests "a trial balloon to see whether we
were so desperate for Chinese business that we would do anything to get it." Although Sollman insisted that U.S. companies
would never agree to such deals, he also warned that, due to
mounting European and Japanese competition, the pressures on
U.S. firms to knuckle under are on the rise. Sollman's account was
confirmed in January 1999 by a report from the Clinton administration's Commerce Department that found that "U.S. high-tech-
nology firms investing in China are under increasing pressure to
transfer commercial technologies and know-how as a condition of
market access and investment approval...." [76]

George David, CEO of United Technologies, told Congress in
June 1999 that "It is . . . perfectly clear to us as an exporter and
competitor in China that our local and joint venture presence is
what got us the Great Hall of the People [air-conditioning installa-
tion] job. Without one, we don't have the other, and it is the foreign direct investment that comes first, always." No doubt the
Chinese requirement that foreign firms make in China much of
what they sell in China is one reason why, of United Technologies'
$1 billion in annual sales to China, exports from the United States
account for only one-fifth. [77]

China's auto industry plan provides an idea of how detailed
local content offsets can be. For example, all auto manufacturing
in China must start with 40 percent Chinese content levels and
move up to 80 percent in three years. Nor is China satisfied to
specify content levels for finished vehicles. Realizing that parts
and components of today's manufactured goods usually consist of
advanced parts and components themselves, China has established 60 percent local content levels for all components. [78] It is possible that China's admission to the World Trade Organization will
reduce or eliminate these and other Chinese trade barriers. However, given their persistence in other longtime members of the organization, the burden of proof clearly is on the optimists.

The importance of local content requirement for creating and
preserving jobs is clear from Thailand's experience. Thailand's
transformation into one of the world's leading automotive pro-

ducers during the 1980s and 1990s (it became the world's second largest manufacturer of pickup trucks) obviously reflected much hard work and significant domestic demand during Thailand's boom years. However, local content requirements have helped considerably, too. According to the Oxford Analytica consulting firm, the country's 54 percent local content rule was instrumental in saving 50,000 jobs in early 1998 when the country's financial crisis cut vehicle sales by some 72 percent.[79]

Korea is another master of technology blackmail. According to a White House report, "'Forced technology transfer' is particularly prevalent in high-tech areas such as telecommunications equipment and services, where the Korean Government is determined to dominate domestically and internationally." The Koreans themselves all but admit this; in the words of the president of the Korean Semiconductor Industry Association, "... Korean device makers actively support foreign equipment makers that directly invest in Korea."[80]

Globalization optimists often argue that the free-market revolution they see unfolding all over the world is already eliminating these obstacles to unfettered trade and investment flows. In 1997, 42 countries accounting for more than 90 percent of the global trade in information technology products signed an agreement to abolish by July 1, 2000, all tariffs on electronics products, including semiconductors, computers, telecommunications equipment, and software. Industrialized countries have also been working off and on on a Multilateral Agreement on Investment, designed to eliminate most barriers to most types of capital flows. As a result, mercantilist governments soon could be legally stripped of many of their most effective nonmarket lures for investment.[81]

Yet even if these agreements can be effectively enforced (and the historical record is not encouraging), the optimists do not seem to realize that much of the damage is already done. U.S. and other multinational companies have been making investment decisions based at least partly on economic barriers for decades. As a result, tens of billions of dollars worth of factories and labs and other facilities now exist in countries that otherwise would have been largely bypassed. These investments represent tremendous sunk costs and are not about to be closed down just because the global playing field legally becomes level once again. In fact, because these investments and costs are so great, they will continue to attract new investment, and to expand or upgrade operations in various ways.

Expansions and other modifications have long been major drivers of foreign direct investment. The head of Ford's operations in Britain has estimated that up to 40 percent of the company's new investment in Europe has come to the United Kingdom because of Ford's decision to expand its sizable existing UK facilities. "It's easier to expand the Bridgend engine plant than to build a new facility somewhere else," he told a reporter. The chairman of the investment firm Salomon Brothers made similar comments about its London European headquarters: "There is real embedded value— we are not all about to close up shop and rebuild somewhere else."[82] The same considerations clearly affect U.S. investments in developing countries.

Moreover, such investments have created another form of embedded value that continually lures ever more investment overseas—extensive supplier bases. Their effects have been especially important in the electronics industry. As explained by analysts such as Michael Borrus and Dieter Ernst of the Berkeley Roundtable on the International Economy, the demise of the U.S. consumer electronics industry by the early 1980s had left a critical void in the U.S. manufacturing base. The skills to develop and manufacture memory chips, displays, precision components, and other essential pieces of electronics systems became increasingly rare in the U.S. economy. However, they were alive and well not only in Japan, but in Southeast Asia, where U.S. multinationals had been outsourcing more and more sophisticated production and technology in order to meet price competition from Japan, and in response to the extensive set of barriers and incentives discussed previously.

As a result, outsourcing decisions soon began to be driven not only by the need to cut costs, but by the simple fact that the supplies of machinery, materials, components, and other inputs needed to develop and manufacture products were to be found overseas. One example is Hewlett Packard's decision in 1994 to choose Singapore for developing and producing its Pentium servers. Singapore had two key advantages in the eyes of HP executives: Its workforce had strong process engineering capabilities, and the suppliers for almost all the components of these devices were located in Southeast Asia, including producers of casings, power supplies, and disk drives. The process works in reverse as well—the establishment of assembly and other manufacturing facilities for final products can lure parts and components makers to that locale.[83]

In 1999, printed circuit board maker Smartflex moved from Tustin, California, across the border to Mexico, in part to be closer to its main customers, the disk-drive manufacturers that have set up shop in Guadalajara. In early 1999, Kulicke & Soffa Industries, a supplier of the bonders used to assemble semiconductors, announced a move from Pennsylvania to Asia because so many of its customers and suppliers had moved there. Even higher up the technology ladder, Lucent has made clear that its decision to develop software for its advanced switching devices in China stemmed directly from its previous decision to produce the switches themselves in China. In addition, according to Advanced Micro Devices, it just established an Integrated Circuit Design Centre in Malaysia because these products are already built and tested there.[84]

D. On Their Own Two Feet

Since the financial crisis struck in the summer of 1997, belittling the economic record of developing Asia has become all the rage. Countries that registered more economic growth for more years than any in history are still being pilloried regularly for rampant corruption, cronyism, bureaucratism, and protectionism. Asian governments obviously have made big mistakes, and in countries like South Korea, Thailand, and Indonesia, growth rates and living standards could remain below precrisis levels for many years. However, blunders in macroeconomic and financial policies should not obscure the low-income Asian countries' success not only in using the technologies brought by foreign multinationals but in developing their own.

Local producers throughout these countries have become important global suppliers of many sophisticated products, have generated important technological advances of their own, and stand at the threshold of future progress. Some of these developments are occurring in other low-income countries as well. The accumulation of such proven wealth-creating capabilities may not be enough to dig these countries out of their current financial holes quickly. However, it will continue to help ensure that Asian workers occupy critical industrial and technological niches instead of U.S. workers.

Some sense of how far this process has advanced is apparent from statistics showing how thoroughly industrialized many of these countries have become. Semiconductors alone comprise 20 percent of South Korea's total exports. In Singapore, the electronics sector employs some 35 percent of the labor force, and its share of the country's manufactures output has been estimated at between 44 and 52 percent. In addition, electronics make up some 60 percent of Singapore's non-oil exports. (Singapore is a major oil refining center.)[85]

According to a World Bank study, Malaysia's exports in 1965 stood at 42 percent of economic output, but 96 percent of these shipments were raw materials, fuels, or metals. By 1990, exports had risen to 79 percent of that resource-rich country's economic output, and 44 percent of these exports were manufactured goods. By 1999, 84.6 percent of Malaysia's total exports were manufactured goods, and 71.8 percent of these were electronics products. As of 1999, manufacturing represented 30.1 percent of the Malaysian economy.[86]

Thailand has made similar progress. Between 1965 and 1990, exports grew from 16 to 38 percent of economic output, and manufactured products rocketed from 3 to 64 percent of total exports. Of these manufactured exports, computers and computer components nearly doubled between 1989 and 1995 alone—from 12 to 21 percent. In the Philippines, electronics exports increased by 33 percent in 1998 alone, and now account for an estimated 75 percent of total exports. In addition, computer chips represent 75 percent of these electronics exports. Electronics products, at least before the financial crisis, were the fastest-rising of Indonesia's non-oil exports—up 30 percent in 1996.[87]

Despite its extremely low wages, China's output and trade are steadily moving up the technology ladder as well. As of mid-1999, 40 percent of China's global exports were electronics and machinery products—surpassing textiles and apparel as China's export leaders. These manufactures made up 70 percent of China's exports to Europe and North America. Beijing is planning a 30 percent increase in high-tech exports by 2002. Including the information technology, biomedical, and new materials industries, achieving this goal would result in such products reaching 14 percent of China's projected total exports.[88]

India is another burgeoning Asian technology powerhouse. According to Harvard economist Jeffrey Sachs, its information technology exports now surpass its overseas sales of the textile and apparel products, for which it has been traditionally known. Part of the conventional wisdom about Mexico's *maquiladora* factories needs revising as well. Once they were generally considered a source of labor-intensive products. Now one in every eight of their workers is a technician.[89]

Developing country technology progress can also be measured by the number of local producers that dominate world markets in specific sectors. In this regard, Taiwan and South Korea are in a class by themselves. Taiwan's companies have lapped the global field in computer hardware such as motherboards (80 percent of world market share in 1994), scanners (61 percent), monitors (56 percent), and keyboards (52 percent). Taiwan producers also held an estimated 46 percent of world market share in notebook computers as of 1999, a remarkable feat considering that engineers consider these devices to be up to 20 times more complex to manufacture than desktop PCs. In 2000, the figure is expected to hit 55 percent. In total, Taiwan has become the world's third largest manufacturer of PC equipment, behind the United States and Japan.[90]

Taiwan has also become the world's fourth largest manufacturer of semiconductors, behind the United States, Japan, and South Korea. As recently as 1993, Taiwan was only number seven. For good measure, the Taiwanese also turn out 30 percent of the world's motherboard chip sets and 85 percent of its graphics chips. A single Taiwanese industrial park alone turns out 10 percent of the world's semiconductors. This reality became abundantly clear in the fall of 1999, when an earthquake that struck the island severely disrupted world personal computers and other electronics markets for months.[91]

Semiconductors have generated many of South Korea's main triumphs as well. Major South Korean producers such as Samsung, Hyundai, and LG have seized nearly 40 percent of world markets for memory chips, which are expected to be a $170 billion industry in the first years of the new century. Samsung alone holds one-fifth of the global market, making it the world leader. Another South Korean firm, Anam, is the world's largest semiconductor packaging and testing company.[92]

Other developing countries are also having major impacts on world high-tech markets. Singapore, for example, produces more than half the world's disk drives, and as of 1993, its three million people generated roughly 20 percent of the computer hardware production of the United States (as well as of Japan). Further, Malaysia was the world's third largest producer of finished semi-conductors and the world's largest exporter as of 1996.[93]

Even in sectors where they are not global leaders, many high-tech producers in developing countries are performing impressively in markets at home and abroad. Malaysia's Proton national car owes much of its 74 percent domestic market share to 100 percent tariffs on vehicle imports into Malaysia. However, the Proton has also been exported to 18 countries, selling 17,000 cars in the United Kingdom and Ireland in 1993. China's strategy to achieve automotive self-reliance is bearing fruit as well. In the first half of 1997, the number of cars China imported fell by 60 percent, and the value of car exports rose by 16.1 percent, to $376 million.[94]

Competitive products made by local companies are also enabling China to reduce computer imports. In 1996, these imports fell by 48,000 units and $490 million. The Chinese company Legend Computer ranks number one in the nation in home sales, and estimates of the domestic market share of Chinese-owned PC makers range from 32 to 40 percent. Some experts reportedly have predicted that Chinese brands' domestic market share would hit 60 percent in the year 2000. Domestic computer makers are grabbing market share from U.S. giants like Compaq in Brazil, too. Chinese firms are also racking up impressive gains in software, and Microsoft executives have predicted in at least two major business publications that these companies will capture some 50 percent of the local market by 2002 at the latest—up from 15 percent in 1997.[95]

Homegrown technological capabilities in low-income countries can also be judged by looking at the individual products made by locally owned companies. South Korea may have taken a major fall in the financial crisis, but as a 1996 study of Asian high-tech activity noted, the country's "transition from labor intensive low-value-added pursuits, to high-level technologies has occurred in less than two decades." This progress, the report added, often "has taken place during periods of domestic unrest."[96]

In 1995, for example, after decades of reliance on Japanese technology, Hyundai Motor Company became the first South Korean automaker to develop a passenger car fully in-house. South Korea has also become the world's third largest auto-making country.[97] In addition, as of mid–1996, South Korean *chaebol* (corporate conglomerates) Samsung, LG, and Hyundai were manufacturing cutting-edge 12.1-inch thin film transistor liquid crystal display screens for notebook computers, one of the most advanced components of personal computer production and one that requires even more high-tech manufacturing expertise than producing notebooks. Japan and Taiwan are currently the only other countries in the world with such large-scale capabilities. (U.S. companies never became significant players in civilian flat panel display markets.) The same firms recently have begun making plasma display panel televisions with 21-to–30-inch screens.[98]

Meanwhile, the semiconductor operations of these companies continue to diversify from memory chips—where they have achieved the highest production yields in the world and have been designing 256-megabit DRAMS since 1994—into logic chips, digital signal processors, and other advanced devices. Hyundai is designing multimedia chips. Samsung has been moving aggressively into products such as large-scale integrated circuits featuring system-on-a-chip technology, logic chips for advanced consumer electronics products such as DVD players and digital televisions, and chips with communications applications. In addition, for most of the 1990s, it went on a shopping spree for U.S. and other foreign high-tech companies and technology in order to consolidate its position in such highly lucrative specialty-chip niches.[99]

South Koreans are keeping up in semiconductor processing technology as well. This is a field in which progress is measured in the tiniest fractions of millimeters—the widths of today's microcircuits. The narrower the individual circuits, the more circuits can be placed onto a single silicon chip, and the more computing power that chip will have. Today, chip makers in the United States, Japan, and Western Europe are producing chips with circuits less than 0.2 microns wide (500 microns is about the width of a typical strand of human hair). Anam's joint venture with Texas Instruments will bring 0.35 micron technology to that South Korean firm. Anam makes its own most critical chip packaging manufacturing equipment, too.[100]

Taiwanese advances in the field of displays for computers are excellent examples of how success in one product area can spawn success further up the technology ladder. Taiwanese prowess in electronics products, starting with televisions and calculators and proceeding to notebook computers, helped create a thriving display industry, including initially the ability to produce thin film transistor liquid crystal displays up to 5.6 inches across. In 1994, Taiwanese researchers rolled out a prototype 10.4-inch screen, which met the standards at that time for notebook computers. Thus, they joined Japan and South Korea in a product with no U.S. presences.

When notebook standards moved up to 12.1-inch screens, Taiwanese manufacturers followed suit. Today the island produces one-fifth of the world's supply of these devices, and its manufacturers are in an excellent position to service enormous new markets such as future generations of notebooks, desktop computer monitors, and flat-screen televisions. The expertise they develop has also proved useful for smaller devices such as personal digital assistants and palm-top computers.[101]

Taiwan's position in packaging technologies for computer chips is strong as well. Taiwanese companies that produce printed circuit boards for components in Intel's Pentium II microprocessors are mass-producing state-of-the-art packaging devices for mounting semiconductors on the boards, and design and manufacture connectors for Pentium IIs. In fact, Taiwan is running right behind world leaders Japan and the United States in most of the latest packaging technologies.[102]

Taiwan has also made great strides in semiconductor processing technology. Taiwanese chip makers began using 0.4 micron technology in 1994, through deals with foreign companies like TI and Japan's Oki. That same year, the Taiwan Semiconductor Manufacturing Company began testing 0.35 micron devices. The company operates the world's largest and most advanced silicon foundry, a facility that etches the integrated circuit designs of other companies onto silicon wafers. Government research labs were aiming at hitting the 0.1 micron target by mid-1999. All told, Taiwanese semiconductor companies are planning to invest $50 billion in new plants through 2007, and unlike other East Asian countries with grandiose development plans, Taiwan was not hit hard by the region's financial crisis.[103]

Yet South Korea and Taiwan face competition as well. The Singapore government's Economic Development Board hopes that the city-state eventually will be home to 25 silicon wafer fabrication plants; plans for the ninth were announced in 1997. In addition, the city-state's Institute of Microelectronics has established a worldwide reputation in mixed-signal integrated circuits, integrated circuit design, and advanced packaging, and the Singapore government is supporting its research in advanced lithography. Singapore is also becoming an important worldwide player in computer software and biotechnology, while Brazilian companies are starting to sell multimedia, internet-related, and factory automation software in the United States.[104]

Asia's giants, China and India, have moved into the highest-tech areas of manufacturing and research and development, too. By mid–1994, China's biggest semiconductor maker, China Huajing Electronics Group, was producing 5-inch silicon wafers with circuit widths of 2 to 3 microns. As of early 1997, China had eight advanced wafer fabrication plants either under construction or in the design phase. Aided largely, but not entirely, by foreign multinationals like Motorola and NEC of Japan, these factories are aiming at Beijing's latest official target of 0.5 micron, 8-inch wafer technology. Huajing's newest production line reportedly already has the potential to produce 0.5 micron products on 6-inch wafers. According to the U.S. embassy in Beijing, Mitsubishi, Mitsui, and Chinese partners are planning to build a wafer factory with 0.35 micron technology just outside Beijing. Despite the prominent role played by foreign companies, China's insistence that foreign joint-venture partners transfer critical technologies in order to sell in the Chinese market practically ensures that entirely Chinese-owned production facilities are not far behind.[105]

Another Chinese government priority is the development and design of application-specific chips. The country's leading integrated circuit design center, in Beijing, has already produced the world's first eight-bit monolithic computer with an all-flash four-kilobyte memory. Moreover, a Shanghai-based institute developed highly advanced gallium arsenide circuitry that foreign governments had been withholding from Chinese manufacturers.[106]

Chinese indigenous software capabilities are becoming formidable as well. The Founder company, for example, produces Chinese-language publishing software, as well as programs to manage the work flow and produce animation for television stations, and to create databases for fingerprinting. China is also in the process of creating a Chinese-language domestic intranet that would use Internet-style Web browsers and communications systems. In addition, the Chinese hardware giant Legend is engaged in software development of its own.[107]

India has made even bigger waves in software. Since the Indian government began a major push in 1986 to develop its domestic industry, some 90 percent of the country's software revenue has come from providing different packages of services—from indi-

vidual consulting engineers to larger and more sophisticated
"turnkey" operations for various clients. However, a major move
into the far more lucrative field of packaged software is well underway. Indian companies have provided the software for the
computer displays at the Barcelona Olympics in 1992; on-line trading programs for local stock exchanges; 13-language translation
programs for the European Commission; the world's fastest, most
advanced computer-assisted design software for machine tools; a
best-selling integrated banking program; and hundreds of other
branded products. In addition, at the end of the 1990s, Indian companies were leaders in providing companies all over the world
with solutions to their Y2K problems [108]

All told, India's software exports nearly tripled from 1995 to
1998 and were expected to grow by 50 percent more in 1999, according to that country's major software industry association.
North America currently imports 61 percent of the total and the
United States (by far the world's largest and most competitive
software market) bought the overwhelming majority of these
products.[109]

Another indication of developing country technological
progress is patenting activity. According to the latest National Science Foundation figures, patents granted in developing Asia to
residents of those countries grew dramatically from 1985 to 1990—
at rates much faster than that of the United States, although from
significantly smaller bases.[110] For the four "tiger" economies of
East Asia—Hong Kong, Singapore, South Korea, and Taiwan—the
numbers nearly doubled, to just under 14,000. In China, they shot
up from 42 to 1,083. (By comparison, the United States awarded
more than 47,000 patents to resident inventors in 1990.) However,
patents awarded to nonresidents are a sign of technological
prowess, too, because they suggest the extent to which an economy can make use of innovations. Here patent awards for the four
countries grew even faster between 1985 and 1990—from 6,796 in
1985 to 18,764.

Patenting by inventors from developing Asia in the U.S. market—the world's most technologically advanced—grew faster still.
In 1981, inventors from the four tiger economies were awarded
134 U.S. patents. In 1991, the number was 1,363. During the same
years, the number of patents granted to inventors from China,
India, Malaysia, and Indonesia rose from 11 to 87 (51 of which

went to Chinese inventors). The fastest growth for all these countries came in electronics.

Still, misconceptions abound about third-world technological progress, and the high-tech job flight it has produced, whether it has been sparked by technology transfers from the industrialized world or has been homegrown. Many supposed experts seem positively clueless, such as Barry Bosworth of the Brookings Institution, who reported that Asian countries still mainly produce "a range of consumer products—particularly clothing—in which the United States does not have a comparative advantage...." (Four paragraphs later, he allowed that Asia "has become the center for the labor-intensive assembly portion of the computer and information-processing industries.")[111]

As Bosworth's second point suggests, commentators also often go through impressive analytical contortions to convince audiences (and maybe themselves) that Asian technological progress is trivial or downright meaningless. Thus *The Wall Street Journal* reporters Bob Davis and David Wessel assured readers that South Asian software workers are "largely left doing the dull work Americans don't want to bother with anyway" and are "stuck in a low-tech rut." Better yet, they noted, "this low-tech programming actually boosts the value of U.S. programmers." The best programming jobs stay in the United States.[112]

These arguments follow a long, strange tradition of what might be called "defining high-tech employment up." For years, globalization optimists have reacted to reports of Japanese or third-world inroads into global technology markets by claiming that the inroads were being made in industries that were not high-tech sectors at all—and certainly not cutting edge. In fact, their very development by foreign scientists and industrialists apparently proved that they had become obsolete at worst and commodities at best—products for which global competition raged and that had become so easy technologically to turn out that profit margins had been cut to the bone. In this way, successive industries from steel and autos and machine tools to computer hardware and most semiconductors have been dismissed by globalization optimists as being beneath Americans' concern. They are viewed as sectors that can be safely lost to the competition because industries more advanced and lucrative (not to mention more fun and exciting) have already emerged or are on the horizon.

Leaving aside the issue of whether advanced flat panel screens and speech recognition software really do represent "the dull work that Americans don't want to bother with anyway," defining high-tech up begs the question of what kinds of jobs do not fall into this category. In other words, what are the exciting, value-laden jobs and industries that the United States and its workers need to hang on to? The only answer the optimists logically can provide—jobs in high-tech industries and fields such as finance that pay superstar salaries and create phenomenal wealth for the world and U.S. economies—is as unrealistic as it is seductive.

It is another way of saying, as demonstrated in Chapter 2, that the only jobs the United States realy needs to retain are those that employ hardly any Americans—and are not likely to for decades, if ever. This is shattering news to the waiters, cashiers, home and health care workers, and tens of millions of other Americans toiling at jobs paying the minimum wage or slightly higher—the very Americans being urged into all the reeducation and retraining programs that the optimists have promised the government or business one day will adequately fund and get right. In other words, unless these workers have genius-level IQs or a Gates-ian knack for business, no matter what careers they prepare themselves for, they will remain trapped in the race to the bottom.

7 FALSE HOPES

P ROBABLY THE MOST IMPORTANT TENET OF THE HIPPOCRATIC Oath that all medical doctors take is the first: Do no harm. This refreshing nod to modesty is one that should be heeded by more economic policymakers, especially since they undoubtedly know less about the domestic and world economies than physicians know about the human body.

Nothing, then, is more depressing than recognizing that globalization enthusiasts inside and outside government seem unaware of this cardinal rule. Not only do they have no clue how to head off the crack-ups looming ahead for American society, the U.S. economy, and the global economy thanks to their policies, but they also seem determined to bring them on sooner. Slightly less depressing is that many of the most perceptive critics of current globalization policies—including those who have insightfully decried the race to the bottom—have lined up behind a series of policy alternatives that could bring the same kinds of results.

The crack-ups will not be averted unless Americans understand what lies behind the world economy's dangerous imbalances. The race to the bottom is only the worst and most important symptom, not the cause, of the global economy's problems. The race is being run in the first place because it is rewarded so lavishly by the way the world economy is set up. The main interlocking mechanisms for generating these rewards are (1) the many and varied policies pursued by governments in the industrialized countries and by international organizations (and lobbied for enthusiastically by multinational corporations) to channel investment into the low-income countries of the third world; and (2) wide-open access for these countries' exports to the markets of the industrialized countries, chiefly the United States.

This investment has different effects in different types of third world countries, and sometimes within the same country. In the export superpowers located mainly in East Asia, it builds the factories and supplies the infrastructure systems that make possible the manufacture of almost endless floods of products—most eventually headed for final markets in Europe and the United States. Because of the mercantilist policies practiced by these countries and IMF financial constraints on many of them and numerous others, the investment flows do not finance enough of the consumption that would enable these countries to buy their share of these products themselves, much less to consume their share of other countries' goods.

In the less successful low-income countries located mainly in Latin America (but now including Russia), investments provided by the world economy finance much export-oriented production. However, much of this investment is simply stolen or wasted by governments. Some of it, to be sure, also finances consumption, but even that modest level of consumption is more consumption than the populations of these countries can sustain responsibly. These populations cannot sustain much consumption because most earn next to nothing, which causes them to live either at the edge of debt or deeply in it. In effect, these countries can import and consume an appropriate share of their own and world output only if they dramatically reduce their output, or if they live far beyond their means. Borrowers that splurge, however, have the rug yanked out from under them all too regularly. Further, because the world sends so much capital their way, when rugs are yanked, financial crises result.

However, one more major imbalance bears responsibility for the world's dangerous financial instability today—the outsized share of the world's imports (and especially the developing world's imports) taken by the United States. It is true that, given the sputtered-out national engines of domestic growth in much of the world nowadays, and given so many countries' insistence on keeping their markets closed, U.S. importing is almost single-handedly keeping the rest of the planet afloat economically. It is equally true, however, that current levels of net importing are driving down living standards in the United States, that they are consequently driving down the real purchasing power that makes significant, responsible levels of importing sustainable to begin with, and that this growing gap between U.S. purchasing power and U.S. imports is bound to make the nation's creditors increasingly reluctant to continue financing these purchases.

Without a sustainable balance between production and consumption, any economic system will sooner or later fall apart. The race to the bottom is inexorably destroying this balance. It is encouraging ever more production by countries and populations that either will not consume or cannot consume for very long. Unfortunately, the race is dependent on ever more consumption by a population whose ability to support consumption with production it is steadily sapping.

A. GROWING THE DEFICITS

For decades, most U.S. leaders and economists responded to concerns about U.S. trade deficits and international payments balances with energetic ridicule. Two notable exceptions were the period from the late–1960s to 1971, when President Nixon ultimately brought down the original post-World War II international monetary system in order to prevent a dollar crash; and 1985, when President Reagan devalued the dollar by 40 percent to reduce merchandise trade deficits to a smaller percentage of the whole economy than today's deficit—and keep them only slightly below levels when international lenders start to worry about repayment.

Today, some academic economists and think-tank types still pooh-pooh the deficits.[1] But political leaders with real-world responsibilities have changed their tune. President Clinton, for example, has run an administration that has long balked even at talking about imports when discussing the effects of U.S. trade flows and trade policies. In February 2000, however, Clinton told reporters, "What bothers me ... is that if we have a trade deficit of this size ... and we have all this personal [and business] debt, all this stuff has got to be financed. And because our personal savings rates are fairly low, about 40 percent of our debt is held by non-Americans." A withdrawal of such financing, the President continued, could seriously damage the economy.[2]

Fed Chair Alan Greenspan has told Congress that although "immigration and imports can significantly cushion the consequences of the wealth effect and its draining of the pool of unemployed workers for a while, there are limits ... that there are limits cannot be open to question."[3]

Unfortunately, all of the old ideas proposed by administration policymakers and the globalizers outside government have failed so far to solve the deficit problem or deal with its effects at home, and none of them has a chance of working in the future. Despite their reluctance to talk about imports or deficits, President Clinton and his aides have consistently emphasized closely related concerns. These have included trade-related measures for improving the international competitiveness of U.S. workers and companies, breaking down foreign trade barriers that hamper even U.S. producers that are competitive, and securing fair trade with Japan in particular, whose companies take advantage of a protected market at home to take business from U.S. firms all over the world.

Aside from promising to work harder than its predecessors to promote U.S. exports directly, the Clinton team touted two major trade initiatives to improve U.S. performance in world markets—concluding the North American Free Trade Agreement and creating the World Trade Organization. The former was supposed to help U.S. companies by giving them one of the big advantages enjoyed by their Japanese and European competition—access to a pool of low-wage workers who could help cut production costs by handling the less sophisticated aspects of modern manufacturing. Just as Japan could profit from using cheap labor in developing Asia, and Western Europe could benefit from utilizing the low-wage workforces in the former Communist countries of Central and Eastern Europe, the United States could counter with Mexican workers.[4]

In other words, NAFTA was supposed to encourage more of the kind of outsourcing and new trade in producer goods that would enable American businesses to boost sales both at home and abroad. Therefore, it would create more jobs at better wages for U.S. workers.[5]

As discussed in Chapter 5, however, there is no reason to think that shifting production to Mexico has benefited U.S. workers or the U.S. trade balance on net. Instead, most U.S. companies have simply increased profit margins by substituting Mexican for U.S. labor. U.S. trade with Mexico, meanwhile, has sunk into deep deficit, while the increase in U.S. global deficit has actually accelerated.

The World Trade Organization was created by the Uruguay Round international trade agreement of 1994, and was also supposed to generate special advantages for U.S. producers. Starting in the late 1940s, the world's major trading powers developed a set of rules designed to encourage fair international economic competition. However, the original General Agreement on Tariffs and Trade that they set up was not enforceable. Morphing the GATT into a new World Trade Organization was supposed to fix this shortcoming. Member states promised to submit their trade complaints and disputes to a new system of international trade courts and to abide by the decisions reached by the judges.

Administration officials and other WTO supporters hailed the new agreement as a watershed for the global economy, and for the United States in particular. Finally, a meaningful, binding set of world trade rules had been established. Finally, free trading countries like the United States had an internationally accepted means to force protectionist countries to mend their ways. Since the WTO was set up to encourage open markets, the United States and the handful of other countries whose trade barriers were already low would have the most to gain.[6] Indeed, simply placing the resolution of trade disputes on a strong legal basis was supposed to work to the advantage of the United States, a law-abiding and traditionally legalistic nation.

What the WTO supporters either forgot or hoped the American people would overlook was that the two main requirements for a fair and reliable quasilegal system for resolving international trade disputes and for promoting free trade norms did not exist. First, there is no strong worldwide consensus in favor of free trade. Not only do most of the third world countries comprising the WTO's majority remain strongly protectionist, as seen in Chapter 4, but Japan and (to a lesser extent) the European Union are still reluctant to open their markets. Moreover, like the developing countries, they also still depend heavily for much of their growth on keeping the U.S. market wide open to their exports.

Just as important, nothing in the WTO's bylaws or structure is capable of ensuring that the system actually can bend protectionist governments to free traders' will. The officials who decide WTO cases are not divine instruments of economic liberalism, devoted to converting humanity to the gospel of free trade. They are flesh-and-blood human beings who are products not only of their particular nation-states but of their histories and cultures and traditions. Consequently, there is no reason to expect them to consistently put the free trade cause ahead of their own national loyalties.

Moreover, unlike the United Nations, the World Bank, or the International Monetary Fund, the United States has no special formal leverage in the World Trade Organization. It enjoys no veto, as in the Security Council. It possesses no special voting power by dint of its budget contributions, as in the international financial institutions. It is one WTO member out of 135. This is another reason to doubt that the judges in its trade courts will reflect a free trading point of view. Most often, these judges will come from the protectionist majority. In addition, the free trade minority can expect simply to be outvoted on crucial matters such as admitting new members.

In other words, contrary to the assumptions of President Clinton and the other WTO supporters, the WTO is like all significant international organizations. It is first and foremost a political institution, not a true legal-judicial institution. The politics, however, are solidly stacked against free trading countries like the United States. Washington has won numerous cases at the World Trade Organization, but none of these cases has affected important economic interests or trade flows. In addition, victory is no guarantee of compliance. One emerging weakness of the WTO that not even critics foresaw was the great loopholes left in the enforcement mechanisms. Even President Clinton has admitted that "a lot of times when decisions are made, they aren't honored."[7] The losers of trade cases have tremendous latitude to drag out appeal proceedings and even actual compliance measures. In a world in which it is constantly repeated that business takes place at the speed of light, this is an obviously fatal flaw.

Meanwhile, U.S. producers have lost a growing number of genuinely important cases, and these cases have set precedents that appear to guarantee more major defeats in the future.[8] Such precedents can be set even when U.S. plaintiffs are handed a victory. Small wonder, then, that since the WTO's creation in 1994, the U.S. trade deficit has ballooned to record heights.

President Clinton's efforts to open the Japanese market have failed as well. In its first year, the administration vowed to avoid the mistakes of its predecessors. No longer would Washington accept meaningless Japanese promises to eliminate the trade protections written into its domestic laws and to reform the monopolistic practices of its businesses. The new administration would understand that the most important Japanese trade barriers have never been written into law, but simply are administered by bureaucrats not accountable even to Japan's elected leaders, much less the

Japanese public or foreign governments. Consequently, the United States would hold the Japanese to measurable results in terms of significantly improved sales in Japan. Finally, the United States would at long last overhaul its strategic priorities. The Clinton team would recognize that the end of the Cold War had freed U.S. diplomats to treat economic concerns on a par with retaining the goodwill of security partners like Japan. Washington would show less tolerance for political friends that acted like economic adversaries. In the words of President Clinton's first U.S. trade representative, Mickey Kantor:

> After World War II and during the Cold War . . . we often opened our market to the products of the world without obtaining comparable commitments from others. As the dominant economic power in the world, we could afford to do so. And as part of a strategy in the Cold War, we needed to do so. . . . But now . . . we will no longer tolerate "free riders" in the global trading system. . . . This is a critical change in the way we view both trade policy and foreign policy.[9]

Japanese leaders, however, soon realized that the Clinton policies were simply talk. For all his rhetoric, the President never consistently focused on Japan trade issues. What plans he had, moreover, never seemed to anticipate simple Japanese obstinacy. The administration never spoke with one clear voice, either. Despite the pledge to realign the nation's security and economic priorities, U.S. national security officials continued to fear that too much U.S. pressure on Japan would disrupt bilateral security relations and throw all of East Asia into turmoil. They even expressed these fears in public.[10]

President Clinton's main economic advisers, meanwhile, never supported a strong drive to open Japan's markets. Drawn largely from Wall Street and academic ranks, they worried that confronting Japan would jeopardize public support for continuing globalization policies that, even as they undermined living standards for most workers, enabled U.S. companies to get lean, mean, and hugely profitable.

Nonetheless, in 1995 short-term political considerations seemed to have convinced President Clinton to authorize a highly publicized campaign to open Japan's automotive markets. Auto trade was a sensible target, as motor vehicles and parts accounted for much of the U.S. trade deficit with Japan. However, the administration's painfully obvious disunity emboldened Japan to just say no. Not only was the Pentagon virtually protesting in public, but the administration's chief economic advisers, led by Treasury Secretary Robert Rubin, had decided that Japan's banking system had become too fragile to withstand the impact of opening a major domestic market—or even continued U.S. hectoring.

Rubin was also worried about the strength of the Japanese yen. Despite a marked slowdown in Japan's growth rates during the 1990s, the continuing rise in Japan's global trade surplus had pushed the yen to all-time highs. However, the strength of the yen threatened the exports that were Japan's only remaining sources of growth. In addition, if Japan's growth slowed further and its surpluses shrank, its capability of continuing to finance America's deficits and overconsumption would falter. Rubin therefore concluded that reducing the yen's value was essential to keeping the U.S. economic party going—at least long enough to ensure President Clinton's reelection the following year.

In the late spring of 1995, Rubin brokered an end to the U.S.–Japan auto dispute. Washington would accept a series of Japanese promises to make good faith efforts to buy more U.S. vehicles and parts, and help U.S. automakers set up more dealerships in Japan. The United States would also help Japan intervene in global currency markets to drive down the yen. In return, Japan would keep lending the United States money at reasonable interest rates.[11]

The agreement enabled Americans to continue enjoying growth and consumption levels they could no longer pay for with their own output and earnings. However, the yen's decline alone guaranteed that U.S. producers in autos and many other industries would stay locked out of Japanese markets indefinitely. It also put added pressure on the exports of the developing Asian countries. Along with China's currency devaluation in 1994, Rubin's deal helped set the stage for the Asian financial crisis. For good measure, the U.S. deficit with Japan has remained at near-record levels, and even the Clinton administration began to complain about Japan's failure to keep its alleged promises on auto trade. At the same time, the President himself began to excuse Japan's failure to keep its promises.[12]

B. IF AT FIRST …

The Clinton administration's reaction to these failures and missteps has been more of the same. NAFTA has shown no ability to improve the global competitiveness of U.S. companies and enrich

U.S. workers, but the President is committed to extending the agreement to the rest of the Western Hemisphere—even though his goal of a Free Trade Agreement of the Americas has been the chief casualty of his failure to secure new trade negotiating authority from Congress. Meanwhile, the President's predilection for trade agreements with low-income countries continues unabated. In 1999 and 2000, two of his highest trade-policy priorities were extending NAFTA to the countries of the Caribbean Basin and Central America and negotiating a trade agreement with the countries of sub-Saharan Africa. In summer 1999, this focus on the destitute reached a truly absurd extreme. U.S. Trade Representative Charlene Barshefsky proudly announced the first steps toward achieving normal trade relations with Vietnam, a country with enough foreign exchange in its treasury to keep importing for all of nine weeks.[13]

President Clinton was also determined to bring China into the World Trade Organization. The President spoke of China exclusively as a huge potential market for exports from the United States. However, U.S. exports to China are dominated by producer goods, and using the protectionist-dominated WTO to combat Chinese protectionism is unpromising at best. Therefore, China's entry is most likely to keep the U.S. market open to the products made in China by Chinese, U.S., and third-country companies. Even the U.S. International Trade Commission has predicted that China's admission to the WTO will increase the bilateral deficit.[14]

The President's initial response to the Asian financial crisis ensured a jump in the U.S. global trade deficit as well. As he explained to an audience in Tokyo in November 1998,

> I made a decision with the full support of my entire economic team that we would do everything we could to leave America's markets as open as possible, knowing full well that our trade deficit would increase dramatically for a year or two. I did it because I thought it was a major contribution we could make to stabilizing the global economy and the economies in Asia.[15]

To be sure, U.S. officials urged other industrialized countries to share the burden of lifting Asia out of recession.[16] Pressured by his labor union supporters, the President also moved to limit the country's role as a dumping ground for steel that neither developed nor developing countries could sell anywhere else. However,

Clinton's burden-sharing pleas went unheeded—just like 20 years' worth of similar efforts by his predecessors.

In the first place, Clinton's campaign fell victim to the phenomenon of free riding. If the President had announced that the United States would take the lead in—and absorb the costs of—sopping up exports from the world's debtor countries, what incentive did that leave for Europe and Japan to join in? In this vein, Clinton also failed to convince U.S. allies that failure to cooperate would bring serious consequences. Second, the President paid for seeking the easy way out in his Japan policy. When his incoherent efforts to open Japan's markets failed, Clinton shifted gears and mainly began to urge Japan to grow faster. If Japan could snap out of its recession, he argued, it would resume its traditional role of leading Asia's growth presumably without having to remove many trade barriers.[17]

The only problem with this strategy was that, precisely because of Japan's trade barriers, Japan had never purchased anywhere near the share of developing Asia's products that its sheer size and proximity would have indicated. Indeed, as shown by IMF figures, Japan is only half as important to developing Asia as an export market as the United States. In fact, it is barely more important than Europe. According to two Lehman Brothers economists who have analyzed this data, although domestic demand from the other industrialized countries and from developing Asia itself "are significant determinants of Asian exports … Japanese domestic demand is not."[18] Japan is certainly capable of leading Asia's debtors out of the financial woods, but only if its trade barriers fall, and President Clinton had already given up on that hope.

In fact, the trade-barrier problem transcends Japan. Catherine L. Mann, economist for the Institute for International Economics, has pointed out that researchers have long recognized that U.S. economic growth pulls in imports much faster than does growth in most other countries.[19] These findings constitute powerful albeit indirect evidence that foreign trade barriers play a major role in channeling too much of the world's output to the United States, and that America's relatively strong growth is only one reason for enormous U.S. trade deficits. They constitute an equally powerful argument that, even if growth rates pick up considerably in other major trading powers, the already dangerous U.S. deficits will continue to widen. If the United States is to remain wide open to trade, removing trade barriers abroad is imperative.

Finally, Clinton's burden-sharing campaign failed because, as with the original Japan trade policy, he never gave it sustained attention. Seeing no consistent presidential follow-through, the Japanese and Europeans understandably viewed Clinton's statements as simple posturing that they could—and did—safely ignore. By late 1999, it was clear that the European Union had decided not only to keep its markets substantially closed but to rely more on exports for stimulating growth. Its main weapon: the weakness of its new common currency, the euro, which gave EU goods sizable price advantages in world markets.[20]

C. THE NEW WELFARE LOBBY

If more of the same has been Clinton's trade policy response to mounting international economic imbalances, his response to the effects at home of the race to the bottom has been considerable talk about reeducation and retraining and offers of welfare. As seen in Chapter 3, counting on reeducation and retraining to solve the U.S. living standards crisis is a pipe dream, given the widespread retraining underway in low-income countries.

Clinton's welfare proposals have taken numerous forms. Some involve employer mandates, for example, for family leave and child care. Others involve incentives to spread the corporate wealth around more evenly.[21] More generally, the President and others who style themselves as progressives have spoken of how greater globalization requires bigger and stronger social safety nets, to provide for those who are left behind. However they are dressed up, Clinton's programs all involve using governmet power to bribe or force businesses to take measures to accommodate workers that businesses would hardly ever take voluntarily and that market forces on their own would not encourage. These programs are entirely consistent with mainstream economic thinking about coping with the "creative destruction" that free markets unavoidably wreak in order to produce more wealth and efficiency overall.

Actually, mainstream theorists would rather not see any interference at all with the hurricane of globalization. The faster it proceeds, they think, the faster and wider its gains will spread. However, if softhearted and softheaded politicians insist on coddling the disadvantaged and especially the displaced, better that they provide out-and-out monetary payments to keep them afloat. As Barry Bosworth of the Brookings Institution wrote somewhat crudely, "It would be far cheaper to simply bribe the losers than pass up the gains from increased trade."[22]

The case for bribing the losers, however, fails dismally on both economic and noneconomic grounds. Above all, it forgets the powerful—and entirely reasonable—consensus that has developed in U.S. society that welfare-type handouts too often are a terrible thing, especially for their recipients. They destroy initiative and self-respect and just about every other quality that most Americans value. In addition, they foster social ills such as street crime, drug abuse, and illegitimate births. In 1996, President Clinton himself decided that welfare—at least as the United States has known it—was so terrible that it had to be abolished. Washington and the states would still support those genuinely in need, but the eligibility for assistance would be greatly restricted. In fact, welfare was deemed to be so terrible that both Washington and the states eventually resolved to spend considerable sums training welfare recipients for jobs that would keep them off the dole. They provided transportation, housing, and child care subsidies to enable them to hold these jobs if (as is often the case) a living wage is not paid, and actually hired them as government workers if they could not find private sector work. *Washington Post* headline writers even consider government hiring to be a "'Welfare-to-Work' Success."[23]

In other words, most Americans have decided that just about anything is better than allowing able-bodied people to get something from the state for nothing. Further, during the present economic expansion, governments can afford to put a great deal of money where their mouths are. How can this record be squared with viewing significantly expanded welfare rolls as an acceptable price to pay for continuing today's globalization policies?

For the record, the globalizers doubt that much welfare will be needed. If *The New York Times* columnist Thomas L. Friedman is any measure, their expectations are quite modest. Friedman starts out by assuming that globalization will continue to benefit the overwhelming majority, and that better education can turn many of the remaining losers into winners. From there, it is easy to reason that whatever safety-net programs are needed "are not all that expensive" and "do not involve radical income redistribution—or lavish compensatory welfare spending programs that would violate the economic rules" that global investors demand. Moreover, the safety net he has in mind is "not a net anyone can live on for long."[24]

Such formulations, however, amount to little more than assuming the problem away. If this globalization pig had wings, it would indeed fly. As seen in Chapter 2, however, three quarters of the U.S. workforce, not a small group of losers, has experienced declining living standards, and today's globalization policies bear much responsibility. Will all the losers get all of the subsidized housing, transportation, and child care they need (let alone all they think they need)? Will they get it if economic growth slows from today's torrid pace? Or will they be content indefinitely with a net that "not anyone can live on for long"?

The final flaw in the welfare approach results directly from the race to the bottom itself. Most of the types of welfare suggested by the globalizers require public expenditures. For those governments that cannot simply print as much money as they need (meaning most governments), these resources have to come from the private sector. However, globalization policies that reduce living standards can also shrink a nation's tax base, and thereby put the flow of resources in jeopardy over the long run. The real tax base could be shriveled as well by the growing concentration of wealth at the top of the income ladder, and by the ability frequently shown by the rich to avoid taxation by wielding political clout. Corporations that can continue to pay the needed taxes, for their part, could well flee to lower-tax locales for doing business.

Business can be expected to react the same way to the various employer mandate proposals. Early in the Clinton years, for example, former Labor Secretary Robert Reich spoke of a "new social contract" among business, government, and citizens to help keep millions of Americans clinging to middle-class lives. According to *BusinessWeek* correspondent Karen Pennar, companies that leave communities in the lurch have "obligations" to prevent those towns and regions from going under. Similarly, "if localities are going to trip over each other to offer tax breaks and other giveaways to companies to set up shop, they ought to demand a hefty quid pro quo in the form of job guarantees from the companies to the community." Friedman would, among other things, "democratize access to capital in America" by using government pressure to urge banks to lend to deprived areas and by launching government-funded venture capital programs.[25]

Anyone perceiving a desperate quality to these proposals is right. How could it be otherwise? As these writers undoubtedly realized, the race to the bottom literally opens up a world of possibilities for companies that would rather not institute family-leave programs or provide free child care for their employees, or for banks and businesses that would rather not bother taking the chance of investing in distressed neighborhoods. The race means that they do not have to. In fact, businesses, especially if they have international reach, are in the driver's seat. Friedman himself wrote of globalization as forcing countries to don a "golden straitjacket" of free-market reforms. This means that adopting a much lighter regulatory touch is the only way of attracting the foreign private capital that is their only reliable engine of growth. However, this very straitjacket would tightly limit government's ability to promote corporate responsibility—or influence corporate behavior in any way. That is why he rightly called it a straitjacket.

D. TRADE AGREEMENTS WITH A DIFFERENCE

Neither globalization's international nor domestic programs, then, will stave off the dangers being created by globalization. On the left end of the American political spectrum, a compelling set of new ideas for running the world economy has emerged in recent years. In fact, these ideas are so compelling that President Clinton has paid considerable lip service to them, especially at the Seattle WTO meeting. So have numerous globalization enthusiasts. Two of these ideas that have received the most attention: (1) incorporating enforceable protections for fundamental labor rights into international trade agreements; and (2) incorporating enforceable protections for the environment into these agreements.[26]

These proposals do have much potential to stop, slow, or transform the race to the bottom. On the labor rights front, most of the ideas suggested would link a country's access to the U.S. market (and in principal to all markets, if the plan is put into effect multilaterally) on its adherence to either its own meaningful labor regulations or to the kinds of labor rights developed at the International Labour Organization (like the right to organize unions independent of governments, and the right to strike).

Contrary to charges from many globalizers, no one with any influence is demanding that countries, particularly developing countries, automatically pay their workers European or North American-level wages, and no one is talking about imposing Western standards and practices on non-Western countries.[27] As correctly noted by the labor rights supporters, measures such as permitting workers to organize would simply give them a realistic chance of securing pay that roughly reflects their productivity, not guarantee undeserved and unrealistic raises. Moreover, many countries that repress workers have either put impressive-sounding labor laws on their books or signed international labor rights conventions. Insisting that they abide by these voluntary commitments should not be the slightest bit controversial.

Besides, countries that felt strongly enough about their right to kill or imprison labor activists (and that includes most of the home countries of the third world intellectuals and politicians protesting the new types of trade agreements) would be free to do so. They just would not be able to repress unions and still trade with countries like the United States. Similar arguments apply to environmental issues. Countries should abide by the environmental agreements they have signed, and they should enforce their own laws. They can assert their sovereignty by refusing if they wish, but they will have to live with the consequences.

Of course, these labor and environmental proposals are not curealls for the race to the bottom. One problem with them is that, due to the heated controversy they have aroused, they have become ends in and of themselves to many of their supporters. Many labor and environmental activists seem to forget that other policy tools are available to countries determined to gain artificial advantages in international trade. As China and others have shown, exchange-rate manipulation can dramatically improve a country's terms of trade. Without provisions to guard against such exchange-rate dumping, U.S. trade partners might be able to offset the tariffs imposed to enforce labor and environmental agreements. Indeed, in order to serve U.S. economic interests adequately, trade agreements would also have to target the numerous ways in which developing countries seek to suppress their own peoples' consumption. Genuinely free trade needs to be free for everyone.

Another problem with pinning so many hopes on labor and environmental provisions is that, even if they work as designed, workers in the United States and other developed countries will remain under tremendous wage pressure. Precisely because wages and environmental standards in developing countries are so low (at least in practice), and precisely because the ongoing global workforce explosion will so powerfully affect wage trends, the pay gap between rich and poor countries will remain too wide for generations no matter what trade agreements require. Therefore, the economic imbalances undermining international financial stability will continue to widen as well. The race to the bottom will at best slow, not stop or change fundamentally. Further, the labor and environmental activists do not pay enough attention to the need to open European and Japanese markets so that these countries share more of the burden for absorbing third world exports.

The most important shortcoming of many of the progressives' globalization ideas, however, is that they ultimately share the globalizers' determination to build the world economy's house of cards ever higher by continuing to subsidize export-led growth—and thus unbalanced trade—in the developing world.

8 TOWARD A NEW RACE

THE SEVERITY AND SPREAD OF THE ASIAN FINANCIAL CRISIS HAS convinced many globalization cheerleaders that something is seriously wrong with the current world economy. Not surprisingly, because the crisis unfolded through financial activity (borrowing and lending), and had its most spectacular effects on the balance sheets of countries or private creditors, experts in and out of government have emphasized its financial characteristics. Indeed, nonfinancial aspects of the crisis have been almost completely ignored.

Certainly the financial aspects are not trivial. As numerous analysts have noted, systems for regulating banks and stock markets in many third world countries have indeed been weak or corrupt. Too many national governments either implicitly or explicitly guaranteed their banks that they would ultimately cover any irresponsible lending; therefore irresponsible lending skyrocketed. Foreigners tried to take advantage as well, counting on these third world governments to insure borrowers indefinitely. In addition, if all failed, many apparently assumed that the U.S. government or the International Monetary Fund would ride to their rescue. President Clinton's bailout of Mexico in 1995 clearly reinforced this notion.

Equally unsurprising is how most suggested responses to the crisis have been financial as well. Some want to impose more controls over global flows of "hot money"—which is usually defined as loans with very short maturities and very high rates of interest, but which is sometimes defined as any investment that can move in and out of a market at a moment's notice.

Hot money has proliferated over the last decade and a half for two main reasons. First, governments around the world opened their financial markets to foreigners, and many governments that were already open deregulated even further. Second, many governments that had gotten into financial trouble or were on the verge became addicted to hot money. Like compulsive gamblers dealing with loan sharks, they borrowed at extortionate rates to pay off past and current debts, but in the process racked up larger future debts that they also wound up "paying off" with yet more hot money. As the financial crisis showed, in the end, their knees were capped all the same.

Other reform ideas have focused on the important role played by exchange rates in the crisis. After all, the trigger for national debt crises turned out to be financial attacks on the debtor countries' currencies by international speculators who became convinced that they were overvalued. Some economists have suggested that institutions called currency boards could prevent a replay. These boards could function like the central banks of countries with better-managed finances, but with one big difference. In central bank systems, allegedly trustworthy appointed technocrats replace allegedly untrustworthy elected politicians as the officials who make the supremely important decisions about that country's money supply and the cost of that money (interest rates). Rather than independently manage their country's monetary affairs, (like the Federal Reserve Board in Washington), currency boards would ensure that the amount of their nation's currency in circulation did not exceed their country's holdings of foreign exchange. When a national currency is strongly supported in this way, speculative attacks would rarely happen.

Some—including prominent Latin American economists and even political leaders—would take the next logical step. They favor "dollarizing" their economies. That is to say, they would adopt the dollar as their national currency, and by so doing, turn control of their money supply and interest rates to the United States. Because dollarization would involve surrendering so much national sovereignty, and because domination by the United States is such a concern, few expect major Latin American or other third world countries to try it any time soon. Further, the United States has not encouraged this—for fear of being held directly responsible for other countries' economic fates. However, some smaller countries, like Panama, are already legally dollarized, and others, like Peru and Uruguay, may as well be. Moreover, it is a mark of Latin America's desperation that important, respectable figures feel free to talk about dollarization openly.[1]

Another group of analysts would dramatically reduce or even eliminate the public sector's role in international financial and monetary policy—at least regarding lending, insuring, and bailing out. These free-market-oriented critics favor abolishing, or radically scaling back, the International Monetary Fund, reasoning that its willingness to fully or partly rescue lenders and borrowers from the consequences of their irresponsible behavior already has generated lots of irresponsible behavior. They believe that free markets are the best means of ensuring that investment capital goes where it belongs, and that if countries are having difficulty attracting investment, it is up to them to become more attractive places to do business.

A. THE REAL ECONOMY CONNECTION

Most analysts of the Asian crisis, however, dance around a fundamental dilemma, especially if they want to avoid stiff controls on both global investment flows and global trade flows. Huge amounts of money have indeed been thrown at many countries that, in retrospect, were unlikely recipients. Thailand, for example, was a country clearly on the rise economically before 1997. However, it was never especially big, and for all its progress, most Thais were not rich. Also, Thailand was not especially stable politically, although it had managed to avoid revolutionary upheaval. Like most of developing Asia, corruption was everywhere. Yet short-term loans to Thailand rose 600 percent from 1990 to 1997. These short-term loans by themselves far exceeded Thailand's foreign exchange reserves and were nearly one-third the size of its total economy. Thailand, of course, also had longer-term debt to pay off.[2]

Indonesia was much bigger, and increasingly successful, too, but its people were even poorer than the Thais and its politics and business even more corrupt. Korea was considerably wealthier than either country, but its domestic markets were tightly closed, its government energetically suppressed consumption even of Korean-made products, and its companies had already taken on unheard of amounts of debt. Some had actually gone belly-up by mid–1997. Yet short-term loans to Korea shot up 325 percent from 1990 to 1997 and also came to exceed the country's foreign exchange holdings. Malaysia and Singapore were both very successful economically, but very small—and Singapore is downright tiny in terms of area and population. Malaysia's short-term borrowing skyrocketed 800 percent between 1990 and 1997.

All told, by mid–1997, Indonesia, South Korea, Malaysia, the Philippines, and Thailand had $274 billion in international bank loans outstanding. Fully $175 billion of this debt was short-term debt, yet their combined foreign exchange holdings equaled only $100 billion.[3]

Capital does not head toward destinations just by chance. In addition, over any length of time, it does not flow for purely financial reasons. Ultimately, capital flows are connected to expectations of profits and returns in the real economy of goods and services. Unless investors thought that most of the wealth-creating opportunities in these small or poor or closed or consumption-averse Asian economies somehow would come from selling to their domestic markets, it becomes obvious that their expectations of big Asian profits were really expectations of continued trade success by these countries. Even the domestic consumption investors may have been eyeing—the glitzy shopping malls and torrid real estate markets of emerging market boomtowns like Bangkok—ultimately were creations of export success.

Developing Asian countries' trade performances were indeed spectacular, and it may have been understandable that their long years of success generated confidence that their progress would continue uninterrupted. However, some trouble signs should have become apparent as well. First, the countries that collapsed, as well as most of their neighbors and other rapidly developing countries like Mexico, were all basing their hopes for economic development heavily on exporting. For example, between 1985 and 1998, exports as a percentage of the total economy rose sharply for most Asian countries. For the Philippines, Thailand, and Indonesia, this ratio more than doubled—to more than 50 percent. Doubling occurred in China as well, but from such a small base that the export ratio was only 22 percent in 1998. (Even so, China's export ratio was nearly double that of another large, continent-sized economy—the United States.) Even Korea and Malaysia, which were both thoroughly globalized by the 1980s, significantly boosted their export ratios.[4]

Second, these countries were all trying to excel in the same product areas. Some of the most prominent are advanced consumer electronics products, computer and electronics parts (including semiconductors), machine tools, steel, telecommunications equipment, machinery, and chemicals (especially petrochemicals). In addition, Japan was determined not to surrender its market share in many of these industries to new competitors. The result was the emergence of overcapacity—more output of these products than world markets could handle.

Third, as mentioned, the Japanese and Chinese currency devaluations created a major price squeeze for the rest of the Asian exporters. Another problem was created by Mexico. Not only did the negotiation of NAFTA, with its preferential access to the all-important U.S. market, help Mexico grab a great deal of business from the East Asians, its own currency devaluation in late 1994 added to the competitive pressure.

Fourth, too many of the developing Asian countries' exports were sent to the United States. In fact, the real origins of the Asian financial crisis can be seen in the following figures, which show developing Asian and other countries' computer parts exports to the United States during the 1990s. Figure 8.1 shows shipments of computer parts (excluding semiconductors) to the United States from the three Asian countries that fell apart financially during the crisis, plus the Philippines, which only narrowly averted disaster.

As this figure makes clear, not only were each of the countries expanding their exports to the United States through 1997, they were all gaining market share as well—most spectacularly, the Philippines. After the crisis hit in 1997, total exports fell off markedly, but their market shares also either stopped growing or, in Korea's case, shrank. As it turned out, mainly for short-term reasons, growth in the U.S. computer market slowed down, and imports in the industry slumped. However, another problem had developed for these countries—other competitors. As mentioned above, China devalued its currency in 1994. Not coincidentally, its own exports of computer parts to the United States began rising shortly thereafter. Both before and after the overall U.S. market slump, as shown in Figure 8.2, China took U.S. market share from some of its four Asian competitors, and helped prevent continued market share growth for others.

Singapore, Taiwan, and Malaysia were big players on the computer parts scene as well, and they had no intention of stopping exports to the United States. After 1997, the competition for a shrinking U.S. market for these products became especially fierce. As shown in Figure 8.3, China, the Philippines, Thailand, and Taiwan maintained export volumes and market share, but market share growth had stopped for all. Korea, Malaysia, and Singapore, meanwhile, began losing out.

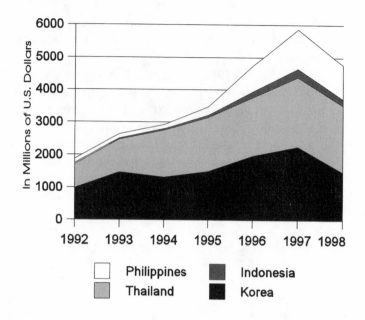

Figure 8.1 *U.S. imports of computer parts (excluding semiconductors) from Asian Crisis "Victims," 1992 to late1998.*

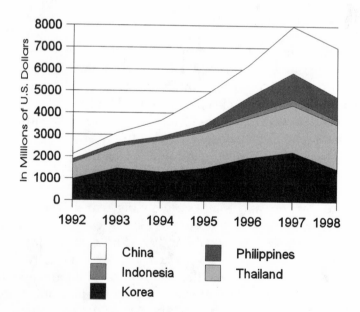

Figure 8.2 *U.S. imports of computer parts (excluding semiconductors) from Asian Crisis "Victims" plus China, 1992 to late 1998.*

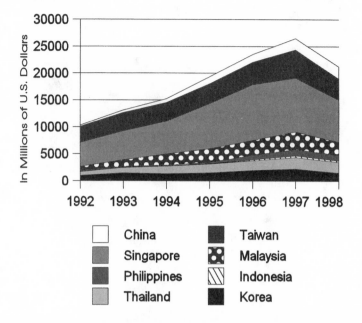

Figure 8.3 *U.S. imports of computer parts (excluding semiconductors) from Asian Crisis "Victims" plus China, Malaysia, Singapore, and Taiwan, 1992 to late 1998.*

The list of competitors did not stop at Asia's shorelines. Mexico, too, had big plans to get into the computer parts business by exporting them to the United States. As shown in Figure 8.4, Mexico began succeeding shortly after NAFTA's signing in late 1993, and the country continued expanding its share even after the overall U.S. market sagged. Also, Mexico's exports to the United States did not exactly slow down after its own currency crash in late 1994.

All these low-income countries, moreover, faced a final, major common problem—high-income Japan. Although U.S. globalizers see no special value to the nation in retaining much high-tech manufacturing, the Japanese economic establishment, rightly or wrongly, completely disagrees. Whereas the Americans have viewed industries like computer parts as sectors that truly advanced countries should be exiting, the Japanese economic establishment sees plenty of value remaining. Therefore, aided significantly by the U.S.-assisted devaluation of the yen in mid–1995, Japan has largely preserved its position in the U.S. computer parts market, despite its high wages. In addition, as shown in the Figure 8.5, whatever the ultimate effect on Japan's economy, the impact on developing Asia and even Mexico has been profound—lost market share and lost opportunities for market share growth.

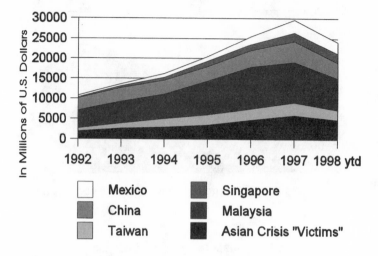

Figure 8.4 *U.S. imports of computer parts (excluding semiconductors) from low-income Asia plus Mexico, 1992 to late 1998.*

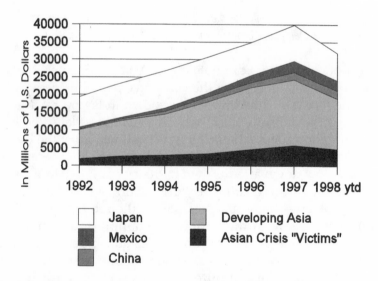

Figure 8.5 *U.S. imports of computer parts (excluding semiconductors) from low-income Asia plus Mexico and Japan, 1992 to late 1998.*

Similar trade patterns hold for many other manufacturing industries. Viewed in this light, the most fundamental causes of the Asian financial crisis—and of the world's growing financial vulnerability—become clear. Not every Asian developing country plus Mexico and Japan could continue to prosper by indefinitely exporting more of the same types of products to a single U.S. market—unless it was reasonable to believe that the U.S. market could keep up its rapid expansion indefinitely. By mid–1997, U.S.-Asian trade had turned into a freeway with too many entrance ramps into the United States and too few vehicles exiting. Eventually, an enormous traffic jam developed.

B. Artificial Markets

It is critical to remember, moreover, that to a great extent, the enormous investment flows to third world exporters are not produced by the spontaneous workings of market forces. Often they are encouraged by governments and by international organizations. In addition, often they are subsidized. American foreign-aid programs play a big role in this regard. As U.S. administrations have reminded skeptical Congresses for decades, many of the dollars appropriated for aid programs go to buying U.S. goods and services. Some of this aid comes in the form of grants, some in the form of loans. Sometimes the loans are paid back, sometimes they are not.

Two U.S. government agencies exist expressly to promote U.S. commerce with countries when market forces signal that such commerce should not take place. The Overseas Private Investment Corporation encourages U.S. companies to invest in politically and economically shaky third world countries by providing insurance for these investments. A good sense of how shaky these countries can be—and of OPIC's intrepid mind-set—was provided by its president and CEO Ruth Harkin several years ago: "Where we are going, in many cases, the risk is so high it is really impossible to calculate. If you look at countries such as the former Soviet Union, there is no track record of doing business."[5] In other words, Washington makes possible numerous investments in the developing world that private enterprise initially viewed as too risky to justify. The investments go ahead because companies are told that, after paying "market" rates for insurance that would never be affordable if offered by the private sector, they can pocket any profits and that taxpayers will cover any losses.

The Export-Import Bank promotes U.S. exports by lending money to third world countries that otherwise could not afford to buy U.S. products. This may sound like a terrific way to boost U.S. jobs and wages, and indeed, the bank helps U.S. companies win contracts over foreign competitors. However, the exports promoted by the Export-Import Bank are generally no different from other U.S. exports. Many consist of producer goods sent back to the United States as final products. Hence, these loans promote outsourcing. Further, many consist of the capital equipment and infrastructure products that build up third world export bases.

Of course, nothing is inherently wrong with making purchases on credit. Most business today could not be conducted in the first place without some form of credit. However, like U.S. foreign aid programs, the Export-Import Bank makes loans to governments and businesses that can't get them at affordable rates from commercial banks, because they are considered bad risks. That is to say, the bank is creating markets that market forces and market institutions themselves say should not exist.

The International Monetary Fund, the World Bank, and the regional development banks subsidize a great deal of third world exporting as well. In fact, these institutions are responsible for much of the third world export boom. Not only have they lavishly financed the creation of export industries in developing countries, they have strongly encouraged these countries to rely heavily on export-led growth for their development.[6]

The U.S. government, aided and abetted by other developed countries, also has given international businesses and financial institutions all manner of subtle and not so subtle signals to encourage commerce with the export-happy economies of the developing world. Of course, businesspeople do not rely on politicians to tell them how to run their enterprises. However, when the President of the United States and his chief trade negotiator say that the United States is a country with few domestic growth opportunities, and when they launch a government-wide campaign to highlight the importance of Big Emerging Market countries in the developing world, one can bet that the private sector stands up and takes notice. Similar messages are sent when presidents focus their trade-negotiating efforts on low-income countries like Mexico and China, give up on market-opening in high-income countries like Japan, and practically ignore market-opening in other high-income regions like Western Europe.

More concretely, Washington has helped boost investment in and trade with South Korea and Mexico by pushing hard and successfully for their entry into the Organization for Economic Cooperation and Development (OECD), a grouping of industrialized countries. Banks lending to OECD countries are not required by the government to set aside as much capital to cover possible losses as they are for loans to non-OECD countries, because OECD countries are by definition supposed to be good credit risks. In fact, loans to OECD countries are officially considered to be risk-free. And in cases like these, perceptions seemed to produce realities. Between 1995 and 1997, the gap (or "spread") between the interest rates charged for emerging market bonds and U.S. Treasuries narrowed significantly.[7] Unfortunately, it took the peso crash and the Korean meltdown to remind investors that honest, competent governments can't be decreed into existence by outsiders.

At the same time, even though recent financial crises have made painfully obvious the risks of hyping and subsidizing commerce with export-oriented developing countries, the hyping and subsidization of such commerce continues unabated. These practices, in fact, have become so pervasive that sometimes they seem to be the very raison d'être of U.S. globalization policy.

It is bad enough to see Wall Street and the media resuming the habit of touting emerging markets as if the Asian crisis never happened. Sometimes the assessments simply do not pass the laugh test. In March 1999, for example—barely seven months after Russia devalued its ruble and shocked the international financial community with the true depths of its problems—*USA Today* reported that "The Russian market represents a good opportunity [for farm equipment sales], but the country's ability to pay is in question." Once upon a time, when prospective customers could not pay for products, it was interpreted as a sign that a market did not exist, not that it looked promising. Similarly ludicrous was the August 1999 *BusinessWeek* article that described Argentina as "one of the world's most attractive emerging markets." At the time, Argentina's economy was shrinking, its unemployment rate was in the teens and rising, and its foreign debt levels equalled nearly half the size of its economy.[8]

President Clinton himself has gotten into the hyping game above and beyond the Big Emerging Markets initiative. In September 1997, shortly after the Thai and Indonesian economies crashed, the President still claimed, in a letter to Congress: "Many foreign markets, especially in the developing world, are growing at tremendous rates. Latin American and Asian economies, for example, are expected to expand at three times the rate of the U.S. economy over the coming years."[9]

This time, however, there was more than talk to the Clinton policies. As previously mentioned, the President kept U.S. markets
wide open to the exports of Asian debtors—in an effort to restore
the very unbalanced precrisis trade flows that led to the crack-up
to start with. United States government agencies also provided actual subsidies to re-create these flows. OPIC and the Export-Import Bank have provided billions of dollars to Thailand, Indonesia,
and South Korea to subsidize purchases of U.S. goods—many producer goods that ultimately get re-exported as final products, or
that aid in export production.[10]

The international financial institutions jumped on the band-
wagon as well. As previously discussed, the IMF bailouts themselves essentially required more net exporting by debtors. In order
to get on the repayment track, countries had no choice but to di-
vert resources from producing and buying for the home market
(especially imports) in order to ramp up export production. These
institutions helped in more specific ways, too. The Asian Development Bank, for example, provided nearly $1 billion worth of credit
for Thai exporters in early 1998.[11]

Finally, with Washington's active encouragement, the international financial institutions have begun not only to subsidize ongoing export-led growth but to pump future growth levels artificially higher. Brazil, Argentina, and Mexico have all been provided
with preemptive bailouts—pledges of capital designed to provide
so much backing for the currencies of these countries that international speculators would never even dream of attacking them. The
Mexican package—the second major rescue of Mexico in less than
five years—also included $4 billion in Export-Import Bank loans.[12]

In the wake of these rescue packages and subsidies, many U.S.
and other international investors have begun to act as if the crises
never happened. For example, in 1999, Moody's, the big credit-
rating agency, upgraded South Korean debt to investment grade.
Did Moody's completely forget that the debt levels of the five
biggest Korean *chaebol* (conglomerates) were still rising, and that
Hyundai and Daewoo in particular were still expanding capacity? Did it forget that Samsung had jumped into the world auto
market in 1998, even though estimates of global overcapacity in
autos is estimated to exceed the United States' enormous 15 million annual demand for cars and trucks? Or did Moody's simply
assume that taxpayers in the United States and other countries
would bail out South Korean companies and their lenders if

boom led to bust once again?[13] For good measure, Moody's announced in February 2000 that it was considering a similar promotion in its rating for Mexico's debt. Shortly after Brazil's devaluation, Merrill Lynch picked the Latin American giant as its favorite equity market in the region—at least for that particular quarter.[14]

As a result, Latin America's debtors have been able to borrow at much lower rates—meaning that international lenders believed that the risks of doing business with them had significantly diminished. By March 1999, the spread between emerging market government bonds and U.S. Treasuries—which had soared fivefold immediately following the Asian crisis' start through the ruble devaluation—were still above precrisis levels but had fallen considerably. Just as revealing, Latin American countries in particular often have been able to return to international capital markets (i.e., to borrow at affordable rates) within days of an announcement of bad news.[15]

Direct investment into emerging markets—mainly factories—has revived as well. U.S. automakers have returned in force to Thailand, along with Lucent, GE, and many other U.S. multinationals. New investment began pouring back into Brazil as well—scant months after Brazil's currency devaluation. In August 1999, just one year after Moscow's shocking and widely blasted ruble devaluation, Ford announced plans for a new auto factory in Russia.[16]

In sum, the Wall Street-funded Institute for International Finance projects that total net flows of private capital (i.e., net of loan repayments) to developing countries will rise from $148.7 billion in 1999 to $193.1 billion in 2000, after slumping dramatically in 1998. Moreover, the strongest pickup is expected to be in portfolio investment—stocks and bonds. In 1999, the Morgan Stanley Emerging Market Stock Index rose faster than the American S&P 500 stock index. A more detailed look at these investment flows by the Deloitte Consulting and Deloitte & Touche firms showed that U.S. manufacturing investment in export-oriented Asian industries like electronics remained strong throughout the financial crisis.[17]

In all these cases, it is obviously too soon to say that the debtors have learned their lessons, and that the internationally mandated reforms have been swiftly and surely implemented. Exactly the opposite message, in fact, was sent in The Wall Street Journal in November 1999. In a single day, the paper reported the two following developments. First, the bellwether Morgan Stanley Capital International index decided to boost its weightings for Taiwan and Malaysia. These expressions of rising or falling confidence by Morgan bankers traditionally have greatly influenced other investors' perceptions. Second, a new survey of 1,200 Asia-based businesspeople "found that company openness—or transparency—actually worsened in Asia in the past year." In other words, even though businesspeople on the ground judged that Asian economies and businesses had actually become more secretive, a major ratings agency was giving the green light to new investment in the region. In other words, it was clearly not too soon for multinational businesses to conclude that national governments and international organizations would continue subsidizing their activities and even bailing them out should trouble erupt again.[18]

These conclusions do not need to be inferred. A senior representative of the international banking community has all but admitted the vital role played by such taxpayer guarantees in international investment decisions. According to Charles Dallara of Wall Street's Institute for International Investment, if plans move ahead to require creditors to bear more of the pain of financial crises—to be "bailed in," as the current jargon calls it—the flow of private capital to emerging markets will shrink. In other words, if implicit and explicit investment subsidies to the third world are stopped, and investors have to pay the consequences for foolish loans, they will want little to do with emerging markets.[19]

The debate over U.S. policy toward third world exporters and international financial reform has been decisively influenced so far by the tendency of many globalization critics to support these bailout and subsidization programs in principle, if not in many details. In particular, U.S. labor unions decided very quickly to support the Clinton administration's efforts to refund the International Monetary Fund and enable the organization to continue offering rescue packages to current and future third world debtors. The unions' rationale: The rescue packages were essential to preserve export markets and U.S. jobs. In a departure from their positions on U.S.-Mexico trade, U.S.-China trade, and new presidential trade-negotiating authority, the unions did not even insist that the IMF refunding include ironclad, enforceable labor rights and environmental provisions.[20] Enough congressional Democrats followed the unions' cues to ensure the refunding's eventual approval.

Perhaps just as important, support for continuing to subsidize dangerous and unsustainable levels of third world growth and trade has been expressed in many of the suggestions for international financial reform coming from these globalization critics' ranks. In its broadest form, these critics have called for a posture of "global Keynesianism" by leading national and international monetary authorities. This approach, named after John Maynard Keynes (arguably the twentieth century's most influential economist), would entail significantly lowering interest rates across the globe. With the cost of money reduced, economic growth and demand for imports would rise, and borrowing and repaying debt would become much cheaper for developing countries.[21]

Specific reform plans show the same determination to sustain artificially high levels of third world economic activity. Harvard economist Jeffrey Sachs, for example, would like to see Asian banks that are loaded down with bad debts sold to foreign investors, but realizes this process would proceed much faster if public funds—presumably from taxpayers in the United States and other wealthy countries—were injected into these banks to establish positive net worth. A coalition of progressive groups throughout the Western Hemisphere, seeks substantial relief for debtor countries and a tax on foreign exchange transactions that would be used for social and economic development (read "foreign aid"). In addition, the coalition insists that "Every agreement between countries at different levels of development must include compensatory financing to allow for achieving the competitiveness that integration implies and to fund social programs" (read "more foreign aid"). Billionaire investor George Soros' various and well-publicized international financial reform proposals are simply more subtle calls for more foreign aid—in this case, taxpayer-funded investment guarantees for loans made by international institutions. As Soros makes clear, his top ultimate priority is restarting "the flow of funds toward the periphery [third world] countries" that had been slowed or suspended by the recent financial crises.[22]

C. STOPPING THE MERRY-GO-ROUND

Transforming economic globalization from a race to the bottom to a winning proposition for the majority of Americans will require fundamental changes in almost every aspect of U.S. foreign economic policy. Trade relations with the industrialized countries,

NAFTA, international financial reform, the World Trade Organization, securing equitable trade with China—U.S. approaches toward all these and more need substantial rethinking. However, needed change on these individual issues is unlikely to take place unless the larger conceptual table is cleared, and a new set of assumptions begins driving U.S. international economic strategy. Once they are adopted, the intellectual (if not yet the political) doors will be open to a variety of new policy measures that can produce durable, broad-based national prosperity. These policy measures, moreover, can be combined in many different ways. There will be no single correct combination. At the same time, the wrong combinations will become much more obvious.

The first assumption involves the place of the United States in the global economy, and the role that international commerce has played and is likely to play in promoting U.S. economic well-being. The Clinton administration and most other globalization cheerleaders believe that international trade and investment deserve most of the credit for the nation's recent economic success. As the President's Council of Economic Advisers contends, nowadays "two features of the U.S. economy are particularly striking. First, it has never been more prosperous and, second, it has never been as integrated into the world economy." Former Commerce Secretary William M. Daley spoke for many when he insisted that the nation's future prosperity will "depend on how well our companies, and our workers, are able to compete in the world economy."[23]

However, the strongest evidence points the other way. Despite decades of policies that have seemed positively obsessed with keeping the U.S. market open and with expanding imports, the nation's total two-way trade still does not exceed 25 percent of its economy. In fact, the 1990s have been especially instructive in this regard. True, U.S. exports have grown significantly. However, as discussed, a large share of these exports simply represent corporate outsourcing, not improved national competitiveness in global consumer markets. More important, the highest U.S. productivity and growth rates in recent years have come during a period when opportunities for traditional exports of finished goods have been drying up, because growth has slowed in most of the world's other major economic regions.

A poignant moment in contemporary U.S. economic history came on September 4, 1998, when Fed Chair Alan Greenspan insisted in a speech that, "it is just not credible that the United States can remain an oasis of prosperity unaffected by a world that is experiencing greatly increased stress."[24] Greenspan's remark had a plaintive tone for a very important reason: Even though the picture of the U.S. economy as an oasis, as still largely self-reliant and independent, is solidly grounded in reality, it rudely and completely undercuts everything Greenspan and other globalization enthusiasts have grown up learning about interdependence and international integration and global cooperation. The facts that were staring Greenspan and others right in the face were destroying their ideology and very worldview. Not surprisingly, even the normally unflappable fed Chair was reduced to pleading for help. In fact, at the very beginning of the new century, events put a striking coda on the globalists' picture of the U.S. international position and prospects: The U.S. growth rate had briefly caught up to China's. The biggest emerging market, it turned out, has been right here at home.

The globalization enthusiasts are missing something else critically important about the U.S. economic position. In terms of its social makeup, the United States is not like a typical advanced industrialized country. For all its size, wealth, and power, the United States has one important and distinctive vulnerability. Alone among the industrialized first world countries, the United States has a large population with what might be called third world levels of education and skills. Other countries can in theory let labor-intensive industries like apparel or traditional manufacturing industries like textiles and steel migrate abroad without undue social fallout. (Keep in mind of course, that the very spread of technology has blurred the line between many so-called low- and high-tech industries.) The United States, however, has more to worry about.

Because improved reeducation and retraining are at best very long-term solutions to the living standards crisis—and because they almost surely will not even be close to total solutions—the wholesale abandonment of these U.S. industries to foreign competition will for generations deny millions of American families any real hope of climbing into the middle class. From a social and moral perspective, this outcome is unacceptable.

Two major policy implications flow from this new picture of the international economic position of the United States. First, the United States has more than enough market power to achieve its essential international economic goals through its own devices. It can secure equitable terms of globalization for its people by unilaterally regulating foreign access to its market. Over the longer run, it can use this same asset to encourage a genuine global consensus on U.S.-style free-market practices and principles. No market on earth approaches the combination of size, wealth, technological sophistication, and dynamism of the United States. The right to do business with Americans is something that no economic actor— government or business—can do without if it expects to become a world-class player. The United States, therefore, does not need any kind of rules-based system of world trade to ensure its citizens' future prosperity, much less today's cumbersome and economically anti-American WTO. The United States does not have the strength to win every showdown with all of its trading partners. However, if it sets realistic priorities and displays a bit of street smarts, it can win the victories it really needs.

Put somewhat differently, the current version of globalization is indeed a powerful force that can evade or run roughshod over the authority of most national governments. However, the United States is not like most other countries. It still approaches the world economy with a virtually unique set of advantages. It can design whatever economic policy straitjacket it wishes to wear—and change it at will. Even President Clinton and his advisers recognize this reality when they repeatedly refer to the United States as the "indispensable nation." Therefore, the United States' best bet for continued national success is focusing on nurturing, enhancing, and using its power and wealth. U.S. political leaders should spend less time simply proclaiming the country's status as an unrivaled superpower and more time acting like one.

A second major new assumption can be seen as the flip side of the first: If the United States is not decisively reliant on international trade and investment for its prosperity, it is even less reliant on markets in or imports from developing countries. Therefore, the United States has no need to subsidize artificially high—and unsustainable—levels of third world trade and growth. It is, in fact, best advised to permit this growth to settle at a more natural, less subsidized, and more sustainable level. Because so many U.S. multinational businesses have become so heavily dependent either on outsourcing to third world countries or on selling abroad to subsidized third world markets, this new policy will unquestionably create some short-term economic costs for the nation. However, these costs pale next to the dangers of building up the world's financial house of cards higher, guaranteeing that the inevitable crash is much more destructive than financial crises to date have been.

The costs to developing countries will of course be greater. However, these could be greatly reduced if Western Europe and

Japan open their markets wider to third world products and relieve the United States of some of the import burden. If the Europeans and Japanese refuse, the United States would have no
choice but to act on behalf of its own interests and the world's
long-term interests in rebalancing trade flows.

With the third world looming smaller in U.S. international economic planning, pressures will build for a new approach to that
portion of the U.S. population with third world education and skill
levels—and to the working poor in general. Because of this population's size and importance, it will become much less acceptable for
U.S. leaders to rely so heavily on opening domestic markets to promote third world development. For decades, decisions to abandon
labor-intensive and traditional industries, and their workforces,
have been justified largely by the need to let developing countries
concentrate on them and thereby start down the road toward industrialization. Much of the support mustered by the sub-Saharan
Africa and Caribbean Basin trade bills stems from such beliefs.[25]

Yet however worthy and important the goal of fostering the mod-
ernization of the developing world, the needs of these populations
should not be placed before those of the working poor of the United
States, and those who initially need to join their ranks. Considerations of equity also demand a new approach. When trade policy is
the chosen tool of U.S. economic development policy, our nation's
most economically vulnerable citizens bear the brunt of the costs. If
significant development assistance is to be continued, more equitable forms—ones that spread the costs more evenly across the entire U.S. economy and electorate—are urgently needed.

A U.S. globalization policy that exploits the nation's command-
ing international position, recognizes the risks of artificially
pumping up the developing world, and works for, not against, its
own low-income population, would find a variety of promising
new, mutually reinforcing policies available to it. By moving unilaterally to promote reasonable global labor and environmental
standards, such a policy would liberate its working class and the
less fortunate from excessive exposure to pauper, repressed labor
and to race-to-the-bottom-style deregulation. By moving unilaterally to open markets in Europe and Japan, moreover, it would relieve its own multinationals of much of the pressure they face to
outsource. If the global commercial playing fields become level,
U.S. firms would be able to exploit worldwide scale economies
while staying at home just as effectively as their European and
Japanese competitors.

Unilateralism would also remove one of the biggest obstacles Americans face when they try to debate globalization productively—the scarcity of reliable data. Washington would be able to require U.S. companies that manufacture and procure internationally to disclose these activities—what products they make abroad, where they are made, how many foreign workers they employ, how much these workers make, and what foreign suppliers they rely on for which parts, components, other inputs, and finished goods. The main objection long voiced by business to such requirements, that this information represents trade secrets essential to their companies' commercial success, would be overcome by requiring disclosure for all companies. When everyone's trade secrets become public knowledge, they lose their strategic value. Of course, foreign-owned enterprises wishing to do business in the United States would have to report the exact same information.

A new U.S. focus on the economies and markets of the industrialized world, meanwhile, would be reinforced by a decision to permit third world economic activity to return to more sustainable levels. The benefits of pushing expanded trade with countries where significant purchasing power already exists—and does not have to be conjured into existence—would become clear. Moreover, a U.S. policy no longer obsessed with artificially pumping up the developing world would more easily recognize the importance of opening the U.S. market to third world products strategically, and according to a realistic set of goals and priorities. A futile attempt to accomplish everything in the developing world all at once would no longer prevent more modest but more effective efforts to do some things within reasonable time frames.

For example, Caribbean Basin and Central American countries have a point when they argue that the trade breaks extended by Washington to Mexico by NAFTA significantly disadvantaged many competing products that they had hoped to sell to the United States—mainly apparel. Unfortunately for American apparel workers, who deserve a chance to earn a livelihood, too, Mexico, Central America, and the Caribbean are not the only third world regions that rely heavily on exporting garments and other textile mill products to the United States. East Asian countries are major exporters as well and have picked up the pace since the financial crisis. The sub-Saharan African countries also would like to start exporting apparel to the United States. Moreover, in 2005, an internationally negotiated WTO quota system for regulating apparel (and textile) trade will expire. Thus, the United States will be deprived of the ability to dole out pieces of its apparel market to favor certain regions for economic, political, or strategic purposes. The competition for U.S. market share will turn into a chaotic free-for-all.

A reasonable U.S. response would be to pull out of the WTO apparel agreement and decide how it wants to divvy up its market. If it really does view Mexico's prosperity and stability as a top national security and economic priority—as NAFTA supporters have long emphasized—it could restrict its market to the Mexicans or the Mexicans plus the other Western Hemisphere countries. In the process, it could require that its neighbors permit workers to organize and help them implement real protection.

Of course, this would involve locking out many Asian countries, but even so, interesting options would be available. U.S. trade policy, for example, could provide some market access to relatively small, militarily weak, and politically friendly developing Asian countries, like Thailand, Indonesia, (nowadays) or the Philippines, or some combination of these. Washington could discriminate against big, unfriendly, militarily worrisome countries like China, or against strongly protectionist countries like South Korea and India. In addition, all this strategic market opening would probably leave some room for new entrants like the African countries—all while limiting the damage to U.S. apparel workers. It is also critical to note that the wider Japan and Western Europe opened their own apparel markets to the third world, the less strategic and selective the United States would have to be.

A U.S. globalization policy that cares about low-income Americans would also recognize the need to make trade-offs between welcoming imports and welcoming immigrants. A nation that decides to protect jobs in labor-intensive and more traditional manufacturing industries from uncontrolled import competition would have more scope to admit relatively large numbers of immigrants. After all, the odds would be increased that the newcomers could find gainful employment without displacing native-born Americans. Alternatively, Washington could decide to continue its open trade policy at home but reduce immigration levels. However, a policy that seeks to open both the immigration and import doors ever wider gives the poor in the United States absolutely no chance.

At this stage of the globalization debate, the specific choices made by Americans are much less important than recognizing that such options exist, mobilizing the will to explore them, and resolving to preserve for future generations the freedom of action Americans still enjoy today. The globalizers' most powerful weapon in the struggle over the place and role of the United States in the world economy may be their very insistence that this nation has lost decisive control over its economic fate and much of the rest of its destiny. As the globalizers see it, resistance to today's globalization is futile—to paraphrase a popular line from the *Star Trek* televison series. In fact, this counsel of defeatism is as wrong as it is fundamentally un-American. The United States cannot single-handedly prop up the ever-increasing international house of cards created by the globalizers. However, it does possess ample power to reshape globalization fundamentally, and to ensure that it serves the interests of the vast majority of Americans. By mustering the national will to match its wallet, the United States also can preserve the priceless legacy of independence for future generations. In the process, it can put the entire global economy on a much safer course.

NOTES

PREFACE

1. The transcript of the program, aired on February 22, 1996, can be found at http://pbs.org/newshour/bb/business/angst_2–21.html.

2. See *America's Small Businesses and International Trade: A Report* (Washington, D.C.: U.S. Small Business Administration, March 1999).

3. "Free Trade: Strip the Myth Away," by James K. Glassman, *The Washington Post*, March 26, 1996.

4. "Mexico: Autoparts Industry—ISA9402," National Trade Data Bank, IT Market 111091162. The remaining 10 percent of Mexican auto parts output is directly exported. Similar numbers—based on information from the Mexican auto parts manufacturers' association, INA—are reported in "Competing in a Lean World: How the Auto Parts Industries in Canada and Mexico Are Responding to the Pressures of Free Trade and Lean Production," by Lorraine Eden, Kaye Husbands, and Maureen Appel Molot, paper presented to panel on "Integrating in a Regionalized World: Adding Cohesion to NAFTA and Beyond," annual convention of the International Studies Association, San Diego, Calif., April 16–21, 1996, p. 5. In 1998, the U.S. Commerce Department's Foreign Commercial Service issued another report on the Mexican auto parts market showing numbers virtually identical to the 1994 study. See "Industry Sector Analysis: Mexico: Automotive Aftermarket Parts Market (1): U.S. and Foreign Commercial Service," November 18, 1998, http://www/globalarchive.ft.com/search-components/ index/jsp.

5. "Excerpts from the President's Remarks at AFL-CIO Convention," September 24, 1997, http://www.pub.whitehouse.gov/uri-res/I2R?uri:pdi://uma. eop.gov.us/1997/9/25/iu.text.1.

6. "Motorola in China," http://www.motorola-asia.com/profiles-china.htm.

7. Big exporters like Motorola claim that once it officially enters the World Trade Organization, China will no longer be able to condition access to its markets on promises to use Chinese suppliers. Yet the World Trade Organization has proven to be a highly ineffective means of protecting U.S. commercial interests. Moreover, as of press time, no U.S. companies doing business with China had announced plans to reduce their use of Chinese suppliers once Beijing is obligated to abide by international trade rules.

8. W. Michael Cox and Richard C. Alm, *Myths of Rich and Poor: Why We're Better Off Than We Think* (New York: Basic Books, 1999).

CHAPTER 1: INTRODUCTION—A TALE OF TWO CITIES

1. "Remarks by the President to the Little Rock Chamber of Commerce," Little Rock, Arkansas, December 10, 1999, http://www.pub.whitehouse.gov/uri-res/I2R?urn:pdi://oma.eop.gov.us/1999/12/10/9.text.1.

2. Many of these survey results are cited and summarized in "A Lack of Support for Free-Trade Policies," by Alan Tonelson, *The San Diego Union Tribune*, May 28, 1997. For more recent results, see "Weighing the NAFTA Tide," by Alan Tonelson, *The Washington Times*, January 14, 1999.

3. For Thai growth and unemployment figures, see "Thailand's Financial Crisis and Progress Towards Recovery—Implications for U.S. Trade," by Karl Tsuji, *International Trade and Technology Review*, U.S. International Trade Commission, October 1999, p. 17. As is the case with such data from many third world countries, the unemployment figure is surely an underestimate. For Thai wage data, see "Thailand," by Frank Flatters, *The Asia Competitiveness Report 1999*, Klaus Schwab and Jeffrey D. Sachs, eds. (Geneva, Switzerland: World Economic Forum, 1999), p. 186.

4. "State of the Union Address," Washington, D.C., January 27, 2000, http://www.pub.whitehouse.gov/uri-res/I2R?urn:pdi://oma.eop.gov.us/2000/1/27/15.text.1.

5. *1995 Annual Report of the President of the United States on the Trade Agreements Program* (Washington, D.C.: Office of the U.S. Trade Representative, 1996), pp. 1–2.

6. For an authoritative account of the launching of the Big Emerging Markets initiative, see Jeffrey E. Garten, *The Big Ten: The Big Emerging Markets and How They Will Change Our Lives* (New York: Basic Books, 1997), especially pp. xii ff.

7. Paul M. Krugman, *Pop Internationalism* (Cambridge, Mass.: MIT Press, 1996), p. 78.

CHAPTER 2: SOME BOOM

1. "Century of Growth," *Investor's Business Daily*, January 14, 2000; "Desperately Seeking a Perfect Model," *The Economist*, April 10, 1999, http://www.economist.com/editorial/freeforall/19990410/fn7756.html.

2. "Household Income at Record High; Poverty Declines in 1998, Census Bureau Reports," Release No. CB–9, U.S. Bureau of the Census, U.S. Department of Commerce, September 30, 1999, http://www.census.gov/Press-Release/www/1999/cb99–188.html; "Yearly Health Review Finds USA's Kids Making Gains," by Steve Sternberg, *USA Today*, April 9, 1999; "Welfare Proposals Hailed as 'Positive,'" by Cheryl Wetzstein, *The Washington Times*, July 20, 1999; "What Are the Poor Doing Tonight?" by Nat Hentoff, *The Washington Post*, July 24, 1999.

3. "US Consumers: Dangerously Overweight?" by Joseph T. Abate, *Global Weekly Economic Monitor*, Lehman Brothers, January 15, 1999, p. 4; "Meet the New Borrowers," by Sandra E. Black and Donald P. Morgan, *Current Issues in Economics and Finance* 5, no. 3, Federal Reserve Bank of New York, February 1999, p. 3;

"US: Consumer Balancing Act," by Joseph Abate, *Global Weekly Economic Monitor*, Lehman Brothers, August 13, 1999, p. 10.

4. For the stock ownership figures, see "The Liquidity Shibboleth," by Jeffrey M. Applegate, *Research Highlights*, Lehman Brothers, March 19, 1999.

5. "Even the Poor Have More," by W. Michael Cox and Richard C. Alm, *Intellectual Capital*, February 25, 1999, http://www.intellectualcapital.com/issues/ issue178/item1337.asp.

6. As noted in a recent *USA Today* editorial, "As long as wealth and income are rising across the board, worries about income inequality are overblown." See "Widening Income Gap Tells Only Part of the Story," *USA Today*, January 21, 2000.

7. "Married Women Joining Workforce Spur 150 Percent Family Income Increase, Census Bureau Finds in 50-Year Review," Release No. CB98–181, U.S. Bureau of the Census, U.S. Department of Commerce, September 29, 1998, p. 2, http://www.census.gov/Press-Release/cb98/181.html.

8. W. Michael Cox and Richard C. Alm, *Myths of Rich and Poor: Why We're Better Off Than We Think* (New York: Basic Books, 1999), p. 4. See also *Wage & Income Inequality*, Background Paper (Washington, D.C.: Employment Policy Foundation), April 30, 1996, p. 7.

9. Lawrence Mishel, Jared Bernstein, and John Schmitt, *The State of Working America 1998–99* (Washington, D.C.: Economic Policy Institute, 1999), p. 248.

10. Ibid., pp. 248–249; "The Anxious Society: Middle-Class Insecurity and the Crisis of the American Dream," by Charles J. Whalen, *The Jerome Levy Economics Institute of Bard College Report 5*, no. 5, October 1995, p. 10.

11. Mishel et al., *The State of Working America*, pp. 250–252.

12. "Hourly Wage Decile Cutoffs, for All Workers, from the CPSURG, 1973–98 (1998 dollars)," *The Datazone*, Economic Police Institute, http://epinet. org/datazone/orghourlyxoffs_all.html; Bob Davis and David Wessel, *Prosperity: The Coming 20-Year Boom and What It Means to You* (New York: Times Books, 1998), pp. 53 ff.; "Why Their World Might Crumble," by Lester Thurow, *The New York Times Magazine*, November 19, 1995, p. 78.

13. Mishel et al., *The State of Working America*, pp. 123 ff. The share of U.S. employees eligible for stock options has risen significantly in recent years, but still stands at only 20 percent. Some three quarters of these eligible workers actually receive options. See "Stock Options Climb Far Down the Corporate Ladder," *The Wall Street Journal*, January 18, 2000.

14. Mishel et al., *The State of Working America*, pp. 147, 148; "Number of U.S. Investors Has Doubled in Seven Years," by Tracy Corrigan, *Financial Times*, February 23, 1997.

15. Mishel et al., *The State of Working America*, p. 146; "More Workers Seen Losing Health Coverage," by Samuel Goldreich, *The Washington Times*, September 11, 1996; "To Reich, There's Ample Room to Give Workers a Raise," by Paul Blustein, *The Washington Post*, August 7, 1996.

16. "In Benefits Ruling, Some See a Promise Broken," by Steven Ginsberg, *The Washington Post*, March 22, 1998; "Retiring? Don't Assume Health Benefits Are Forever," by Albert B. Crenshaw, *The Washington Post*, November 3, 1996.

17. "U.S. Trade Competitiveness and Workforce Education and Training," Testimony of Robert B. Reich, Secretary of Labor, before the House Ways and Means Committee Subcommittee on Trade, July 25, 1996, pp. 3, 4.

18. Davis and Wessel, *Prosperity*, p. 55; Thomas L. Friedman, *The Lexus and the Olive Tree: Understanding Globalization* (New York: Farrar, Straus and Giroux, 1999), pp. 270–71.

19. Mishel et al., *The State of Working America*, p. 157; Davis and Wessel, *Prosperity*, p. 154.

20. Mishel et al., *The State of Working America*, p. 157; "Wake Up and Smell the Latte: College Still Pays, Mostly," by Steven Pearlstein, *The Washington Post*, January 11, 1996; "Overeducated and Underpaid," by Thomas Geoghegan, *The New York Times*, June 3, 1997; "Sharp Increase Along the Borders of Poverty," by Jason DeParle, *The New York Times*, March 31, 1994.

21. Friedman, *The Lexus*, pp. 270–71.

22. *Digest of Education Statistics, 1999* (Washington, D.C.: U.S. Department of Education, 2000), http://nces.ed.gov/pubs2000/digest99/chapter 3.html; "The Menace to Prosperity," by Robert Reich, *Financial Times*, March 3, 1997; "Colleges' Failure to Resolve Funding May Bar Millions from Attending, Study Finds," by Rene Sanchez, *The Washington Post*, June 18, 1997; Friedman, *Prosperity*, p. 253.

23. The following BLS wage and employment figures are available on the BLS Web site, http://www.bls.gov/webapps/legacy/cesbtabl/htm. Price levels since 1947 can also be found on the site, at "Consumer Price Index—All Urban Consumers," Series ID CUSR000USA0, seasonally, adjusted, http://146.142.4.24/cgi-bin/drsv.

24. Employment figures come from "Nonfarm Payroll Statistics from the Current Employment Statistics (National)," at the BLS Web site, http://146.142.424/cgi-bin/dsrv.

25. *Digital Economy 2000* (Washington, D.C.: U.S. Department of Commerce, June 2000), p. 48.

26. "Software Engineers Lead Tech Wage Gains," by Peter Behr, *The Washington Post*, April 8, 1999.

27. "The Perceived Shortage of High-Tech Workers," by Clair Brown, Ben Campbell, and Greg Pinsonneault," http://heather.cs.ucdavis.edu/ClairBrown.html.

28. The ITAA study and its major findings are cited in an article on the organization's Web site by its president. For an updated version, see *Help Wanted 1998: A Call for Collaborative Action for the New Millennium*, http://www.itaa.org/workforce/studies/hw98.htm. Although Congress has already raised the limit once and is likely to do so again, the Department of Commerce—which, unlike the ITAA, has no vested interest in finding a worker shortage—has confirmed that "the evidence on IT labor market imbalances remains ambiguous." See also *Digital Economy 2000*, p. 49.

29. "Silicon Valley's Temps See Relevance in UPS Strike," by David Kline, *San Jose Mercury-News*, August 25, 1997. A marked recent decrease in the numbers of full-time computer-industry jobs in Silicon Valley has also been found in research by Michael P. Smith of the University of California at Davis' Applied Behavioral Sciences Department and the private National Planning Association. See "A Critical Look at Immigration's Role in the U.S. Computer Industry," by Norman Matloff, July 11, 1996, p. 10, ftp://heather.cs.ucdavis.edu/pub/svreport.

html, and "High-Tech Workers Need to Unionize," by Rebecca Eisenberg, *San Francisco Examiner*, May 31, 1998.

30. These and the following employment projection figures are found in or derived from "Occupational Employment Projections to 2008," by Douglas Bradduck, *Monthly Labor Review*, November 1999, pp. 51–77.

31. "Ambassador Charlene Barshefsky, ISAC Plenary Session," May 6, 1998, pp. 5–6.

32. "U.S. Trade Competitiveness and Workforce Education and Training: Testimony by Leo Reddy, President, National Coalition for Advanced Manufacturing," Subcommittee on Trade, Committee on Ways and Means, U.S. House of Representatives, July 25, 1996, p. 1. For other such statements, see Geza Feketekuty and Bruce Stokes, eds., *Trade Strategies for a New Era* (New York: Council on Foreign Relations, 1997), pp. 3, 35.

33. Good journalistic treatments of this skills shortage include "Help Wanted," by Murray Hiebert, *Far Eastern Economic Review*, June 6, 1996; "Skills Wanted," by Salil Tripathi, *Asia, Inc.*, December 1995/January 1996; "The Asia Boom: Training," by Teresa Watanabe, *The Los Angeles Times*, November 29, 1994; and "Failing Grade," by Gordon Fairclough, *Far Eastern Economic Review*, September 29, 1994.

34. Figures come from Jean Johnson, *Human Resources for Science and Technology: The Asian Region*, NSF 93–303 (Washington, D.C.: National Science Foundation, 1993), pp. 61, 63, 69.

35. "NASSCOM for Immediate Action to Increase Supply of Knowledge Workers," National Association of Software and Software Companies, April 17, 2000, http://www.nasscom.org/template/pressrel.htm; "Best of Both Worlds: Emerging Opportunities in Hong Kong and China," by Christine Keck, U.S. Information Technology Office, unpublished; "Information Technology in South Korea," by Alex Schultz, http://gurukul.ucc.american.edu/MOGIT/as8961a/html; "Government Policy Regarding IT in Singapore," by Julie Johnson, http://gurukul.ucc.american.edu/MOGIT/as8961a.html; "IT in Singapore: Government Policy Regarding IT in Singapore," by Julie Johnson, http://gurukul.ucc.american.edu/MOGIT/jj7134a/govepage.html.

36. "SM Spells Out Major Role of Unions," *The Straits Times*, April 29, 1995; "Daily-Rated PUB Worker Promoted After Taking Course," *The Straits Times*, May 11, 1995; "Managing Technology for Development," *The Straits Times*, July 2, 1996; "Third-Wave Reform," *Free China Review*, June 1995; "Basic Background Report," National Taskforce on Information Technology and Software Development, http://it-taskforce.nic.in/vsit-taskforce/bgr15.htm.

37. "Survival Lessons," by Michael Vatikiotis, *Far Eastern Economic Review*, December 30, 1993–January 6, 1994; "Training in IT Vital to Manufacturing Sector," by Shyla Sangaran and Wendy Lee, *New Straits Times*, June 17, 1996; "Nod for More Science and Technology Courses," by Hussaini Dahalan and Ahmad Kushairi, *New Straits Times*, August 17, 1995; and "'Tigers Show Signs of Aging," by Michael Richardson, *International Herald Tribune*, May 17, 1995.

CHAPTER 3: WHAT'S GLOBALIZATION GOT TO DO WITH IT?

1. *Economic Report of the President* (Washington, D.C.: U.S. Government Printing Office), February 1998, p. 241.

2. See, for example, Jagdish Bhagwati and Marvin H. Kosters, eds., *Trade and Wages* (Washington, D.C.: American Enterprise Institute, 1994); "On the Labor

Market Effects of Immigration and Trade," by George Borjas, Richard Freeman, and Lawrence Katz, *Immigration and the Workforce* (Chicago: University of Chicago Press and National Bureau of Economic Research, 1992), pp. 213–44; Paul Krugman, *Technology, Trade, and Factor Prices*, NBER Working Paper 5335 (Cambridge, Mass.: National Bureau of Economic Research, 1995); Robert Z. Lawrence, *Single World, Divided Nations? International Trade and OECD Labor Markets* (Paris: Organization for Economic Cooperation and Development and Brookings Institution Press, 1996); "Income Inequality and Trade: How to Think, What to Conclude," by J. David Richardson, *Journal of Economic Perspectives 9*, no. 3, Summer 1995, p. 36; "Does Globalization Lower Wages and Export Jobs?" by Matthew J. Slaughter and Phillip Swagel, *Economic Issues* 11, International Monetary Fund, 1997, http://www.imf.org; and "Inequality Amid Prosperity," by Laura D'Andrea Tyson, *The Washington Post*, July 9, 1997.

3. The Lawrence and Slaughter conclusion is found in "International Trade and American Wages in the 1980s: Giant Sucking Sound or Small Hiccup?" by Lawrence and Slaughter, *Brookings Papers on Economic Activity: Microeconomics 2*, p. 165. Similar conclusions are found in "Changes in the Demand for Skilled Labor Within U.S. Manufacturing: Evidence from the Annual Survey of Manufactures," by Eli Berman, John Bound, and Zvi Griliches, *Quarterly Journal of Economics 109*, May 1994, pp. 367–97; "Trade, Jobs, and Wages," by Paul Krugman and Robert Z. Lawrence, *Scientific American*, April 1994, pp. 22–27; and Robert Z. Lawrence, *The Impact of Trade on OECD Labor Markets*, Occasional Paper 45 (Washington, D.C.: Group of Thirty, 1994). For the Krugman statement on leveling, see "E-Mail to the Editors," *Slate*, August 14, 1997, http://www.slate.com.

4. Bob Davis and David Wessel, *Prosperity: The Coming 20-Year Boom and What It Means to You* (New York: Times Books, 1998), p. 209.

5. "Casualties of the 'Rising Tide,'" by Robert J. Samuelson, *The Washington Post*, August 31, 1994; "Gephardt vs. Gore," by Thomas L. Friedman, *The New York Times*, April 3, 1997. See also "Where Have the Good Jobs Gone?" by Mortimer B. Zuckerman, *U.S. News & World Report*, July 31, 1995, p. 68.

6. Paul M. Krugman, *Pop Internationalism* (Cambridge, Mass: MIT Press, 1996), p. 66; "U.S. Trade Policy Turning into Game of Tug of War," by Bill Mongelluzzo, *Journal of Commerce*, July 1, 1997.

7. "The Magic Mountain," by Paul M. Krugman, *The New York Times*, January 23, 2000.

8. For Bhagwati quotes, see "Fast Track: Not So Fast," *The Wall Street Journal.*, September 10, 1997; "Skilled Workers Watch Their Jobs Migrate Overseas," by Keith Bradsher, *The New York Times*, August 28, 1995; "The Challenges of an Emerging World," by Jeffrey Garten, *Financial Times*, May 21, 1997.

9. "The New American Politics," *The New York Times*, November 13, 1997; Thomas L. Friedman, *The Lexus and the Olive Tree: Understanding Globalization* (New York: Farrar, Straus & Giroux, 1999), p. 269.

10. "The World's View of Multinationals," *The Economist*, January 29, 2000; "Remarks by the President at World Economic Forum," Davos Switzerland, January 29, 2000, http://www.whitehouse.gov/uri-res/I2R?urn:pdi://oma/eop.gov.us/2000/1/31/13.text; "Remarks by the President at the Democratic Leadership Council Gala," Omni Shoreham Hotel, Washington, D.C., October 13, 1999, http://www.pub.whitehouse.gov/uri-res/I2R?urn:pdi://oma.eop.gov.us/1999/10/14/10.text.1.

11. "Capitalism Isn't Broken," by Michael C. Jensen and Perry Fagan, *The Wall Street Journal.*, March 29, 1996.

12. "The Myth of High-Wage Service Jobs," by Alan Tonelson, *Intellectualcapital.*, June 17, 1999, http://www.intellectualcapital.com/issues/issue249/item 5413.asp. According to researchers at the Economic Policy Institute, when non-wage benefits are factored in, the gap has been considerably wider. See Lawrence Mishel, Jared Bernstein, and John Schmitt, *The State of Working America 1998–99*, "Table 3.28: Employment Growth by Sector, 1979–97" (Washington, D.C.: Economic Policy Institute, 1999), p. 173.

13. Eamonn Fingleton, *In Praise of Hard Industries: Why Manufacturing, Not the Information Economy, Is the Key to Future Prosperity* (New York: Houghton-Mifflin, 1999), p. 7; Davis and Wessel, *Prosperity*, p. 240.

14. The trade figures in this and the following paragraphs are found in "Table 3: U.S. Trade in Goods, 1972–1999," posted on the Web site of the International Trade Administration of the U.S. Department of Commerce, http://www.ita.doc.gov/td/industry/otea/usfth/aggregate/H99t03.txt. The employment figures come from "National Employment, Hours, and Earnings," BLS Web site, http://www.bls.gov/webapps/legacy/cesbtabl/htm. The wage figures come from Mishel et al., *The State of Working America*, pp. 182–83. The Economic Policy Institute also contends that some 80 percent of the jobs lost in manufacturing during this period were attributable to trade flows. See Robert E. Scott, Thea Lee, and John Schmitt, *Trading Away Good Jobs: An Examination of Employment and Wages in the U.S., 1979–94*, Briefing Paper (Washington, D.C.: Economic Policy Institute), October 1997, p. 2.

15. See, for example, Krugman, *Pop Internationalism*, p. 48.

16. *BusinessWeek* report cited in "Trade Fact of the Month," *Trade Deficit Monitor 3*, no. 10, AFL-CIO Public Policy Department, December 1997, p. 3. Although America's services trade is still in healthy surplus, rising services import levels are noteworthy as well. According to Assistant Secretary of Commerce Patrick A. Mulloy, imports of goods and services currently are increasing at twice the healthy rate of American economic growth. See "Prepared Statement of the Honorable Patrick A. Mulloy, Assistant Secretary of Commerce for Market Access and Compliance, before the U.S. Trade Deficit Review Commission," December 10, 1999, p. 2.

17. "The Global Jobs Crisis," by Ray Marshall, *Foreign Policy 100*, Fall 1995, pp. 53–54. For similar analyses, see Craig Elwell, *The U.S. Trade Deficit in 1998: Data and Analysis*, CRS Report for Congress (Washington, D.C.: Congressional Research Service), June 1, 1999, p. 7; "Take a Close Look at Those GDP Numbers," *BusinessWeek*, May 3, 1999, p. 35. Economists at Bankers Trust, like some others, view the trade deficits effects on manufacturing in a positive light. The deficits, they argue, are acting as a safety valve for the U.S. economy, "siphoning production away from potentially overheating domestic industries and thus helping keep inflation at bay." See "With Assets Pumped Up, Few Worry About Inflation," by Louis Uchitelle, *The New York Times*, May 23, 1999.

18. Trade figures calculated from the U.S. International Trade Commission's Trade DataWeb, http://dataweb.usitc.gov; "U.S. Commodity Trade with 80 Largest U.S. Trde Partners, 1995-1999, http://www.ita.doc.gov/td/industry/otea/usfth/top80cty/top80cty.html; and "U.S. Commodity Trade with World," http://www.ita.doc.gov/td/industry/otea/usfth/geoarea/cworld.txt.

19. Detailed qualitative descriptions of foreign trade barriers are published every year by the U.S. Trade Representative's office in surveys titled *National Trade Estimate Reports on Foreign Trade Barriers.*

20. One of the most elaborate statements of this position is J. David Richardson and Karin Rindall, *Why Exports Matter: More!* (Washington, D.C.: Institute for International Economics and the Manufacturing Institute, 1996).

21. Scott et al., *Trading Away Good Jobs*, pp. 9–11.

22. Manufacturing's share of the economy is found in Gross Domestic Product by Industry in Current Dollars, 1993-98, Industry Accounts Data, Bureau of Economic Analysis, Department of Commerce, http://www.bea.doc.gov/bea/dn2/gpoc.htm#1993-98. National Employment, Hours, and Earnings Series IDs:EEU0500001, EEU00300001, Bureau of Labor Statistics, Department of Labor, http://146.142.4.241/cgi-bin/dsrv.

23. Alan V. Deardorff, *Technology, Trade, and Increasing Inequality: Does the Cause Matter for the Cure?* Discussion Paper No. 428, Research Seminar in International Economics, School of Public Policy (Ann Arbor, Mich.: The University of Michigan), June 17, 1998, p. 6, http://www.spp.umich.edu/rsie/workingpapers/wp.html; "US: deflation@internet.com," by Joseph T. Abate and Ethan S. Harris, *Global Weekly Economic Monitor*, Lehman Brothers, April 12, 1999, p. 10.

24. See "An Even Stronger Case for Big Caps," by Jeffrey M. Applegate, *Research Highlights*, Lehman Brothers, January 15, 1999, p. 2. Clinton cited in "… And No; Labor Rights and the Environment First," by Jerome I. Levinson, *The Washington Post*, December 6, 1999.

25. Economist David Blanchflower has calculated that American union workers enjoyed a nearly 15 percent wage premium from 1985 to 1993. See "Do Unions Still Matter?" by Stephanie Flanders, *Financial Times*, May 26, 1997. The Economic Policy Institute has calculated that unions generate a 23.2 percent premium for wages and as much as a 35.9 percent premium for total compensation (which includes benefits). See Mishel et al., *The State of Working America*, p. 183. Even the business-sponsored Employment Policy Foundation agrees that the decline of unionization has helped widen wage inequality. See "Wage and Income Forum Concludes That Raising Productivity Growth Is Critical.," *Fact & Fallacy 2*, no. 1, Employment Policy Foundation, May 1996, p. 3.

26. For American union membership numbers, see "Labor Can't Keep Pace," by Timothy Burn, *The Washington Times*, January 26, 1999. For private sector figures, see "Is This Really Labor's Day?" by William Serrin, *The Washington Post*, September 1, 1996.

27. For union election results, see "The 'Worker Backlash' Shibboleth," by Jeffrey M. Applegate, *Lehman Brothers Research Reports*, June 24, 1996, pp. ii–iii. For strike figures, see "Work Stoppage Data: Work Stoppages Idling 1,000 Workers or More Beginning in Period," and "Work Stoppage Data: Days of Idleness from WIS in Effect in Period, as % of Total Estimated Working Time," both at the Bureau of Labor Statistics Web Site, http://146.142.4.24/cgi-bin/surveymost.

28. For foreign union membership numbers, see "Union Membership Drops Wolrdwide, UN Reports," by Steven Greenhouse, *The New York Times*, November 4, 1997. For quote, see "UN Report: Increased Trade Flows Spur Big Changes in Labor Relations," by John Zaracostas, *Journal of Commerce*, November 4, 1997.

29. "Final Whistle: A GM Plant Closes, Scattering Workers Around the Country," by Rebecca Blumenstein, *The Wall Street Journal.*, June 26, 1996; "GM's Labor

Hawks Are Getting Tough With UAW to Fulfill Plans to Cut Costs," by Rebecca Blumenstein and Gabriella Stern, *The Wall Street Journal.*, April 22, 1996.

30. The poll results are cited in "Going South: Mexican Wages and U.S. Jobs After NAFTA," by Harley Shaiken, *The American Prospect*, Fall 1993, p. 63.

31. See Kate Bronfenbrenner, *Final Report: The Effects of Plant Closing or Threat of Plant Closing on the Right of Workers to Organize*, submitted to the Labor Secretariat of the North American Commission for Labor Cooperation, 1996. The report has not yet been officially released by the commission. See also "We'll Close! Plant-Closing Threats, Union Organizing and NAFTA," *Multinational Monitor*, March 1997, pp. 8–13.

32. "The Economy in a Nutshell," by Stephen D. Slifer, *Research Highlights*, Lehman Brothers, April 30, 1999, p. 11. Influential *Wall Street Journal* reporter Alan Murray evidently agrees. See "The Economy Is New; Human Nature Isn't," *The Wall Street Journal.*, May 24, 1999. For the Clinton remarks, see "Clinton Shares Credit for Longest Boom," by John M. Berry, *The Washington Post*, February 2, 2000.

33. See, for example, "Importing Poverty," by Robert J. Samuelson, *The Washington Post*, July 10, 1996, and Brookings Institution economist Gary Burtless' statements in Center for Immigration Studies and Center for Public Policy Issues, *Immigration and the Labor Market*, CLA Paper 9 (Washington, D.C.: Center for Immigration Studies), November 1, 1994, pp. 6, 16.

34. Borjas et al., "On the Labor Market Effects of Trade and Immigration," pp. 213–44; "The New Economics of Immigration," by George Borjas, *Atlantic Monthly* 278, no. 5, November 1996, pp. 72–80; Jordan Commission quoted in "A Nation in Search of Answers," by Donald L. Bartlett and James B. Steele, *The Philadelphia Inquirer*, September 22, 1996.

35. "Greenspan Holds Forth Before a Friendly Panel," by Richard W. Stevenson, *The New York Times*, January 27, 2000.

36. For another concession by globalization enthusiasts about the wage-depressing effects of immigration, see "Wage and Income Forum," p. 3.

37. "By the Numbers: U.S. Immigration," by Roger Doyle, *Scientific American*, September 1999, http://www.sciam.com/1999/0999numbers.html; "INS Shifts 'Interior' Strategy to Target Criminal Aliens," by William Branigan, *The Washington Post*, March 15, 1999; "Immigrants' Growing Role in U.S. Poverty Cited," by Michael A. Fletcher, *The Washington Post*, September 2, 1999.

38. On the 1965 changes, see "U.S. Immigrant Level at Highest Peak Since '30s" by Heather Knight, *The Los Angeles Times*, April 9, 1997. For the 1980s levels, see "Immigration Study Urges New Curbs and Criteria," by Patrick J. McDonnell, *The Los Angeles Times*, September 15, 1997. The amnesty provisions of the 1986 laws are found in Branigan, "INS Shifts 'Interior' Strategy." For the 40 percent figures, see "How Immigration Harms Minorities," by Norman Matloff, *The Public Interest* Summer 1996, p. 62. In October 1997, the Jordan Commission specifically recommended cutting current immigration levels to 550,000 and reducing the commitment to unite extended families. See "Immigration Panel Urges Focus on Unity," by Jodi Wilgoren and Patrick J. McDonnell, *The Los Angeles Times*, October 1, 1997.

39. See "Immigration Policies Threaten U.S. Growth," by Nancy Cleeland, *The Los Angeles Times*, April 11, 1999; "Los Angeles Apparel Industry Facing Shift in Trend and Major Challenges," PR Newswire, May 12, 1999; "Going, Going,

Gone: U.S. Says Adios to Jobs and Balance in Trade as High-Tech Manufacturing Moves to Mexico," by Dean Culbreath, *San Diego Union-Tribune*, July 25, 1999. For a report from *The Los Angeles Times* itself on how such job flight to Mexico and Asia has affected the area's wages, see "L.A. County Jobs Surge Since '93, but Not Wages," by Don Lee, *The Los Angeles Times*, July 26, 1999.

40. Fletcher, "Immigrants' Growing Role."

41. See "U.S. Cos. Sued Over Saipan Sweatshops," Associated Press, January 13, 1999; "Lawsuits: Retailers, Factories Mistreat Offshore Workers," by Paula L. Green, *The Journal of Commerce*, January 14, 1999; "Pregnant Saipan Workers Get Support from EEOC," by Alison Maxwell, *Women's Wear Daily*, July 6, 1999.

42. "United States: Immigration Politics," *Oxford Analytica*, October 23, 1998.

43. *Executive Summary of Labor Department Inspector General Audit of Employment-Based Permanent and Temporary Labor Programs*, published in *Daily Labor Report*, no. 72, Bureau of National Affairs, April 15, 1996, pp. E, 9, 10.

44. "A Critical Look at Immigration's Role in the U.S. Computer Industry," by Norman Matloff, May 19, 1997, p. 19, ftp://heather.cs.ucdavis.edu/pub/svreport.html; "United States: Immigration Politics."

45. "Piled Higher and Deeper," by Edwin S. Rubenstein, *American Outlook*, fall 1999, http://www.hudson.org/American_Outlook/articles_faa999/rubenstein.htm.

Chapter 4: The Global Workforce Explosion

1. Population figures and growth rates can be found at the Population Reference Bureau's Web site, http://www.prb.org./pubs/wpds99/wpds99_1.htm.

2. See *World Development Report 1995: Workers in an Integrating World* (Washington, D.C. and New York: World Bank and Oxford University Press), pp. 210–11. The Mexico estimates are found in "NAFTA: Off with the Rose–Colored Glasses," *The Christian Science Monitor*, October 18, 1999; and "NAFTA Gives Mexicans New Reasons to Leave Home," by Robert Collier, *San Francisco Chronicle*, October 15, 1998.

3. "Aegis and Kathie Lee," by Jorge A. Banales, *The Washington Times*, November 18, 1996; "Analysts Question Pakistan's Child Labor Plan," by N. Vasuki Rao, *Journal of Commerce*, July 19, 1996.

4. William Wolman and Ann Colamosca, *The Judas Economy: The Triumph of Capital and the Betrayal of Work* (Reading, Mass.: Addison-Wesley, 1997), pp. 33–34.

5. World Development Report, pp. 1, 7, 9.

6. Ibid., p. 72.

7. For the open Mexican unemployment figures, see *Avancia de Informacion Economica*, INEGI, February 1996. For the U.S. embassy view, see "Mexican Unemployment in 1995," U.S. Embassy, Mexico City, http://www.sils.umich.edu/~imi/mexunemp36/html.

8. The ILO's analysis of Russian jobless figures is found in "Grim Jobs Picture Emerges in Russia," by John Thornhill, *Financial Times*, February 6, 1997. For the recent unemployment figure, see "Global Economy Watch," Bloomberg News, March 15, 2000.

9. For the South Africa figure, see "South Africa Health Service on Critical List," Reuters, March 13, 2000. For current Eastern and Central European unemployment rates, see "Polish Central Bank Today," Bloomberg News, March 14,

2000; "Czech February Consumer Prices Rose 3.7% in Year," Bloomberg News, March 8, 2000; and "Bulgarian National Bank Today," Bloomberg News, March 10, 2000. East and Central European figures from 1990 to late 1994 can be found in *World Employment 1995* (Geneva: International Labor Organization, 1995), p. 110. For the Latin America figures, see "UN: Joblessness Up in Latin America," Associated Press, August 22, 1999.

10. For the U.S. government estimate of Indian joblessness, see "India Fact Sheet," http://www.mac.doc.gov/INDIA/ind-fact.htm. On job-related concerns in India, see "Voters in India Focus on Unemployment," by Kenneth J. Cooper, *The Washington Post*, May 4, 1996. For the south Asia estimate, see *World Employment Report*, p. 68.

11. "Indonesia: Investment Climate Statement," *Indonesian Economic News and Reports* (Jakarta, Indonesia: Economic Section, U.S. Embassy, Jakarta), May 1997, http://www.usembassyjakarta.org/econ/investment.html; Interview, September, 1997.

12. See "Global Unemployment Crisis Continues, Wage Inequalities Rising," *The Magazine of the ILO: World of Work*, no. 18, December 1996. For a more recent assessment, see "Decent Work and Poverty Reduction in the Global Economy," papers submitted by the International Labour Office to the Second Session of the General Assembly on the Implementation of the Outcome of the World Summit for Social Development and Further Initiatives, April 2000, http://www.ilo.org/public/english/bueau/exrel/papers/2000/globalec.htm.

13. The overall Chinese unemployment rate appears in "17 pc of China Out of Work," Associated Press, January 18, 1999. The Standard & Poor's shift is reported in "Buy Time, Not Guns," by Thomas L. Friedman, *The New York Times*, July 29, 1999.

14. For the World Bank estimates, see "Hope: Buoyant Exports and Healthy Investment in Fixed Assets May Not Be Enough to Overcome the Structural Weaknesses Underlying Seven Consecutive Years of Slowing Growth," by James Kynge, *Financial Times*, December 29, 1999. Rawlski's assessment is found in "China's Move to Market: How Far? What's Next?" by Thomas G. Rawlski, prepared for the Cato Institute conference "Whither China? The PRC at 50," (Washington, D.C.), September 29, 1999, p. 9. The fears of China's leaders are cited in "Unemployed Ranks Threaten China," by Charles Hutzler, Associated Press, December 25, 1997.

15. "Capitalism Isn't Broken," by Michael C. Jensen and Perry Fagan, *The Wall Street Journal.*, March 29, 1996; "The Lonely Americans, Isolated in a Trade War," by Nathaniel Nash, *The New York Times*, May 26, 1995. More recent examples include Bob Davis and David Wessel, *Prosperity: The Coming 20-Year Boom and What It Means to You* (New York: Times Books, 1998), pp. 6, 221, 222.

16. "The Big Lie of Global Inequality," by Martin Wolf, *Financial Times*, February 9, 2000.

17. See "A Larry King Special—Ross Perot Debates V.P. Al Gore on NAFTA," *Larry King Live* Transcript 961, November 9, 1993, p. 2.

18. "Remarks by the President to Farmers, Students from the Seattle-Tacoma Area Who Study Trade, and Area Officials," Seattle, Washington, December 1, 1999, http://www.pub.Whitehouse.gov.

19. "Free Trade: Knocking Down Barriers to U.S. Business," http://www.uschamber.org/frame/frame/frame.html. See also "Revitalizing U.S. Leaderhip," http://www.uschamber.com/policy/8-newmarkets/issues/other/intl2.htm.

20. See "East, Southeast Asia Make Huge Strides in Reducing Poverty, World Bank Says," by Eduardo Lachica, *The Wall Street Journal.*, August 27, 1997. For the one dollar per day figure, see "Huge Strides" and "India's 5 Decades of Progress and Pain," by John F. Burns *The New York Times*, August 14, 1997. For the rise in the numbers of impoverished, see "World Bank Says Poverty Is Increasing," by Paul Lewis, *The New York Times*, June 3, 1999.

21. See "Even If You Build Them ... the Chinese May Not Come to Theme Parks," by Seth Faison, *The New York Times*, August 3, 1999. The $6,000 threshhold is specified in "Long March to Mass Market," by James Harding, *Financial Times*, June 25, 1997. The cheapest Chinese cars and Chinese income levels are described in "China Hopes to Enter Auto Industry," by Elaine Kurtenbach, Associated Press, December 28, 1997. A similar analysis can be found in "Carmakers Take a More Critical Look at China's Prospects," by James B. Treece and David Murphy, *Automotive News*, June 23, 1997. The Kodak information is found in "Kodak, Fuji Face Off in Neutral Territory: China's Vast Market," by Craig S. Smith, *The Wall Street Journal.*, May 24, 1996.

22. "India Consumer Market 'Set to Treble,'" by Mark Nicholson, *Financial Times*, May 28, 1997; *Investment Policies of South Asian Countries: A Critical Review* (Lahore, Pakistan: Lahore Chamber of Commerce & Industry), undated, p. 2, http://www.lcci.org.pk/lcciweb/serv02.htm.

23. "Such a Deal! The Much-Maligned Mexico Bailout Is Looking Smart— and Not Just for Mexico," by David Hale, *The Washington Post*, June 2, 1996.

24. "Trade Surplus Cheers Brazil," by John Barham, *Financial Times*, June 2, 1999; "Latin Markets Fall as Brazil Rejects Reform," by Diana Jean Schemo, *The New York Times*, December 4, 1998.

25. Zedillo quoted in "Mexico's Export-Led Economic Decline," by Roberto Salinas-Leon, *The Wall Street Journal.*, May 24, 1996. Mexico's new tighter budget and tax policies are described in "Mexico: Economic Programme," Oxford Analytica, June 13, 1997 and "Zedillo's budget battle," by George W. Grayson, *Journal of Commerce*, November 20, 1997. Mexican export figures appear in "Look Homeward, Asia," by Pierre Goad, *Far Eastern Economic Review*, June 10, 1999, http://www.feer.com/9906_10/p10cover.html. For accounts of Brazilian responses to international financial pressures, see "Shock Waves Run Deep over Brazil Import Restrictions," by Kevin G. Hall, *Journal of Commerce*, April 1, 1997; "Brazil: No Bombshells on the Radar," by James C. Cooper, *BusinessWeek*, October 10, 1997; "Brazil's Radical Fiscal Package Welcomed," by Geoff Dyer, *Financial Times*, November 11, 1997; and "Brazil Plan Is Bitter Pill for U.S. Multinationals," by Matt Moffett, Rebecca Blumenstein, and Nichole M. Christian, *The Wall Street Journal.*, November 13, 1997. Malaysian responses are described in "Malaysia May Defer Imports," by James Kynge, *Financial Times*, August 13, 1997; and "Vancouver Summit," Oxford Analytica, November 5, 1997. Camdessus' comments on Malaysia cited in "IMF Chief Praises Malaysia," *Journal of Commerce*, March 27, 1998. Tighter Indian fiscal policies—including an increase in effective tariff rates, are discussed in "Delhi Moves to Plug Fiscal Gap," by Mark Nicholson, *Financial Times*, September 18, 1997. A description of India's export drive is found in "India Trade Sec: Likely to Meet 12% FY Export Growth Aim," by Denny Kurien, Dow Jones Newswires, January 14, 2000. For new South Korean and Thai measures, including import restrictions, see "Thai Fiscal Rescue Plan Draws Mixed Reaction,"

by Ron Corben, *Journal of Commerce*, October 16, 1997, and "South Korea Banks Curb Some Loans to Importers," *Journal of Commerce*, November 14, 1997.

26. See "Mexico: Economic Programme," Oxford Analytica, June 13, 1997; "Brazil car sector shunts into reverse," by Richard Cowper, *Financial Times*, November 14, 1997; "Thailand's Go-Go Economy Stopped Cold by Dramatic Downturn," by Keith B. Richburg, *The Washington Post*, August 10, 1997; "No One's Driving," by Rodney Tasker, *Far Eastern Economic Review*, October 30, 1997; "Paper Tiger?" by Paul A. Eisenstein, *Investor's Business Daily*, November 6, 1997; and "Slow Boat in China," by Stephen Butler and Brian Palmer, *U.S. News & World Report*, December 15, 1997. For more recent reports, see, "Mazda Closes Thai Plant," by Paul Abrahams, Alexandra Harney, and William Barnes, *Financial Times*, July 27, 1999; "Brazil Car Sales Fall 6% as Prices Depress Demand;" Bloomberg News, December 6, 1999; and "Argentine Auto Sales Drop in October as Discounts Reduced," Bloomberg News, November 4, 1999.

27. "Hourly Compensation Costs for Production Workers in U.S. Dollars, All Manufacturing, 1975 and 1987–97," *Hourly Compensation Costs for Production Workers in Manufacturing, 29 Countries or Areas, 40 Manufacturing Industries, 1975 and 1986–97, Unpublished Data*, Office of Productivity and Technology, Bureau of Labor Statistics, U.S. Department of Labor, May 24, 1999, ftp://ftp.bls.gov/pub/special.requests/ForeignLabor/industry.txt.

28. *World Development Report 1995*, pp. 174–75.

29. See, for example, "Penang Finds It Tough Staying on Top," by James Kynge, *Financial Times*, August 14, 1996; "Wage Scales May Lose Investor Appeal.," by N. Vasuki Rao, *Journal of Commerce*, February 12, 1997; and "Let This Be a Lesson," by Nayan Chanda and Michael Vatikiotis, *Far Eastern Economic Review*, June 12, 1997.

30. Indonesia's minimum wage cited in "Nike Workers Stage Strike in Indonesia," by Tim Shorrock, *Journal of Commerce*, April 24, 1997. As the article makes clear, minimum-wage laws are frequently violated by the country's employers. For the World Bank assessment, see "Car Makers Get the Jitters," by Manuela Saragosa, *Financial Times*, June 25, 1996. The Singapore analysis is in "Chasing the Lion," by Murray Hiebert, *Far Eastern Economic Review*, February 27, 1997. The Singapore wage cuts are cited in "CPF Cut May Be Restored Earlier if Recovery Lasts," by Irene Ng, *Straits Times*, July 7, 1999.

31. These and other examples of low-wage Asian countries losing jobs to even lower-wage countries are found in "Zycon Corp Deems Low-Wage Labor Still Important, Finds It in Malaysia," by G. Paschal Zachary, *The Wall Street Journal.*, June 13, 1996; "Economic Triangle Faces Shift in Focus; Singapore's Neighbors Move Away from Plan for Labor-Intensive Bases," *The Nikkei Weekly*, July 22, 1996; "Have We Hit Baht-tom Yet?" by Greg Gardner and Barbara McClellan, *Ward's Asia-Pacific Auto Industry News*, November 30, 1997; and "Treasure Island: Asia's Economic Storm Seems to Have Skirted Penang," by Murray Hiebert, *Far Eastern Economic Review*, December 18, 1997. See also "Malaysian July Trade Surplus Widens to 5.8Bn Ringgit," Bloomberg News, September 1, 1999 and "U.S. and Philippine Companies: Joined at the Chip," by Robert Frank, *The Wall Street Journal.*, September 2, 1999. For the South Korea report, see "South Korea Looks North to Augment Workforce," by John Gittings, *The Washington Times*, June 25, 1996. The article also discusses South Korea's imports of workers from poorer Asian countries, a practice long engaged in as well by Singapore, Malaysia, and

other countries with shortages in specific segments of their labor markets. For the Latin American developments, see "Unilever, GM Among Cos. Leaving Argentina for Brazil," Bloomberg News, December 27, 1999. For analyses that more generally blame rising wages for debt problems in developing Asia, see "Complacency Gives Way to Contagion," by John Ridding and James Kynge, *Financial Times*, January 13, 1998; "Tigers Declawed," by Fred Hiatt, *The Washington Post*, September 8, 1997; and "Let This Be a Lesson," by Nayan Chanda and Michael Vatikiotsis, *Far Eastern Economic Review*, June 12, 1997.

32. For the Southeast Asian figures, see "Investors Shy of Asean Region," *Financial Times*, July 5, 1996. China's lower-wage competition is mentioned in "Mexico Sews Up U.S. Title As Top Textile Supplier," by Paula N. Green, *Journal of Commerce*, April 7, 1997. For the new competition facing China, see "China's Trade Regime at the End of the 1990s: Achievement, Limitations, and Impact on the U.S.," by Barry Naughton, prepared for the Cato Institute conference "Whither China? The PRC at 50," Washington, D.C., September 29, 1999, p.12.

33. "Remarks by Chairman Alan Greenspan: Implications of Recent Asian Developments for Community Banking," Annual Convention of the Independent Bankers' Association of America, Honolulu, Hawaii, March 3, 1998, p. 1, http://www/bog/frb.fed.us/boarddocs/speeches/1998/19980303.htm.

34. For new Thai and Chinese rural investment, see "In Thailand, the Companies Are Migrating to the People," by Ted Bardacke, *Financial Times*, June 25, 1996; and "Rise of Market Economy Dents 'Iron Rice Bowl,'" by Edward Cody, *The Washington Post*, January 4, 1997. For similar Indonesian trends and policies see "Indonesia Govt Offers Income Tax Breaks to New Investors," by I Made Senatana, Dow Jones Newswires, January 26, 1999.

35. Ulrich Lachler, Education and Earnings Inequality in Mexico, unpublished, p. 6.

36. For the recent wage increases and the 1994 and 1999 comparisons, see "Mexico's Wages Rise—for Now," by Monica Gutschi, *Miami Herald*, October 19, 1999. The employment figures are reported in "Maquiladora Industry Said to Contribute to Dynamic Job Growth in Mexico," by Kurt Anderson, *Regulation, Law & Economics*, Bureau of National Affairs, December 15, 1999. For the trade figures, see "U.S., Mexico Reach Deal on Factory Tax," by James F. Smith and Chris Kraul, *The Los Angeles Times*, October 20, 1999.

37. For regional apparel wage figures, see "Hourly Labor Cost in the Apparel Industry," Werner International, unpublished, 1999. For overall regional wage trends, see the Interamerican Development Bank's various "Country Economic Assessment Reports," http://www.iadb.org/regions/re2.htm.

38. See "Thailand," by Frank Flatters, "Korea," by Jong-Wha Lee, "Indonesia," by Stephen C. Radelet, "Philippines," by Ruiz Fernholz, and "China," by Wing Thye Woo in *The Asia Competitiveness Report 1999*, Klaus Schwab and Jeffrey D. Sachs, eds., (Geneva, Switzerland: World Economic Forum, 1999), pp. 108, 130, 146, 168, 186. For the change in Chinese pension policy, see "Is China Headed for a Crash?" by Hugo Restall, *The Wall Street Journal.*, September 2, 1999.

39. The Wise and Pastor findings are in "NAFTA Backer's Flawed Excuses," by Alan Tonelson, *The Washington Times*, March 28, 1997. The steelworkers figures are in "Breaking the Cycle of Exploitation," United Steelworkers of America, undated; "Does Trade with Low-Wage Countries Hurt American Workers?" by Stephen Golub, *Business Review*, Federal Reserve Bank of Philadelphia,

March/April 1998, p. 10; James Burke, *U.S. Investment in China Worsens Trade Deficit* (Washington, D.C.: Economic Policy Institute, 2000), pp. 6–7.

40. See "Remarks by Chairman Alan Greenspan: Implications of Recent Asian Developments." Intel managers, for their part, say that productivity at their new semiconductor assembly and testing plants in the Philippines is nearly equal to that of comparable factories in Arizona. See Frank, "U.S. and Philippine Companies: Joined at the Chip."

41. "Interview: John S. McKennirey," by Dianne Solis, *Dallas Morning News*, July 19, 1998.

42. "Forecast Summary 2000," for individual Asian countries in "Pacific Basin, Second Quarter 2000," Wharton Econometic Forecasting Associates, unpublished. Adjusting these exchange rates to reflect world trade patterns—a process known as trade weighting—does not change them significantly. See "Nominal World Trade-Weighted Exchange Rates, Levels," Annual Averages, Ibid.

43. For the Singapore figure, see "Does Singapore Invest Too Much?" by Kenneth Kasa, *FRBSF Economic Letter* 97–15, Federal Reserve Board of San Francisco, May 15, 1997, p. 1, http://www.frbsf.org/econrsrch/wklyltr/e197–15.htm.

44. The Asian investment figures are found in L. Randall Wray, *Policy Notes: Goldilocks and the Three Bears* (Annandale-on-Hudson, N.Y.: The Jerome Levy Economics Institute, 1998), p. 5.

45. "The Challenge Now Is Trade," by David Hale, *Financial Times*, November 7, 1997.

46. For Malaysia's savings rate, see "Malaysia: Industrial Transformation," Oxford Analytica, Asia Pacific Daily Briefing, February 24, 1997. For Singaporean and South Korean rates, see "Asian Miracle," Oxford Analytica, October 30, 1996. Rates for the other Asian countries are in "Doubts Raised Over Health of Vietnamese Banking," by Jeremy Grant, *Financial Times*, August 21, 1996. Other developing-country efforts to boost savings are found in "Mexico: Economic Programme," Oxford Analytica, June 13, 1997; and the following *Financial Times* articles: "Manila Tries to Boost Savings," by Edward Luce, August 29, 1996; "Ramos Warned Over Economy," by Edward Luce, November 14, 1996; "Growth Chicken or Savings Egg?" by Stephen Kidler, November 14, 1996; "India Set to Maintain Growth Level This Year," by Mark Nicholson, February 26, 1997; "Thais Face Compulsory Savings," by Ted Bardacke, March 25, 1997; and "Brazil's Coming of Age," by Richard Lambert, Stephen Fidler, and Geoff Dyer, October 28, 1997.

47. For general tax policies in these two emerging market countries, see *Country Reports: Barriers to Trade* The Chrysler Corporation, unpublished, December 17, 1996. For foreign vehicle taxes, see "International Business Practices: Region 3: Asia and the Pacific Rim: Indonesia," and "Region 1: North and South America: Brazil," International Trade Administration, U.S. Department of Commerce, September 30, 1996.

48. See "Argentine Auto Sales Drop"; "Brazil Car Sales Seen Doubling in March After Tax Reduction," Bloomberg News, April 6, 1999; and "Thai May Car Sales Surge 43% on Tax Cut, Promotions," Bloomberg News, June 14, 1999.

49. Lachler, *Education and Earnings Inequality in Mexico*, p. 10; *Labor Standards: Try a Little Democracy*, by Aaron Bernstein, *BusinessWeek*, December 13, 1999.

50. Except where specified, the following descriptions of developing country trade barriers draw on the 1998 edition of *National Trade Estimate Reports on Foreign Trade Barriers*, a report submitted to Congress each year by the Office of the

U.S. Trade Representative. Although specific countries change specific trade barriers year in and year out, the overall protectionist posture remains.

51. For the 120 percent figure, see *Country Reports*, p. 8. For a detailed look at China and its protections, see China "China's Evolving Automotive Industry and Market," by Laura Polly, *Industry, Trade, and Technology Review*, U.S. International Trade Commission, June 1998, pp. 1–21.

52. See "China Carmakers Expect Continued Protection After WTO: Analyst," AFX News, January 10, 2000.

53. See Naughton, "China's Trade Regime at the End of the 1990s," p. 19.

54. The Indian report is quoted in "India's New Rulers Cast Doubt on Reform," by Miriam Jordan, *The Wall Street Journal.*, June 6, 1996. As of early 2000, India's effective peak tariff remains at 45 percent, according to "U.S. Firms Say India Too 'Cautious' in Promoting Trade in Budget for FY 2000," by Gary Yerkey, Bureau of National Affairs, Asia/Pacific Rim, *Trade Policy* 17, no. 10, March 9, 2000, p. 386.

55. The number of banned consumer goods is found in "U.S. to Go to WTO Over India's Ban on Consumer Goods Imports," by Mark Nicholson, *Financial Times*, October 8, 1997. The trade deal is described in "U.S. Companies Say India Trade Pact Won't Yield Gains for Years," Bloomberg News, January 11, 2000.

56. See "Mercosur Trade Fell 32% on Slow Growth, New Barriers, IDB Says," Bloomberg News, November 5, 1999.

57. See "Mr. and Mrs. High-Spender Become Pariahs," by John Burton, *Financial Times*, August 5, 1996; "U.S. Companies Crack South Korean Market," by Michael Schuman, *The Wall Street Journal.*, September 11, 1996.

58. *The Economic Implications of Liberalizing APEC Tariff and Nontariff Barriers to Trade*, Publication 3101 (Washington, D.C.: U.S. International Trade Commission), April 1998, p. 1.

59. "Appendix 2—Country Reports, People's Republic of China," *1998 "Special 301 Review," Policies and Practices of Foreign Countries Regarding Intellectual Property Rights*, submitted to the Office of the U.S. Trade Representative, Washington, D.C., March 10, 1998, http://www.spa.org/gvmnt/iprt/9830.htm.

60. See "EU Warns Seoul on Campaign Against Imports," by John Burton, *Financial Times*, April 4, 1997; "EU Supports US in Complaints over South Korea's 'Frugality Campaign,'" by John Zaracostas, *Journal of Commerce*, March 12, 1997; "Implications of the Asian Financial Crisis," testimony by Andrew H. Card, Jr., President and Chief Executive Officer, American Automobile Manufacturers Association, House Banking Committee, April 9, 1998, p. 6; "Angry S. Koreans Target Foreign Cars," by Don Kirk, *The Washington Post*, March 12, 1998.

61. The investment and growth rate comparison is from "Over-Capacity Stalks the Economies of Asian Tigers," by Peter Montagnon, *Financial Times*, June 17, 1997. The Korean businessman is quoted in "Asian Investment Floods into Mexican Border Region," by Joel Millman, *The Wall Street Journal.*, September 6, 1996.

62. Except where noted, these descriptions of export pressures and incentives are drawn from *The National Trade Estimate Report on Foreign Trade Barriers.*

63. For the Kodak requirements, see "High-Tech Chinese Charge Sweeps American Electronics," by Lorraine Woellert, *The Washington Times*, April 9, 1997. For the doubling of tax rebates, see "China Paid NY7.5B In Tax Rebates to Boost Exports—Report," Dow Jones Newswires, December 30, 1999.

64. See "The Binational Importance of the Maquiladoras Industry," by Lucinda Vargas, Southwest Economy 6, Federal Reserve Bank of Dallas, November/December 1999, http://www.dallasfed.org/htm/pubs/swe/11–12–99.html.

65. See "The Indian Software Advantage," by Dewang Mehta, http://www.software.india.com/swindust.htm; "Software Technology Parks: NSIC—Software Technology Park," http://www.nic.in/nsic/ste.htm; and "Madras Export Processing Zone," http://www.mepz.com/mepz1.htm.

66. *Malaysia: Investment in the Manufacturing Sector: Policies, Incentives and Facilities* (Kuala Lumpur, Malaysia: Ministry of International Trade and Industry), January 1996, pp. 7, 14–15, 17–18. Thailand's similar export promotion policies are mentioned in "Thailand's Financial Crisis and Progress Towards Recovery—Implications for U.S. Trade," by Karl Tsuji, *International Trade and Technology Review*, U.S. International Trade Commission, October 1999," p. 18.

67. "Total Auto Production in Korea: 1990-1999" and "Korean Passenger Car Exports," both fax communications to author from the Korean Economic Institute, Washington, D.C., July 27, 2000 and August 3, 2000. "IMF Bailout for Korea Must Include Structural Reform of Trade Practices," United States Senate Republican Policy Committee, December 2, 1997, p. 2; "Chips with Everything," by Charles S. Lee, *Far Eastern Economic Review*, June 27, 1996.

68. "Ford: Mexico Needs Big Sales for Small Cars," *Ward's South American Auto Industry News*, http://198.110.248.165/samerica/0724small_cars.htm; "U.S. and Mexican Companies Poised to Gain Global Benefits," by Tim Shorrock, *Journal of Commerce*, November 14, 1997.

69. "The Republic of PCs," by Lore Levin, *Electronic Business Asia*, March 1997; "Taiwan Textile Industry Pins Hopes on WTO Accession," by Y. H. Sun, Dow Jones Newswires, January 20, 2000.

70. *Economist*, January 4, 1999. Malaysia, for its part, seems to be keeping the ringgit artificially low in order to boost exports. See "Malaysia Ends Most Controls on Investment," by Mark Landler, *The New York Times*, September 2, 1999.

71. "Remarks by the President at the Democratic Leadership Council Gala," Omni Shore Hotel, Washington, D.C., October 13, 1999, http://www.pub.whitehouse.gov.

CHAPTER 5: A NEW KIND OF TRADE

1. For a discussion of these data problems and the global statistics that follow, see Alexander J. Yeats, *Just How Big Is Global Production Sharing* (Washington, D.C.: World Bank), undated, especially pp. 3–4, 10.

2. For South Korean consumer goods imports, see "Korean Currency Slide Shakes Economy," by John Burton, *Financial Times*, November 12, 1997. 1980–1995 figures are from the Korea International Trade Association, fax communication to author, November 13, 1996. Indonesian figures from "Changing Patterns of Trade in Goods and Services in the Pacific Region," by William E. James, *Business Economics*, April 1994; and from "Table 9. Leading Non-oil Imports Down One-Third in 1998." *Indonesia Economic Trends 1999—Signs of Life*, U.S. Embassy, Jakarta, Indonesia, http://www.usembassyjakarta.org/econ/trends 99–2.htm/ reports. Thai figures for 1996 come from "A Few Familiar Symptoms," by Ted Bardacke,

Financial Times, August 9, 1996. Thai figures for the 1980s come from James, "Changing Patterns of Trade in Goods."

3. "Taiwan 1999 Foreign Trade Figures," Bloomberg News, January 7, 2000.

4. Information on Malaysia's imports is found in James, "Changing Patterns of Trade in Goods"; the Embassy of Malaysia in Washington, D.C., fax communication to author, August 1, 1996; and "Malaysian July Trade Surplus Widens to 5.8Bn Ringgit," Bloomberg News, September 1, 1999. The Philippine Central Bank governor is quoted in "Philippine Trade Deficit Widens," by Edward Luce, *Financial Times*, August 16, 1996. More recent Philippine trends are described in "Philippine August Trade Surplus Widens to Record, Imports Fall," Bloomberg News, October 15, 1999.

5. See "The Growing U.S. Trade Imbalance with China," by Thomas Klitgaard and Karen Schiele, *Current Issues in Economics and Finance 3*, no. 7, May 1997, pp. 4, 6.

6. "China's Trade Regime at the End of the 1990s: *Just How Big Is Global Production Sharing*, p. 11.

7. "Boom in Computer Related Trade," *China Daily*, March 24, 1997, http://www.cbw.com/business/quarter1/computer.htm; "PC Legend in the Making: U.S. Companies Lag As Chinese Firm's Market Share in China Soars," by Julie Schmitt, *USA Today*, December 21, 1999.

8. Derived from U.S. International Trade Commission's Trade Dataweb http://dataweb.usitc.gov. The U.S. government classifies imports according to "end-use categories," among other schemes but distinguishes between "consumer goods" and "automotive vehicles, parts and engines," even though most imported finished vehicles clearly are consumed. The 35.5 percent figure adds finished vehicle imports to the consumer goods imports total. But it still undoubtedly underestimates actual consumer goods import levels, because it does not include food imports.

9. Menes' analysis appears in "U.S. Sees Growth in Face of Turmoil," by Mark Suzman, *Financial Times*, November 22–23, 1997. The Swedish report is summarized in "East Asian Countries Competing Unfairly on Exports, Says Study," by Guy de Jonquieres, *Financial Times*, June 25, 1996.

10. "Global Strategy: Asia—Playing the Improvement Via Multinationals," by Markus Rosgen and Deborah Weinswig, Morgan Stanley Dean Witter, November 17, 1998, p. 20; "Why Trade with Asia, Benefits the U.S. Economy," by Barry Bosworth, in Selig S. Harrison and Clyde V. Prestowitz, Jr., eds., *Asia After the Miracle* (Washington, D.C.: Economic Strategy Institute, 1998), p. 103. For a discussion of how many of Taiwan's exports to Asia wind up in the United States see "Taiwan 1999 Foreign Trade Figures: Tables," Bloomberg News, January 7, 2000.

11. See *America's Interest in the World Trade Organization: An Economic Assessment*, A Report by the Council of Economic Advisers, The White House, November 16, 1999, unpublished, p.12.

12. "Part A: Seasonally Adjusted. Exhibit 10. Exports and Imports of Goods by Principal End-Use Category (Constant Dollars Basis): January 1998 to December 1999, 1996 Constant Dollar Basis," Foreign Trade Division, U.S. Bureau of the Census, U.S. Department of Commerce, http://www.census.gov/foreign-trade/Press-Release/current_press_release.exh10.txt.

13. "Remarks by the President to the Little Rock Chamber of Commerce," Statehouse Convention Center, Little Rock, Arkansas, December 10, 1999,

http://www.pub.whitehouse.gov/uri-res/I2R?urn:pdi:oma.eop.gov.us/
1999/12/10/9.text.1.

14. Figures derived by adding "Part A: Seasonally Adjusted. Exhibit 10," to
"Part B: Exhibit 18. Not Seasonally Adjusted. Exports and Imports of Motor Vehicles and Parts by Selected Countries Data," http://www.census.gov/ foreign
trade/Press-Release/current_press_release/exh18.txt. To be sure, as previously
discussed, not all auto parts exports are used in original auto manufacturing. Many
are used to supply the "after market" as replacement parts. Therefore, these auto
parts are best seen as consumer goods.

15. "The Changing Face of North America in the Global Economy," remarks
by Jeffrey E. Garten, Under Secretary of Commerce for International Trade Before
the Americas Society and the Council of the Americas, May 17, 1994, p. 7.

16. "A Larry King Special—Ross Perot Debates V.P. Al Gore on NAFTA,"
Larry King Live Transcript 961, November 9, 1993, pp. 2, 12.

17. *Study on the Operation and Effects of the NAFTA: Executive Summary* (Washington, D.C.: The White House), July 1997, p. iii.

18. All Mexican import figures from the Web site of the Mexican statistics
ministry ("Imports by Type of Goods"), http://www.inegi.gob.mx.

19. "Pace of Imports Slows in Mexico, May End Slowdown, Economist
Says," *Daily Report for Executives*, Bureau of National Affairs, February 23, 1999.
Imports rose again in 1999—thereby once more raising the specter of unsustain-
able consumption and a currency collapse.

20. For confirmation of this point, see the NAFTA analysis performed by
David Gould, Jeremy Nalewaik, and Lori Taylor of the Federal Reserve Bank of
Dallas: "Texas-Mexico Trade After NAFTA," *Southwest Economy,* no. 5, Septem-
ber/October 1996, p. 2.

21. Raul Hinojosa Ojeda, et al., *North American Integration Three Years After
NAFTA: A Framework for Tracking, Modeling, and Internet Accessing the National and
Regional Labor Market Impacts* (Los Angeles, Calif.: North American Integration
and Development Center, UCLA School of Public Policy and Social Research),
December 1996, p. 9.

22. "Excerpts from the President's Remarks at AFL-CIO Convention."

23. See "Cheap Labour Loses Its Allure for Investors," by Guy de Jonquieres,
Financial Times, July 15, 1996; "Major U.S. Companies Expand Efforts to Sell to
Consumers Abroad," by G. Pascal Zachary, *The Wall Street Journal.,* June 13, 1996.

24. "U.S. Multinational Companies: Operations in 1997," by Raymond J.
Mataloni, Jr., *Survey of Current Business,* July 1999, http://www.bea.doc.gov/
bea/ai/0799mnc/maintext.htm; Lawrence Chimerine, Andrew Z. Szamosszegi,
and Clyde V. Prestowitz, Jr., *Multinational Corporations and the U.S. Economy*
(Washington, D.C.: Economic Strategy Institute), July 1995; Matthew J. Slaughter, *Global Investments, American Returns: A Report on the Domestic Contributions of
American Companies with Global Operations* (Washington, D.C.: Emergency Committee for American Trade, 1998); Marcus Noland, *Trade, Investment, and Economic Conflict Between the US and Asia*, Working Papers on Asia Pacific Economic
Cooperation, no. 96–11 (Washington, D.C.: Institute for International Economics,
1996).

25. Noland, *Trade, Investment, and Economic Conflict*, pp. 23, 5, 3. Another
statement of this position can be found in "International Economics: America's

Hidden Export Strength," by Joseph P. Quinlan and Andrea L. Prochniak, Morgan Stanley Dean Witter, January 13, 1999, p. 16.

26. These and the following figures come from *U.S. Direct Investment Abroad: Operations of U.S. Parent Companies and Their Foreign Affiliates, Preliminary 1997 Estimates* (Washington, D.C.: U.S. Department of Commerce, Bureau of Economic Analysis), July 1999, especially Tables III.F2, 3, 4, 7, 8.

27. "Real Gross Product of U.S. Companies' Majority-Owned Foreign Affiliates in Manufacturing," by Raymond J. Mataloni, Jr., *Survey of Current Business*, April 1997, http://www.bea.doc.gov/bea/a:/0497iid/maintext.htm.

28. "An Even Stronger Case for Big Caps," by Jeffrey M. Applegate, *Research Highlights*, Lehman Brothers, January 15, 1999, p. 3.

29. "Mexico Exports—By Country of Destination," faxed communication to author from American Automobile Manufacturers Association, June 18, 1998. Phone calls in the spring of 1997 revealed that the American Electronics Association and the Pharmaceutical Manufacturers Association, whose members also have sizable investments in Mexico, did not keep comparable figures.

30. "The Real Truth About the Economy," by Michael J. Mandel, *BusinessWeek*, November 7, 1994, p. 112.

31. See "Still Unscathed," by Juliam Baum, *The Far Eastern Economic Review*, January 8, 1998. Explaining why Taiwan's electronics industry is unlikely to be affected by the Asian financial crisis, Baum uses arguments similar to those made by Jonathan Menes in the U.S. Commerce Department regarding U.S. exporters: "The main destinations for Taiwanese electronics products are the United States and Europe, not Asia or Taiwan's small domestic market. Even exports of components to regional customers, typically Taiwan-invested factories in China and Southeast Asia, are destined for re-export to the U.S. and Europe." The same goes for Thailand, according to the U.S. International Trade Commission. See "Thailand's Financial Crisis and Progress Towards Recovery—Implications for U.S. Trade," by Karl Tsuji, *International Trade and Technology Review,* U.S. International Trade Commission, October 1999, p. 37.

32. "Study: Asian Skid Poses Little U.S. Threat," by James Kim, *USA Today*, November 17, 1997.

33. "Company News: MEMC Sets Up South-East Asia's First Fully Integrated Silicon Wafer Manufacturing Plant in Malaysia," *Malaysia Industrial Digest*, October-December 1996, p. 11.

34. "Exports and Re-Exports of Merchandise: Item by Country," faxed communication to author from the Commercial Section, Consulate General of Malaysia, New York, N.Y., August 10, 1998.

35. "Cleaning up: Delphi Wiring JV Aims for 70% of Market," *Ward's Focus on China*, August 1, 1996, p. 3.

36. Slaughter, *Global Investments, American Returns*, p. 62.

37. "Foreign Investment, Outsourcing, and Relative Wages," by Robert C. Feenstra and Gordon H. Hanson, in Robert C. Feenstra, Gene M. Grossman, Douglas A. Irwin, eds., *The Political Economy of Trade Policy: Papers in Honor of Jagdish Bhagwati* (Cambridge, Mass.: MIT Press, 1995), p. 107.

38. Michael Borrus, *Left for Dead: Asian Production Networks and the Revival of U.S. Electronics*, BRIE Working Paper 100 (Berkeley, Calif.: The Berkeley Roundtable on the International Economy), April 1997, pp. 8–9, http://www.brie.org.

39. "The Ex-Im Files," by William Greider, *Rolling Stone*, August 8, 1996, pp. 52–53.

CHAPTER 6: HIGH-TECH JOB FLIGHT

1. United States International Trade Commission, *Production Sharing: Use of U.S. Components and Materials in Foreign Assembly Operations, 1991–1994 (U.S. Imports Under Production Sharing Provisions of Harmonized Tariff Schedule Heading 9802)*, USITC Publication 2966, Investigation No. 232–237 (Washington, D.C.: U.S. International Trade Commission), May 1996, pp. 1–1, 2–1.

2. "A View from the Helm: Laura D'Andrea Tyson," *Technology Week*, May/June 1994, p. 55; "The Left's Wrong Turn: Why Economic Nationalism Won't Work," by Jay Mandle, *Dissent*, Spring 1998, p. 78.

3. Bob Davis and David Wessel, *Prosperity: The Coming 20-Year Boom and What It Means to You* (New York: Times Books, 1998), p. 220.

4. "High-Tech Jobs All Over the Map," by Pete Engardio et al., *BusinessWeek*, November 18, 1994, p. 112.

5. The U.S. auto industry's consumption of semiconductors is discussed briefly in *The Future of the Auto Industry: It Can Compete, Can It Survive?* (Washington, D.C.: Economic Strategy Institute, 1992), p. 26. The lunar module point was made by "The 300 mm International Initiative," presentation by William Spencer, CEO, SEMATECH, at "New Vistas in Transatlantic Science and Technology Cooperation," conference of the Board on Science, Technology, and Economic Policy, National Research Council, Washington, D.C., June 9, 1998.

6. For auto trade barriers around the world, see USTR Trade Barriers report, any year, plus "China's Evolving Automotive Industry and Market," by Laura Polly, *Industry, Trade, and Technology Review*, U.S. International Trade Commission, June 1998, pp. 11, 19–21; "U.S. complains to WTO, India Defends Restrictions; Official Cites 'Clear Violation' of WTO Rules," by John Zaracostas, *The Journal of Commerce*, June 10, 1999. For U.S.-Mexico vehicle flow, see "Part B: Not Seasonally Adjusted. Exhibit 18. Exports and Imports of Motor Vehicles and Parts by Selected Countries Data," http://www.census.gov/foreign-trade/PressRelease/current_press_release/exh18.txt.

7. See "Brazil's Jobless Rate Declines to 8%," Bloomberg News, December 22, 1999; and "GM Is Building Plants in Developing Nations to Woo New Markets," by Rebecca Blumenstein, *The Wall Street Journal.*, August 4, 1997.

8. "GM Agrees Polish Car Plant," by Kevin Done, *Financial Times*, June 27, 1996.

9. See "Continuing Asian Crisis Stalls GM Thai Plant," by Ronald Corben, *The Journal of Commerce*, May 19, 1998; "General Motors Drives Some Hard Bargains with Asian Suppliers," by Robert L. Simison, *The Wall Street Journal.*, April 2, 1999.

10. "Madras Revs Up to Achieve Car Ambitions," by Mark Nicholson, *Financial Times*, April 10, 1997. For Nasser's views, see "Indian Auto Cos Say Used Vehicle Imports Will Kill Industry," by Denny Kurien, Dow Jones Newswires, January 13, 2000.

11. "SAIC and GM Sign Contracts to Form New Automotive Company in China: U.S. Vice President Al Gore and China's Premier Li Peng Witness Sign-

ing," General Motors Corporation, March 25, 1997; "Paying to Enter China's Shop; Economists Question Boeing, GM Contract Concessions," by Paul Blustein, *The Washington Post*, March 29, 1997; "Big Three's Plans for China," *USA Today*, December 16, 1996; telephone interview with Thomas Hoyt, Ford Motor Co., May 22, 1998. By no means do all of the non-Chinese parts for GM's Shanghai factory however, come from the United States. Some of the contractors for the Shanghai Buick plant are South Korean and Japanese. See Simison, "General Motors Drives Some Hard Bargains."

12. "Delco Electronics Singapore Pte. Ltd.," http://www.singapore.com/companies/delco/, p. 1; "Delphi Builds Battery Plant in Saudi Arabia," *Automotive Engineering*, September 1996, p. 38; "Motorola in China—Facts 96," http://www. mot.com/General/China/facts96.htm, p. 2. "AlliedSignal Names Wong to Head Operations in China," September 25, 1996, http://www.AlliedSignal.com/corporate/media_kit/press_release/1996/Sep25_96.html.

13. See "Going, Going, Gone: U.S. Says Adios to Jobs and Balanced Trade as High-Tech Manufacturing Moves to Mexico, by Dean Culbreath, *San Diego Union Tribune*, July 25, 1999; "Kodak Relocates One Production Unit," *The New York Times*, August 2, 1998; "Malaysia, Luring Manufacturers, Likely to Keep Currency Fixed," Bloomberg News, October 14, 1999.

14. See "Kansas Mulls GM Tax Break; Package Could Be Worth Millions to KCK," by John A. Dvorak and John L. Petterson, *The Kansas City Star*, February 10, 2000; and "Navistar to Spend $45 Million on Tulsa School-Bus Chassis Plant," Bloomberg News, December 6, 1999.

15. See "A Boom Built on Big Wheels," by Robyn Meredith, *The New York Times*, June 3, 1999; and "GM Officials Argue That Jobs Shift to Mexico Is Largely Completed," by Robert L. Simison and Gregory L. White, *The Wall Street Journal.*, July 23, 1998.

16. "Success Stories: Pfizer Inc.," U.S.-China Education Foundation, http://www.uschinatrade.org/success/pfizer.html.

17. "Editorial Backgrounder, AlliedSignal Aerospace News and Events," November 4, 1996, http://www.allied.com/aerospace/news96/asia.html.

18. "Will It Fly?" by John McBeth and Nigel Holloway, *Far Eastern Economic Review*, November 24, 1994, p. 123; "Two-Way Trade," by Michael Westlake and Susumu Awanohara, *Far Eastern Economic Review*, March 10, 1994, p. 39; "GE in Russian Jet Engine Link," *Financial Times*, June 4, 1996; "Welch's March to the South," by Aaron Bernstein, *BusinessWeek*, December 8, 1999, p. 74.

19. "China Broadens Foreign Aviation Ties," by P. T. Bangsberg, *The Journal of Commerce*, November 14, 1996; Randy Barber and Robert E. Scott, *Jobs on the Wing: Trading Away the Future of the U.S. Aerospace Industry* (Washington, D.C.: Economic Policy Institute, 1995), p. 66; "Boeing in China," http://www.boeing.com/companyoffices/aboutus/Boechina97.html, p. 2.

20. Ibid.; Barber and Scott, *Jobs on the Wing*, p. 62; "Hyundai Sues Boeing for $750 Million," by Michael Schuman and Jeff Cole, *The Wall Street Journal.*, July 8, 1999; Westlake and Awanohara, "Two-Way Trade," p. 39.

21. Barber and Scott, *Jobs on the Wing*, p. 62.

22. Ibid., pp. 14, 42.

23. For a comprehensive description of Lucent's activities in China, see "Lucent in China," http://www.lucent.com/intl/ap/china.html; "Good News, Bad

Timing for Russia's Chip Industry; Incentives Go Begging During Semiconductor Slump," by Drew Wilson, *Electronic Business*, August 1998.

24. "Motorola in China—Facts 96", p. 2; "China's Business," *Online Newshour*, April 16, 1999, http://www.pbs.org/newshour/bb/asia/jan-june99/zhu_4-16.html; "Motorola to Build Pager Plant in Mexico," *The Journal of Commerce*, August 1, 1996; "Telecom Roundup—Motorola Chooses Singapore for R&D," *Newsbytes*, June 12, 1997, www.nb-pacifica.com/headline/telecomroundupmotorol_985.shtml; and "Motorola Set to Build Second Plant in China," *The Journal of Commerce*, October 22, 1997.

25. *Export Controls: Sale of Telecommunications Equipment to China*, U.S. General Accounting Office Report to the Chairman, Committee on National Security, House of Representatives, GAO/NSIAD–97–5 (Washington, D.C.: U.S. General Accounting Office), November 1996, p. 4; telephone interview with GAO staff member Karen Zuckerstein, May 22, 1998. For one of the most comprehensive descriptions of U.S. high-tech investment in China, see Alan Tonelson, *Factories, Not Markets: Why U.S. Multinational Firms Really Want "Normal Trade" with China* (Washington, D.C.: U.S. Business and Industry Council Educational Foundation, 2000).

26. Dieter Ernst, *From Partial to Systemic Globalization: International Production Networks in the Electronics Industry*, BRIE Working Paper 98 (Berkeley, Calif.: Berkeley Roundtable on the International Economy), April 1997, http://brie.berkeley.edu/~briewww/pubs/wp/wp98.html.

27. Except where noted, the following descriptions are taken from Michael Borrus, *Left for Dead: Asian Production Networks and the Revival of U.S. Electronics*, BRIE Working Paper 100, (Berkeley, Calif.: Berkeley Roundtable on the International Economy), April 1997; http://brie.berkeley.edu/~briewww/pubs/wp/wp100.html.

28. "Apple Places OEM Orders with Taiwan PC Makers," *Nikkei Asia Business Technology*, May 24, 1999.

29. "Compaq to Step Up Procurement from Taiwan by 20 Pct. In 2000," *Nikkei Asia Business Technology*, December 15, 1999.

30. "Intel Malaysia," http://www.intel.co.jp/my/eng/compinfo/, p. 3; "Xerox Delivers Desktop Color Laser Printing in China," News from Xerox, May 28, 1996, http://www.xerox.com/PR/NR960528-China.html; "Motorola in China—Facts 96", p. 2; "Motorola Eyes China Expansion," *Newsbytes*, January 3, 1997, http:// www.nb-pacifica.com/headline/motorolaeyeschinaexpa_825.html; "Brazil's Jobless Rates Declines to 8%," Bloomberg News, December 22, 1999; "Gateway Inks Vitech Deal to Tap Brazil's PC Market," Reuters, September 22, 1999.

31. "Hard Disk Drives," by David McKendrick, in David C. Mowery, ed., *U.S. Industry in 2000: Studies in Competitive Performance* (Washington, D.C.: National Academy Press, 1999), p. 312.

32. The following discussion of Seagate and IBM is based on Ernst, *From Partial to Systemic Globalization, pp. 28–29, 30–32.*

33. "Seeding Plants for a Global Harvest," by Andrew Bartmess and Keith Cerny, *The McKinsey Quarterly*, 1993, no. 2, pp. 115–118.

34. See "IBM Cuts 1,100 Jobs in California," Associated Press, June 25, 1999.

35. *U.S. Semiconductor Manufacturers: Competing for World Leaderhip: U.S. Ownership Matters* (San Jose, Calif.: Semiconductor Industry Association), July 1993, p. 7.

36. "Site Description: Introducing Intel and Our Operations in Malaysia," http://www.jobstreet.com.my/1997/i/intelmal.htm, p. 5; "Construction Begins On Intel's Costa Rica Assembly and Test Site," April 24, 1997, http://www.intel.com/pressroom/archive/releases/AW042497.HTM; "Another San Jose Finds Its Way to Software Fame," by James Wilson, *Financial Times*, January 27, 2000; "Intel Chairman Andy Grove Opens Shanghai Flash Memory Factory," May 7, 1998, http://www.intel.com/pressroom/archive/releases/AW050698.HTM.

37. Ernst, *From Partial to Systemic Globalization*, p. 24; "The Philippines' New Face," by Mark L. Clifford, *BusinessWeek*, April 1, 1996; "Hewlett-Packard (Malaysia) Sdn Bhd," The Online Career Directory, undated; "Information Technology in Malaysia: Competitive Analysis," http://gurukul.ucc.american.edu/ initeb/to2115a/analysis.htm.

38. Clifford, "The Philippines' New Face."

39. Ernst, *From Partial to Systemic Globalization*, p. 43. See also ITC, *Production Sharing*, pp. 4–9 for confirmation of this point.

40. "Site Description: Introducing Intel," p. 3; "Intel Announces New Areas of Technology Commitment to China," June 2, 1995, http://channel.intel.com/ pressroom/archive/releases/china.htm; "AMD Invests in Training Center," *Malaysia Industrial Digest*, April–June 2000, p. 10; "Hewlett-Packard Singapore (Pte) Ltd," The Online Career Directory, undated; "Delco Electronics Singapore Pte. Ltd.", p. 2.

41. "Motorola in China—Facts 96", p. 2; "Risky Hi-Tech Leap," by Charles S. Lee, *Far Eastern Economic Review*, October 31, 1996; "Taiwan: At the Gateway to Silicon Stardom—A Comprehensive Look," by David Manners, *Electronics Weekly*, March 15, 1995; "TI to Sell Memory Chip Unit to Micron," by Bill Richards and Evan Ramstad, *The Wall Street Journal.*, June 19, 1998; "Turning Around a Battleship," by Huang Hsiao-ling, *Electronic Business Asia*, March 1997, p. 23; "New U.S. Partners in Alliance Program," *Free China News*, June 7, 1996; "Empire Building," by Michael Bordenaro, *Electronic Business Asia*, January, 1997, p. 18.

42. "India: Asia's New Chip Hub," by Robert Riselhueber, *Electronic Business Today*, April 1997, p. 30; "Companies Target India for R&D Operations," by Siddharth Rastogi, *The Tinet Report*, http://www.institute.ieee.org/INST/oct95/ tinet.html#2; "Product Groups," http://www.novell.com/offices/asiapac/ india/npgb/p_group.html; "Cisco Opens a Development Site in India," by Jeff Ferry, *Computer News Daily*, http://nytsyn.com/live/Latest/223_081197_ 172202_28727.html; "Sun Microsystems to Develop Software in India," Reuters, August 6, 1998.

43. "Microsoft in Plan for India Software Base," by Mark Nicholson and Paul Taylor, *Financial Times*, November 15–16, 1997; Davis and Wessel, *Prosperity*, p. 227; "IBM Builds Global Software Team," by Paul Taylor, *Financial Times*, February 18, 1997; "The Data Highway May Be a Route for Exporting U.S. White-Collar Jobs," by Michael Schrage, *The Washington Post*, September 23, 1994.

44. "IBM and Tsinghua University Joint Venture Deliver Object Technology Solutions for Commerce on the Web," IBM News, May 14, 1996, http:// ibm.co.jp/IBMGCG/IBMPRC-E/Newsfeed/96-5/96051.html; "Lucent Technologies Establishes Bell Laboratories Communications Regional Technical Center," *News and Investor Info*, July 6, 1998, http://www.lucent.com/press/ 0798/98076.bla.html; "Novell to Set Up Software JV in China," *Asia Computer Market Update* 2, no. 1, January 27, 1998, Office of Computers and Business Equip-

ment, International Trade Administration, U.S. Department of Commerce, Bryan.Larson@mail.doc.gov.

45. "Around the Globe," *Washington Trade Daily 6*, no. 151, July 30, 1997, p. 3.

46. "Asia: The Asian Explosion—Electronics Market," *Electronics Weekly*, January 18, 1995, Reuters Textline Version.

47. See Ernst, *From Partial to Systemic Globalization, p. 27; and "Running with the Low-Cost Crowd: Disk Drive Giant Seagate Has Cut Cycle Time and Costs by Moving Design to Asia,"* by Craig Addison, *Electronic Business Asia*, July 1999.

48. Blumenstein, "GM Is Building Plants in Developing Nations"; Donald H. Dalton and Manuel G. Serapio, Jr., *Globalizing Industrial Research and Development*, Office of Technology Policy, Asia-Pacific Technology Program (Washington, D.C.: U.S. Department of Commerce), October 1995, p. 87; "Newsbriefs: New Name in Singapore," *AutoSmart*, Summer 1995, http://www.delco.com/ autosmart/95-summer/newsbriefs.html; "Delco Electronics Singapore Pte., Ltd.", p. 2; "AlliedSignal Aerospace Wheel And Brake Joint Venture Receives Design Authority from Russia," *Allied Signal News & Events, 1996 Releases*, October 22, 1996, http://www.allied./com/aerospace/news96/rubix.html.

49. "China to be GE's Global Manufacturing Center for Medical Scanners," *Asia Pulse*, December 30, 1999; "Russia's Rybinsk Motors Agrees to Engine Venture," *The Wall Street Journal.*, June 4, 1996; "Schering-Plough Will Build a Research Plant to Make a New Hepatitis C Drug," by Siti Andriane, *Straits Times*, November 5, 1999.

50. "AT&T, China Sign Technology Transfer and Manufacturing Deals," AT&T News Release, August 3, 1995, http://www.att.com/press/0895/950803.cib.html; "Ten Leading Academies in China Join Cisco Networking Academy Progam," http://www.cisco.com/warp/public/146/january99/13.html; "TI Co-operates with China's Ministry of Education to Promote Math and Science Educational Tools and DSP Technology," News Release C–98051, http://www.ti.com/corp/docs/pressrel/1998/c98051.htm;   "Telecom Roundup—Motorola Chooses Singapore for R&D," *Newsbytes*, June 12, 1997, http://www.nb-pacifica.com/headline/telecomroundupmotorol_985.shtml; "Motorola Singapore's Product Innovations," *Singapore EDB Investment News: Electronics R&D Supplement*, http://www.sedb.com.sg/sinews/supp_jul95/jul13.html; "Motorola to Shift into Software, Systems, and Networks," *Malaysia Industrial Digest*, April–June 2000, p 9; "Motorola in China—Facts 96," p. 2; Bangsberg, "China Broadens Foreign Aviation Ties."

51. "Intel Malaysia," pp. 2–3; "Site Description: Introducing Intel", p. 5; Borrus, *Left for Dead*, p. 8.

52. "Motorola in China—Facts 96," p. 2; "China Information Technology: Beijing Information Base Offers Advantages for Foreign High-Tech Investment," undated, U.S. Embassy, Beijing, courtesy of Christine Keck, U.S. Representative, U.S. Information Technology Office.

53. "Designed to Please," *About Motorola ASPG: Manufacturing*, p. 2, http://www.apspg.com/design.html.

54. "Intel Malaysia," p. 2; "Site Description: Introducing Intel", p. 5; "AMD Invests in Training Centers," p. 10; Borrus, *Left for Dead*, p. 8; Julie Johnson, *IT in Singapore: Government Policy Regarding IT in Singapore*, p. 2, http://gurukul.ucc.american.edu/MOGIT/jj7134a/govepage.html; "India: Asia's New Chip Hub," p. 30;

"Alpha-TI Semiconductor Joint Venture Announcement: Remarks by Thomas En-gibous, Executive Vice President, Financial Analyst Briefing," *TI's Virtual Library*, December 9, 1995, http://www.ti.com/corp/docs/library/thai.htm; "China Infor-mation Technology"; "New IBM China Research Laboratory Ushers in the Year of Technology and Partnership," *IBM Research News*, September 21, 1995, http://www.research.ibm.com/research/press/china1.htm.

55. "Motorola in China—Facts 96," p. 2; "China Information Technology"; "India: Asia's New Chip Hub," pp. 29–30; Julie Johnson, *IT in Singapore;* "Asia's Race to Go Digital.,"by Charles Bickers, *Far Eastern Economic Review*, July 1, 1999; Brenda Leszkiewicz, *Brazil: Computer Hardware and Software*, http://gurukul.ucc.american.edu/MOGIT/bl5783a/ linkpage. html.

56. "Intel Announces $50 Million China Research Center," May 5, 1998, http://www.intel.com/pressroom/archive/releases/AW50598B.HTM; "Intel Chairman Andy Grove Opens Shanghai Flash Memory Factory"; "Lucent Tech-nologies Establishes Global Design Center in China for 5ESS(R) AnyMedia (TM) Switch Software in Development," November 8, 1998, http://www.lucent.com/press/1198/981109.nsa.html; "Lucent Technologies Establishes Bell Laboratories Communications Regional Technical Center in China," July 6, 1998, http://www.lucent.com/press/0798/980706.bla.html.

57. Dalton and Serapio, *Globalizing Industrial Research and Development*, pp. 25–26. The National Academy of Sciences claims a less dramatic increase, but its study provides no details on developed versus developing country work. See "America's Industrial Resurgence" by David C. Mowery, in Mowery, *U.S. Indus-tries in 2000: Studies in Competitive Performance*, p. 9.

58. Engardio et al., "High-Tech Jobs All Over the Map," p. 114.

59. *U.S. Semiconductor Manufacturers*, p. 2.

60. For extensive discussions of these U.S. policy decisions, see "Beating Back Predatory Trade," by Alan Tonelson, *Foreign Affairs*, July/August 1994, pp. 49–61; and Lawrence Chimerine et al., *Can the Phoenix Survive: The Fall and Rise of the Amer-ican Steel Industry* (Washington, D.C.: Economic Strategy Institute), June 1994.

61. *Malaysia: Investment in the Manufacturing Sector: Policies, Incentives and Fa-cilities* (Kuala Lumpur, Malaysia: Ministry of International Trade and Industry), January 1996, pp. 7–9, 13; *List of Promoted Activities and Products Which are Eligible for Consideration of Pioneer Status and Investment Tax Allowance under the Promotion of Investment Act 1986* (Kuala Lumpur, Malaysia: Ministry of Trade and Industry), January 4, 1995.

62. "Mahatir Unveils Multimedia 'Super-Corridor,'" by James Lynge, *Finan-cial Times*, August 2, 1996. For a recent—decidedly upbeat—progress report on the project, see "Tech Mecca," by Simon Elegant and Murray Hiebert, *Far Eastern Economic Review*, March 16, 2000, http://203.105.48.721/p48economies. html.

63. "Indonesia to Offer Investors Tax Breaks," by Sander Thoenes, *Financial Times*, October 17, 1997; "Indonesia Govt Offers Income Tax Breaks, to New In-vestors," by I. Made Senatana, Dow Jones Newswires, January 26, 1999;" "Thai-land: Special Report—Making Sure the Tax Man Only Bites Once," *Bangkok Post*, July 15, 1996; Johnson, *IT in Singapore;* Done, "GM Agrees Polish Car Plant"; Nicholson, "Madras Revs Up." For more on tax breaks for foreign investors in India and its neighbors, see *Investment Policies of South Asian Countries: A Critical Review* (Lahore, Pakistan: Lahore Chamber of Commece and Industry). For excellent treat-ments of China's elaborate policies as of the mid–1990s, see "China's Trade Regime

at the End of the 1990's," by Barry Naughton, paper prepared for the Cato Institute Conference "Whither China? The PRC at 50," Washington, D.C., September 29, 1999;" and Ding Lu and Zhimin Tang, *State Intervention and Business in China: The Role of Preferential Policies* (Cheltenham, United Kingdom: Edward Elgar, 1997).

64. "Penang Finds It Tough Staying on Top," by James Kynge, *Financial Times*, August 14, 1996; "Singapore Attracts Record Investment Inflow," by James Kynge, *Financial Times*, January 31, 1997; Johnson, *IT in Singapore*, "Singapore to Revise Trade Priorities," by James Kynge and Elizabeth Robinson, *Financial Times*, January 21, 1997.

65. "Brazil Warned of WTO Probe into Car Tariffs," by Geoff Dyer, *Financial Times*, April 7, 1997; "Brazil Sets Low Auto Tariffs, But Critics Are Not Appeased," *The Journal of Commerce*, August 22, 1996; "WTO Criticizes Brazil for Straying from Reform," by John Zarocostas, *The Journal of Commerce*, November 1, 1996; "Brasilia Rocks the Boat," by Jonathan Wheatley, *Financial Times*, February 4, 1997; "South American Trade Pact Is Under Fire," by Michael M. Phillips, *The Wall Street Journal.*, October 23, 1996.

66. "Poland Curbs Car Part Imports," by Christopher Bobinski, *Financial Times*, August 29, 1996.

67. See Polly, "China's Evolving Automotive Industry," esp. pp. 11–19. See also Thomas R. Howell, Jeffrey D. Nuechterlein, and Susan B. Hester, *Semiconductors in China: Defining American Interests* (Washington, D.C.: Semiconductor Industry Association and Dewey Ballantine, 1995), p. 64. China's agreement with the United States securing its admission into the World Trade Organization cuts auto tariffs from the current 80–100 percent level to 25 percent by 2006—still formidable in an industry mired in excess capacity and engaged in cutthroat global competition. Moreover, Washington's record of enforcing trade agreements with China is notoriously poor. See "Summary of U.S.–China Bilateral WTO Agreement," China Trade Relations Working Group, The White House, February 2, 2000, http://www.chinapntr.gov/bilatsumm.htm.

68. *Offsets in Defense Trade: Report to Congress*, Office of Strategic Industries and Economic Security, Bureau of Export Administration (Washington, D.C.: U.S. Department of Commerce), August 1997, p. 2; *Military Exports: Offset Demands Continue to Grow*, GAO/NSIAD–96–95 (Washington, D.C.: U.S. General Accounting Office), April 1996; *Offsets in Defense Trade 1999: Executive Summary*, http://www.doc-bxg.bmpcue.org/odtir_99report.html.

69. See, for example, "The U.S. Aircraft Industry in a Global Market," by Robert Trice, Vice President, International Business Development, Lockheed Martin Corp., in Charles W. Wessner and Alan Wm. Wolff, eds., *Policy Issues in Aerospace: Report of a Workshop*, Board on Science, Technology, and Economic Policy, National Research Council (Washington, D.C.: National Academy Press, 1997), p. 4.

70. Quoted in Manufacturers Alliance, *Offsets in Foreign Sales of Defense and Nondefense Equipment: A Manufacturers Alliance Review*, Economic Report ER–395 (Arlington, Va.: Manufacturers Alliance), February 1997, p. 11. Ms. Bath acknowledged that her assessment only covered prime aerospace contractors—the giant companies that produce the final aircraft—and not the large group of subcontractors whose workforces and operations could be more dramatically affected by these practices. Unfortunately, reliable employment data for the full set of subcontractors does not exist.

71. "Buyers of U.S. Arms Toughen Demands," by Jeff Cole and Helene Cooper, *The Wall Street Journal.*, April 16, 1996.

72. *Offsets in Defense Trade 1997*, p. 1; Barber and Scott, *Jobs on the Wing*, p. 37.

73. Ibid., p. 38.

74. "Future Shape of Commercial Aircraft Market in the Pacific Region," by Dr. Yang Ingbao, speech to the 29th International General Meeting of the Pacific Basin Economic Council, Washington, D.C., May 20–22, 1996, pp. 3–4.

75. William Greider, *One World, Ready or Not: The Manic Logic of Global Capitalism* (New York: Simon and Schuster, 1997), pp. 131–132.

76. "China Pushes for Tech Swap with U.S.," by Peter Tirschwell, *The Journal of Commerce*, November 27, 1996; "China's Demand for Commercial Technology Poses Dilemma for U.S. Companies: Commerce Report Finds," Bureau of Export Administration, U.S. Department of Commerce, http://www.bxa.doc.gov/press/99/PRCTech.html.

77. "Statement of George David, Chairman and Chief Executive Officer, United Technologies Corporation, Hartford, Connecticut, and Member, Board of Directors, U.S.-China Business Council, on behalf of the Business Coalition for U.S.-China Trade," Testimony Before the Subcommittee on Trade of the House Committee on Ways and Means, Hearing on United States-China Trade Relations and the Possible Accession of China to the World Trade Organization, June 8, 1999, pp. 1–2, http://www.house.gov/ways_means/trade/106cong/6–8–99/ 6–8davi.htm.

78. See "China's Evolving Automotive Industry," p. 11.

79. For Thailand as the world's runner-up pickup truck producer, see Thomas L. Friedman, *The Lexus and the Olive Tree: Understanding Globalization* (New York: Farrar, Straus and Giroux, 1999), p. 246. For the jobs figures, see "Thailand: Automobile Slump, *Asia-Pacific Daily Brief*, Oxford Analytica, July 8, 1998.

80. Susan Hammer and W.L. Lyons Brown, *Recommendations on Asia of the President's Advisory Committee for Trade Policy and Negotiations* (Washington, D.C.: The White House), September 14, 1995, p. 2; "Korea, U.S. Share Future in Semiconductor Sector," by Kim Chi-luck, *The Korea Herald*, June 22, 1995.

81. For brief descriptions of the Information Technology Agreement, the Multilateral Agreement on Investment, and other trade liberalization agreements and initiatives see, "Testimony of Ambassador Charlene Barshefsky, United States Trade Representative before the Senate Finance Committee," June 3, 1997, pp. 5–6.

82. "U.S. Says 'Yes, Prime Minister,'" by Richard Waters, *Financial Times*, July 24, 1997.

83. See Borrus, *Left for Dead*, pp. 6–9; Ernst, *From Partial to Systemic Globalization*, p. 37; "Components Producers: The Supplier Moves Next Door," by Richard Wolfe, *Financial Times*, July 24, 1997.

84. Culbreath, "Going, Going, Gone: U.S. Says Adios to Jobs and Balanced Trade"; "Kulicke Will Shift Some Output to Asia," *The New York Times*, February 3, 1999; "Lucent Technologies Expands Facility in China for 5ESS ANYMEDIA (TM) switch production," *News & Investor Info*, December 11, 1998, http://www.lucent.com/press/1298/981211.nsa.html; "AMD Invests in Training Centres," p. 10.

85. "Producers Ask Korea to Remove Chip Tariffs," by Tim Shorrock, *The Journal of Commerce*," September 14, 1996; "It Gets Tougher at the Top in SE Asia," by James Kynge, *Financial Times*, November 14, 1996; and "Singapore to Revise

Trade Priorities," by James Kynge and Elizabeth Robinson, *Financial Times*, January 21, 1998.

86. "Technology Strategy in East Asian Developing Economies," by Carl J. Dahlman, unpublished, (Washington, D.C.: The World Bank), July 1994, p. 19; "Variety of Factors Slows Down Asia's Exports," by Peter Montagnon, *Financial Times*, July 4, 1996; "Malaysian July Trade Surplus Widens to 5.8 Bn Ringgit," Bloomberg News, September 1, 1999; "Performance of the Manufacturing Sector," *Malaysia Industrial Digest*, April–June 2000, p. 3.

87. Dahlman, "Technology Strategy," p. 19; "Let This Be a Lesson," by Nayan Chanda and Michael Vatikiotis, *Far Eastern Economic Review*, June 12, 1997; "U.S. and Philippine Companies: Joined at the Chip," by Robert Frank, *The Wall Street Journal.*, September 2, 1999; "Philippine November Exports Rise 19% From Year Ago," Bloomberg News, January 4, 2000; "Non-Oil/Gas Exports up Nine Percent," Indonesia Economic News in Brief, *Indonesian Economic News and Reports*, The Economic Section (Jakarta, Indonesia: U.S. Embassy Jakarta), April 1997, p. 1.

88. "China Plans to Increase Hi-Tech Exports by 30 Percent Annually," Agence France Press, July 29, 1999.

89. "Missing Pieces," by Jeffrey Sachs, *Far Eastern Economic Review*, February 25, 1999; "Maquiladora Industry Said to Contribute to Dynamic Job Growth in Mexico," by Kurt Anderson, *Regulation, Law & Economics*, Bureau of National Affairs, December 15, 1999.

90. Borrus, *Left for Dead*, p. 7; "Taiwan to Grab 20 Pct. of Global TFT-LCD Panel Market," *Nikkei Asia Business Technology*, November 5, 1999; "Taiwan Is Thinking Big," by Richard Lawrence, *The Journal of Commerce*, October 10, 1997; "Taiwan Bets Its Chips on IC Production," by Ken Liu, *Business Taiwan*, May 8, 1995; "Taiwan PC Makers Rely More on China," by Russell Flannery, *The Wall Street Journal.*, October 21, 1999.

91. "Taiwan PC Makers Squeezed by Quake," Reuters, November 5, 1999; "Shaken, Not Stirred: Taiwan's Hi-Tech Firms Recover Speedily from Quake," by Julian Baum, *Far Eastern Economic Review*, October 7, 1999, http://www.feer.com/9910_07/p91economies.html.

92. "Top South Korean Producers Plan to Cut Chip Supplies," by Jack Burton, *Financial Times*, February 5, 1997; "Chip Wars," by Charles S. Lee, *Far Eastern Economic Review*, September 23, 1999.

93. Lee, "Risky Hi-Tech Leap"; "Singapore: Tough Lap Ahead on Ambitious Marathon," by James Kynge, *Financial Times*, February 18, 1997; Johnson, *IT in Singapore*; ITC, *Production Sharing*, pp. 3–7.

94. "Proton Pushes up Sales," *Global Press Advertisement*, undated; "Emerging Trends in China's Foreign Trade," *Asia-Pacific Daily Briefing*, Oxford Analytica, November 10, 1997.

95. "Decrease in Market Share for Foreign Computer Producers," *China Business and Investment Update*, March 1, 1997, http://www.china-invest.com/cbiu.htm; "China Sold 1.8 million PCs Last Year," *PC Week*, January 27, 1997; "Increased Demand for Computers in China," *China Economic News*, March 1, 1997; and "Domestic Computer Manufacturers to Produce 4–5 Million Units Annually," *China Economic Information*, February 3, 1997; all cited at http://www.cbw.com/business/quarter1/computer.htm. Legend still held the Chinese pc market share lead as of mid–1999. See "WTO Entry Would Make

China Cos More Competitive," by Trish Saywell, Dow Jones Newswires, May 12, 1999. For Brazil computer sales trends, see "Battling for Brazil," by Cristina Adams, *US/Mexico Business*, November, 1997. For Chinese software developments see "Softly, Softly," by Trish Saywell, *Far Eastern Economic Review*, December 11, 1997; and "Move Over, Microsoft," *BusinessWeek* (International Edition), November 18, 1996.

96. *Workshop on Semiconductor and Electronics Manufacturing in the Pacific Rim*, International Technology Research Institute, JTEC/WTEC Program (Baltimore, Md.: Loyola College, 1996), p. 115.

97. "Asian Countries Aim to Boost Research," by Dan Biers, *The Wall Street Journal.*, October 24, 1995; "Korea's Foreign Exchange Crisis and Its Implications for U.S.-Korean Trade," by William L. Greene, *Industry, Trade, and Technology Review*, U.S. International Trade Commission, March 1999, p. 1.

98. Ibid., pp. 92, 110; "The End of the Drought," *Electronic Business Asia*, January 1997.

99. "Blazing New Trails," by Hordon Kim, *Electronic Business Asia*, February 1997; *Samsung Corporation: Acquisitions and Alliances*, CSW, Inc., unpublished, January 1997, p. 13; *Workshop on Semiconductor and Electronics Manufacturing*, p. 107; Lee, *"Chip Wars"*; "Samsung Rides Licensing To High-End Chipmaking," by Gene Koprowski, *New Technology Week* 10, no. 34, August 19, 1996.

100. Spencer, "The 300 mm International Initiative"; Kim, "Blazing new trails"; *Workshop on Semiconductor and Electronics Manufacturing*, p. 107.

101. "LCDs: Moving the Goalposts," by Alice Yu, *Electronic Business Asia*, January 1997; "Taiwan: ERSO Pushes Toward Vanguard of Integrated Circuit Development," by Ken Liu, *Business Taiwan*, October 17, 1994; *Workshop on Semiconductor and Electronics Manufacturing*, p. 97; Baum, "Shaken, Not Stirred"; "Taiwan PC Makers Squeezed by Quake."

102. "Still Unscathed," by Julian Baum, *Far Eastern Economic Review*, January 8, 1998; *Workshop on Semiconductor and Electronics Manufacturing*, p. 69.

103. "Taiwan: Targeting Silicon Wafer Production," *Business Taiwan*, November 28, 1994; Lawrence, "Taiwan is thinking big."

104. "Squeezed at Home, Companies and Officials Are Looking Abroad," *The Journal of Commerce*, November 4, 1997; "Aiming High," by Mee-Ling Soo, *Electronic Business Asia*, December 1999; "Technology Underpins Tiger's Hopes," *Financial Times*, December 4, 1996; Biers, "Asian Countries Aim to Boost Research"; "Tech group targets U.S. from Pembroke Pines Offices," by L. A. Lorek, *Sun Sentinel*, December 18, 1997.

105. Howell et al., *Semiconductors in China*, [au: supply ref] pp. 37; "China: Great Progress Has Been Made But More Investments are Needed," *Channel*, February 1997, http://www.semi.org/Channel/1997/feb/features/qa.html; "China Fab Turns to Foundry Market," by Mark Carroll, *EE Times*, May 1, 1998, http://pubs.cmpnet. com/eet/nerws/98/1006news/china.html; "China Information Technology."

106. *Semiconductors in China*, p. 59.

107. "In China, Professor Leads a High-Tech Revolution," by Steven Mufson, *The Washington Post*, June 10, 1998; "PRC Net Dreams: Is Control Possible?" *Asia Computer Market Update* 1, issue 4, October 21, 1997; "China Information Technology."

108. See "Indian Software Products: Prospects, Trends, New Initiatives," ATIP97.80, Asian Technology Information Program, http://www.atip.or.jp/public/atip.reports.97/atip97.080.html; "Success Stories," http://www.nasscom.org/success.htm.

109. "Indian IT Software and Services Industry," http://www.nasscom.org. "India's Infotech Industry Grows in 97/98," *The San Jose Mercury News*, July 22, 1998; "India's Computer Industry Set to Benefit from E-Commerce," by N. Vasuki Rao, *The Journal of Commerce*, July 19, 1999.

110. The following figures come from Lawrence Rausch, *Asia's New High-Tech Competitors*, NSF 95–309 (National Science Foundation: Arlington, Va.), pp. 41–55.

111. "Why Trade with Asia Benefits the U.S. Economy," by Barry Bosworth, in Selig S. Harrison and Clyde V. Prestowitz, eds., *Asia After the "Miracle"* (Washington, D.C.: Economic Strategy Institute, 1998), pp. 103–4.

112. Davis and Wessel, *Prosperity*, pp. 16, 224–5.

CHAPTER 7: FALSE HOPES

1. For such a perspective from a political conservative, see "Causes of the Trade Deficit," John H. Makin, American Enterprise Institute, Testimony to the Trade Deficit Review Commission, August 19, 1999, unpublished. For such a perspective from a political liberal., see "Our Friend, the Trade Deficit," by Robert G. Murphy, *The Washington Post*, May 21, 1999.

2. "Clinton Shares Credit for Longest Boom," by John M. Berry, *The Washington Post*, February 2, 2000.

3. "Fed Chairman Discusses the 'Limits'" to the Economy," by Richard W. Stevenson, *The New York Times*, January 14, 2000.

4. For an early discussion of such thinking see Clyde V. Prestowitz, Jr. and Robert B. Cohen, et al., *The New North American Order: A Win-Win Strategy for U.S.-Mexico Trade* (Washington, D.C. and Lanham, Md.: Economic Strategy Institute and University Press of America, 1991), esp. pp. ii and 52.

5. See, e.g., "A View from the Helm," by Laura D'Andrea Tyson, *Technology Week*, May/June 1994, p. 55.

6. A typical statement of this argument is found in *America's Interest in the World Trade Organization: An Economic Assessment*, report by the President's Council of Economic Advisers, The White House, November 16, 1999, unpublished, esp. pp. 2, 24, 30.

7. "Transcript of Interview with President Clinton," *Seattle Post-Intelligencer*, December 1, 1999, http://www.seattlep-i.com/national/trans01.shtml.

8. See "We Told You So: The WTO's First Trade Decision Vindicates the Warnings of Critics," by Alan Tonelson and Lori Wallach, *The Washington Post*, May 5, 1996.

9. "Remarks Prepared for Delivery, National Press Club, March 23, 1995, Ambassador Michael Kantor," http://www.ustr.gov/speeches/kantor/kantor_1.html.

10. The most important of these public warnings came in *United States Security Strategy for the Asia-Pacific Region* (Washington, D.C.: U.S. Department of Defense), February 1995, p. 10.

11. For as definitive an account as possible of this critical phase of U.S.-Japan economic diplomacy, see R. Taggart Murphy, *The Weight of the Yen: How Denial Imperils America's Future and Ruins an Alliance* (New York: W. W. Norton, 1996).

12. See *Report to President William Jefferson Clinton of the Interagency Enforcement Team Regarding the U.S.-Japan Agreement on Autos and Auto Parts* (Washington, D.C.: U.S. Department of Commerce, Office of the U.S. Trade Representative), June 3, 1999, http://www.ustr.gov/reports/99-iet.html. For Clinton's excuses, see "Clinton: Japan Options Limited," Associated Press, September 22, 1998.

13. For the Vietnam figure, see "Vietnam Trade Balanced in July vs Year Ago $120 M Deficit," by Catherine McKinley, Dow Jones Newswires, July 26, 1999.

14. *Assessment of the Economic Effects on the United States of China's Accession to the WTO, Executive Summary*, Investigation No. 332–403, Publication 3228 (Washington, D.C.: U.S. International Trade Commission), August 1999, p. xii.

15. "Remarks by the President to American and Japanese Business Leaders, Tokyo, Japan," The White House, Office of the Press Secretary, November 20, 1998. See also "President Clinton Will Not Ask Asia to Cut Exports to U.S. Despite Trade Deficit," by Gary Yerkey, *Daily Report for Executives*, Bureau of National Affairs, November 16, 1998.

16. Media commentators have demanded allied cooperation, too—for example, see *BusinessWeek*'s editorial insistence that "A Unified Europe Must Shoulder Global Responsibilities with a New Global Attitude." See "It's Bigger Than Bananas," *BusinessWeek*, March 22, 1999, p. 122.

17. See, e.g., "Remarks by the President to Opening Ceremony of the 1998 International Monetary Fund/World Bank Annual Meeting, Washington, D.C.," The White House, Office of the Press Secretary, October 6, 1998, p. 3.

18. "Asia: Recovery Without Japan?" by Robert Subbaraman and Matthew Poggi, *Global Weekly Economic Monitor*, Lehman Brothers, April 30, 1999, pp. 4, 5. Unfortunately, the IMF and the two Lehman economists forgot that much intra-Asian trade is trade in producer goods that eventually winds up being consumed outside of Asia.

19. See "Is the U.S. Trade Deficit Sustainable? Prepublication excerpt: Chapters 2 and 8 for the Trade Deficit Review Commission Briefing, August 19, 1999," by Catherine L. Mann, unpublished, pp. 8.7–8.8.

20. France even openly praised the weak euro as an export-driver. See "France's Economic Council Sees Faster Growth, Praises Euro Fall," Bloomberg News, December 14, 1999.

21. See "Clinton Proposes Plan to Compensate Parents for Time Off for Childcare," Jeanne Cummings, *The Wall Street Journal.*, May 24, 1999; and "Clinton Touts 'New Markets' Plan," by Charles Babington, *The Washington Post*, May 12, 1999.

22. "Why Trade with Asia Benefits the U.S. Economy," by Barry Bosworth, in Selig S. Harrison and Clyde V. Prestowitz, Jr., eds., *Asia After the "Miracle"* (Washington, D.C.: Economic Strategy Institute, 1998), p. 105.

23. A good summary of new state programs for welfare alumni and other low-income Americans, and their costs, is found in "Welfare Law Buoys the 'Working Poor,'" by Richard Wolf, *USA Today*, June 9, 1999. The *Post* headline is in "'Welfare-to-Work' Success," by Stephen Barr, *The Washington Post*, August 2, 1999. For more on government hiring of welfare alumni, see "Recipients of Welfare Are Fewest Since 1969," by Katherine Q. Seelye, *The New York Times*, April 11, 1999.

24. Thomas L. Friedman, *The Lexus and the Olive Tree: Understanding Globalization* (New York: Farrar, Straus and Giroux, 1999), pp. 358, 361.

25. "Reich, Redefining 'Competitiveness,'" by Frank Swoboda, *The Washington Post*, September 24, 1994; "A Helping Hand, Not Just an Invisible Hand," by Karen Pennar, *BusinessWeek*, March 24, 1997, p. 71; Friedman, *The Lexus and the Olive Tree*, p. 361.

26. For Clinton's highly controversial statement endorsing the use of sanctions to enforce these provisions, see "Transcript of Interview with President Clinton"; *The Wall Street Journal* reporters Bob Davis and David Wessel favor "[making] labor issues a part of trade negotiations" but appear to oppose using sanctions to enforce protections. See Bob Davis and David Wessel, *Prosperity: The Coming 20-Year Boom and What It Means to You* (New York: Times Books, 1998), pp. 361–362.

27. One of the sharpest and highest-profile recent attacks on linking trade expansion with worker protections came in a speech by then Mexican President Ernesto Zedillo at a January 2000 international economics and business conference. See "Clinton Shift on Trade: 'Wake-Up Call,'" by Joseph Kahn, *The New York Times*, January 21, 2000.

CHAPTER 8: TOWARD A NEW RACE

1. For good introductions to the dollarization issue, see "Crisis Starts Debates on Dollarisation," by Richard Lapper, *Financial Times*, March 12, 1999 and "'Dollarization' in Latin America," by David Ignatius, *The Washington Post*, April 28, 1999.

2. For the short-term borrowing figures, see Ramon Moreno, Gloria Pasadilla, and Eli Remolona, *Asia's Financial Crisis: Lessons and Policy Responses*, Working Paper PB98–02, Center for Pacific Basin Monetary and Economic Studies, Economic Research Department, Federal Reserve Bank of San Francisco, San Francisco, Calif.: July, 1998, pp. 9, 25.

3. "Missing Pieces," by Jeffrey Sachs, *Far Eastern Economic Review*, February 25, 1999.

4. "Asian Trade Is Turning Around," by Robert Subbaraman, *Global Weekly Economic Monitor*, Lehman Brothers, August 13, 1999.

5. "Q&A: Ruth Harkin," *The San Diego Union-Tribune*, April 21, 1996.

6. A groundbreaking treatment of this subject is "No More NICs," by John Cavanagh and Robin Broad, *Foreign Policy* 72, Fall 1988.

7. For the benefits of OECD status, see "Fed Rule Gives U.S. Banks Holding South Korean Loans a Break," by Lorraine Woellert, *The Washington Times*, January 30, 1998. For information on emerging market and U.S. Treasury yields,"Figure L. Brady Bond Index Stripped Yields versus U.S. Tresury Bond Yields 1994–January 2000," in *Emerging Market Outlook and Strategy,* Salomon Smith Burney, May 2000, p. 5.

8. "U.S. Farm-Equipment Firms Head to Russia," *USA Today*, March 23, 1999; "Argentina: The Unfinished Revolution," by Ian Katz and Beth Rubenstein Keaveny, *BusinessWeek* (International Edition), August 16, 1999, http://www.businessweek.com/1999/99_33/b3642011.htm.

9. Letter accompanying transmission to Congress of the "Export Expansion and Reciprocal Trade Agreements Act of 1997," The White House, Office of the Press Secretary, September 16, 1997.

10. "Thailand's Financial Crisis and Progress Towards Recovery—Implications for U.S. Trade," by Karl Tsuji, International Trade and Technology Review, U.S. International Trade Commission, October 1999, p. 30; "Korea's Foreign Exchange Crisis and Its Implications for U.S.-Korean Trade," by William L. Greene, Industry, Trade, and Technology Review, U.S. International Trade Commission, March 1999, p. 9; and "Clinton's Moves to Repair Global Economic Crisis Bring Mixed Grades for Successes and Setbacks," by Michael M. Phillips, The Wall Street Journal., April 21, 1999.

11. Moreno et al., Asia's Financial Crisis, p. 13.

12. See "Buenos Aires 'Close' to Deal on Fresh IMF Loan," by Ken Warn, Financial Times, January 27, 2000 and "Mexico Prepares for Election with Financing," by Jonathan Friedland, The Wall Street Journal., June 16, 1999. For an oddly triumphalist discussion of Brazil's preemptive and actual bailouts and their effects, see "Yes, Investors Panicked, But Brazil Didn't," by Larry Rohter, The New York Times, May 23, 1999. The gist of Rohter's analysis is that Brazil's success in beginning to "right itself" with the help of $41.5 billion in international aid shows that the country's "underlying strengths" had been overlooked by foreign financiers.

13. "Asia: How Real Is the Recovery?" by Bruce Bremner, BusinessWeek, May 3, 1999, p. 58; Robert J. Myers, The Faltering Economic Reforms of South Korea, Working Paper no. 51 (Cardiff, Calif.: Japan Policy Research Institute), November 1998, p. 3; "Battle of Wills," by Charles S. Lee, Far Eastern Economic Review, August 26, 1999, http://www.feer.com/9908_26/p10cover.html; "More Manufacturers Face Race to Survive As Cup Runs Over in the Industrial World," by Marcus W. Brauchli, The Wall Street Journal., November 30, 1998. Some capacity has been cut in countries such as South Korea. See, for example, "Worldwatch," The Wall Street Journal., November 25, 1998.

14. "Mexico Isn't Investment-Grade Yet," by Geri Smith, BusinessWeek, March 13, 2000, p. 140; "Brazil Makes Progress Toward Economic Recovery," by Peter Muello, USA Today, March 29, 1999. For some welcome expressions of Wall Street skepticism about emerging markets, see "Russia's Revival May Be Shaky," BusinessWeek, March 13, 2000, p. 28.

15. "The World Economy: On the Edge," The Economist, September 5, 1998, http://www.economist.com/editorial/freeforall/19980905/sfl128.html; "Taking Action to Avoid Domino Effect," by Richard Lapper, Financial Times, March 12, 1999; Capital Flows to Emerging Market Economies (Washington, D.C.: Institute for International Finance), January 24, 2000, pp. 6–7.

16. "Tsuji, Thailand's Financial Crisis," pp. 26, 32; "Lucent Technologies Invests $40 Million in Manufacturing Facilities in Thailand," News & Investor Info, June 8, 1999, http://www.lucent.com/press/0699/990608.cob.html; Rohter, "Yes, Investors Panicked"; "Ford Gambles on Russia," by Greg Myre, The Washington Times, August 17, 1999.

17. Capital Flows to Emerging Market Economies, pp. 1, 8; Foreign Direct Investment Trends of U.S. Manufacturers: 1999 Annual Report, advanced unedited draft, pp. 8ff., http://www.dc.com/research.

18. "MSCI Adjusts for Malaysia, Taiwan" and "Asian Companies Became Less Open with Information," by Robert Frank, both *The Wall Street Journal.*, November 30, 1999.

19. Dallara is quoted in "Opening the Money Tap," by G. Pierre Goad, *Far Eastern Economic Review*, October 7, 1999, http://www.feer.com:10071/9910_07/p84/economies.html.

20. See, for example, "The New Internationalism," John J. Sweeney, speech to the Council on Foreign Relations, New York, New York, April 1, 1998, http://www.aflcio.org/pub/speech1998/sp0401.htm.

21. See, for example, Robert A. Blecker, *Taming Global Finance: A Better Architecture for Growth and Equity* (Washington, D.C.: Economic Policy Institute, 1999), esp. pp. 137ff.

22. Sachs, "Missing Pieces"; *Alternatives for the Americas*, p. 36; Alliance for Responsible Trade, Common Frontiers, Red Chile por una Iniciativa de los Pueblos, Red Mexicana de Accion Frete al Libre Comercio, and Reseau Quebecois sur l'Integration Continentale, *Alternatives for the Americas: Building a Peoples' Hemispheric Agreement*, Discussion Draft 2, November, 1998, p. 37. George Soros, *The Crisis of Globalism [Open Society Endangered]* (New York: Public Affairs Press, 1998), esp. Chapter 8. The reference to restarting the flow of funds is on p. 182.

23. *America's Interest in the World Trade Organization: An Economic Assessment*, report by the President's Council of Economic Advisers, The White House, unpublished, November 16, 1999, p. 1; "U.S. Secretary of Commerce William M. Daley Designates November 10 as National Dialogue on Trade Day," U.S. Department of Commerce, November 2, 1999, http://204.193.246.62/public.nsf/docs/nted-main.

24. "Remarks by Chairman Alan Greenspan at the Haas Annual Business Faculty Research Dialogue, University of California," Berkeley, California, September 4, 1998, http://www.federalreserve.gov/board/docs/speeches/1998/19980904.htm.

25. See "Don't Punish Africa," by Thomas L. Friedman, *The New York Times*, March 7, 2000.

INDEX